The Football Managers

Tony Pawson

THE FOOTBALL MANAGERS

Eyre Methuen
London

First published 1973
© 1973 Tony Pawson
Printed in Great Britain for
Eyre Methuen Ltd
11 New Fetter Lane, London EC4P 4EE
by Clarke, Doble & Brendon Ltd
Plymouth

ISBN 413 30370 5

Contents

Acknowledgements 6
Preface 7
1 The Winners and the Workers 11
2 The Managerial Revolution 26
3 The National Interest 44
4 The Magnificent Seven 63
5 The Supporting Cast 91
6 The Tactics of Success 97
7 Training for Victory 117
8 Players and Captains 134
9 Maintaining the Team 141
10 The Money-Go-Round 162
11 The Business Game 178
12 It's Tough at the Bottom 185
13 Looking to the Future 197
Appendix Plymouth Argyle Job Descriptions 211
Index 217

Acknowledgements

I am grateful to the *Sun* for permitting the inclusion of a quote by Lou Macari, and to the *Sunday Telegraph* for two quotes by Bobby Charlton. For the early history of Management I have been indebted to material from:

N. L. Jackson, *Association Football* (George Newnes Ltd)
Pickford and Gibson, *Association Football and the Men Who Made It* (Ballantyne Press)
Football – A popular handbook of the game (Religious Tract Society, 1887)
Herbert Chapman on Football (Garrick Publishing Co.)

Preface

Gordon Jago was preparing Queen's Park Rangers for two games over Christmas 1972 on which might hinge their return to the First Division. How should he get them to train without resentment on both Sunday and the following morning, Christmas Day?

Ron Jones, the International sprinter who organises Rangers' stamina training, expressed his own very definite view that they should come to the Ruislip training ground both days. Jago then took the decision to issue kit after Saturday's game so that they could train at home on Sunday and come in only on Christmas Day. The players welcomed his trust and readily accepted the lesser alternative after the harsher proposal. Both matches were won and a four-point gap was opened over the chasing clubs.

The scene stirred memories for both of us. Jago, an apprentice with Charlton, had received no instruction for Christmas 1952 and indulged himself in turkey, plum pudding and feet before the fire. The agony of the Boxing Day game for the reserves left its scar.

That same weekend Jimmy Seed, Charlton's Manager, asked me to play my first First Division game at White Hart Lane. It was a bold decision, as his only knowledge of my play was a Scout's report on a televised Pegasus Amateur Cup match. I endured a calorieless Christmas interrupted by runs up a steep hill outside Maidstone.

Boxing Day was happy fantasy. Entering the well-ordered world of professional football I waited expectantly for the detailed briefing. There was no word about our tactics or Tottenham's. The club doctor prescribed a tot of whisky to calm the nerves. Benny Fenton, now Millwall's Manager, asked me to kick my corners to the far post – which happened to be beyond my range on a dry ground, let alone in the cloying mud in which White Hart Lane then specialised. After twenty minutes I had run myself breathless. We were two down. Came a corner at last. In the intensity of effort my left foot skidded away, the right sent the ball sliding diagonally back towards the centre circle. Twenty players stared incredulous. Inside-right Kiernan hit it smoothly into the net.

Thereafter Kiernan kept drawing the back, slipping me the ball, finally heading home a centre. At half-time I thanked him for the excellent service. 'Thank the Scout who recommended you. He has promised to murder me if you don't have a good game.'

That induction started me wondering how haphazard or how professional was football Management. Other incidents from early experience hinted at the potential and the limitations of a Manager's effect on a player. Vic Buckingham, later to take West Bromwich Albion so close to the double, managed our Pegasus team to their first Amateur Cup win. Buckingham, debonair, happy-go-lucky, articulate, was an ideal man to motivate a University side. Before facing Bishop Auckland and a hundred thousand crowd at Wembley his instructions were brief: 'Whether you are playing well or badly, *want* the ball all the time. Don't worry about what they will do, make them worry about what you will do. If you can sprint off the field at the end you haven't given of your best.'

'Want the ball' was a simple phrase that conditioned the right mental approach in most of us. Before that match the Tottenham team played us on their training pitch at Cheshunt, with Arthur Rowe and Billy Nicholson giving us two hours of coaching. That is not long to improve on the habits of a lifetime, but they gave a new perception of opportunities. Practice of a simple positional switch perfected a move from which came the two goals that won the match.

Jimmy Hill, coaching the Great Britain team for the Helsinki Olympics, touched another chord when he said, 'It took me sixteen years to realise this is a passing, not a dribbling, game.' That suddenly illumined my own chief failing.

In twenty years of watching and writing on the game one has seen the Manager's job cocooned in mystique as if everything is planned, nothing spontaneously achieved by players.

How could Dave Sexton be such a failure with Orient, so successful with Chelsea? Or Alec Stock work wonders with Orient and be so ineffective with Arsenal? Was this the pattern that accounted for Tommy Docherty's appointment to Manchester United when his previous club record was so uninspiring?

Why do the public regard the Manager as the embodiment of the club when the Secretary is the Chief Executive Officer, the Chairman the ultimate power?

Managers keep telling us that football is show business. So far as the show is concerned it is action in the goalmouth that most excites the customer, yet modern sophisticated tactics often confine play to twenty yards either side of the half-way line. So far as business is concerned, while the cry is of financial crisis, two clubs at the bottom of the First Division happily spent nearly two million pounds between them in 1972-3 in the struggle to avoid relegation. And some players with a working week of twenty hours can earn over £10,000 per annum from their football alone.

Over a million pounds of football talent transferred from Scotland to England in 1972. Is the drain of players bad for Scottish clubs, or the drain of money a drag on English development? It is accepted dogma that Scottish footballers have to raise their pace to play in the English League, yet Celtic has the best record in Europe. Is the higher standard of English League fact or fiction, Scottish Management shrewder or less sophisticated?

This book is a personal look at football Management and Managers and at their job in clubs at all levels. One Manager commented: 'Professional footballers are the most inconsiderate group you can meet. The club organises everything for them so they never cultivate the habit of thinking of others.' But when the footballer changes to Manager he changes to long hours, to the pressures of responsibility, to thinking ceaselessly about his players. Perhaps that is why so many were so considerate and helpful to me, and I have been most grateful for their assistance.

My thanks are also due to Bob Wilson, Danny Blanchflower, John Rafferty of the *Scotsman*, Ian Archer of the *Glasgow Herald*, Arthur Hopcraft, Terry O'Neill and Barry Norman for contributions from their special knowledge, to *The Observer* for allowing me time and material, and to Marguerite Rogers for typing the manuscript. I am indebted to Bryan Smith for research into Apprentices and to Don Kendan for helpful information.

The Winners and the Workers

'Free tickets, free tickets' – the cry attracts a group of frustrated Liverpool fans breasting against the rising current of crowd that swirls round Wembley's concrete stands. For the final against Arsenal the black market price of a seat has soared as high as £50 and even the cheapest is beyond their range.

Curiosity, rather than hope, channels them to the small untidy man on the grassy slope beyond 'D' block, waving his handful of printed cards like some Derby tipster. The free tickets prove to be for heaven if sin and Shankly are renounced.

'Shankly is our God' is the answering shout, prelude to a good-humoured argument, rather than the violence momentarily threatened.

This minor incident on the fringe of football's showpiece spotlights the emotive power of the Manager.

In the high dressing-rooms beside the stone corridor the players fidget with their laces or stamp their feet on the tiled floor to get the feel of their boots. Mee and Shankly talk to relax the tension, give the final instructions to key them for the vital opening minutes. At 2.48 they lead their teams up the dark tunnel into the sunlight and the shock-wave of cheers. Small men both, their sober clothes add to the impression that they are dwarfed by the players in their bright track-suits. Yet as they wave to the crowd there is no mistaking that these are the father figures embodying the hopes of their side and their supporters.

Such moments are the highlights of a Manager's career. Some will call them genius if their team win, fool if they lose, though the game may be decided by the bounce of a ball or the inspiration of a player.

For the footballer, action brings relief of anxiety. For the Manager there is only the concentrated suspense of watching.

Matt Busby found the pleasure and pain more intense as United Manager than City player. In the 1933 Cup Final Manchester City arrived too early at Wembley, the ninety-minute wait in the dressing-rooms a tense prelude to humiliating defeat by Everton. The bitter memory was happily erased next season as Fred Tilson 'plonked in two' against Portsmouth to make good a half-time promise to Frank Swift and bring City the Cup.

But the footballing moment that still rankles in his mind, overshadowing the Best affair, is McParland's charge on Wood that snatched the double from his team of all the talents. With the League won, the 1956 Final seemed formality if all his players were fit. Aston Villa surely were no match in ability or confidence for Duncan Edwards, Jackie Blanchflower, Tommy Taylor, Bobby Charlton and their peers. The relief as they took the field at full strength let him watch the opening minutes with relaxed enjoyment. Then McParland's reckless run shattered his composure and Wood's cheekbone. With the goalkeeper concussed there was only bitter resentment for him as the game slipped away from United. Adding insult to injury it was McParland whose two goals destroyed his team.

But Wembley relented in that night of emotion, of lilting happiness as the European Cup was won at last by an English team. The United side was close to decline, Busby near to handing over as Manager. This was their last chance of football's greatest prize, a game that stirred the crowd as only the Matthews' final before. Surely not even Benfica could deny these two folk heroes of football, Matt Busby and Bobby Charlton. Not at Wembley. Not against that passionate surge of shared excitement. Not after Bobby Charlton's glancing header slid so neatly into the net. But there was the unfeeling Graca hitting home the equaliser. With minutes left Eusebio galloped clear down the centre. The dream turned nightmare as Europe's most gifted marksman hit his shot low and true. Busby felt again the desolation of defeat as the ball arrowed for the net. But Stepney, yards from his goal, feet from Eusebio, stretched instinctively for the ball – and held it. It was a save unmatched even by that of Banks from Pelé, and Busby knew now that it was his night. Before the game went into extra time he pin-pointed the weakness that had lost United control. Asking for tighter marking and firmer tackling in mid-field he lifted the players with his own quiet confidence, watched with total fulfilment as Benfica were swept away in the storm of United's fervour.

Bobby Brown, Scotland's first full-time Team Manager, experienced the power of Wembley to centre the crowd's joy or frustrations on the Manager.

For Scots the game against England still stirs a deep intensity of feeling. Brown's moment of elation was the 3–2 win in 1967, his team as rampant as the lions on the wildly waving banners of the ecstatic supporters. Ramsey's World Cup side was taunted and humiliated by their showy skills. But it was not Brown's earnest tactics talk which inspired that proud display. Baxter, deaf to technical niceties, cut through the long briefing with a scornful 'They canna play nane'. Then he strode out to take delight in proving his point, the flaunting arrogance of his play firing his side. Brown was lifted by his players, the style of their football easing the national resentment that it should have been England who won the World Cup.

Four years later he was destroyed by them, their football as fumbling at his own tactical substitutions. While England coasted to victory, Wembley resounded to the deafening catcalls of 30,000 infuriated Scots. Brown was their one target, the ritual sacrifice demanded to ease their own heartache. They wanted colour, character, success. When Brown could not satisfy the craving they turned to Docherty.

But Don Revie is the one who best appreciates the sharp twists of fortune's knife. As player he has three Cup Final medals. In 1949 he steered Second Division Leicester City to Wembley, the outstanding forward in their semi-final defeat of the League leaders, Portsmouth. Yet even the losers' medal was his only by special request. For injury kept him a frustrated spectator in the stands as Wolverhampton took charge. And injury snuffed out hope when he returned with Manchester City six years later.

Milburn and Mitchell, the pride of Tyneside, decided the game in the first twenty minutes. Milburn so strong of shot, so weak in the air, headed a goal that surprised himself as much as the defenders. Then Mitchell's sleight of foot contorted right-back Meadows, broke his leg as the studs caught in the lush turf.

The following season Manchester City were again in the Final but with Revie now dropped from the side. On the very morning of the match Spurdle developed boils, and Revie was reinstated to dominate the game, destroy Birmingham. All this he accepted with composure. As Manager he was more vulnerable. It was late in extra time before St John's agile header snatched the Cup from Leeds in 1965. Revie sat head in hands in silent bitterness as the Stadium reverberated to the joyous chants of the Liverpool fans.

Against Chelsea six years later his team played the best football of any final, on a sandy beach of a pitch, the worst ever seen at Wembley. When they took the lead six minutes from the end the game was theirs if they stayed cool. As the players exulted, Revie had a sudden sense of disaster, had to be physically restrained from dashing on to the pitch to warn them. The rest, the equalising goal, the long-drawn agony of the replay lost late in extra time, was all the more poignant for being foreseen. It was third-time-lucky for him as Manager as it had been as player. Yet even success turned sour when Arsenal were beaten in the Final. In the last move of the game Jones fell heavily over the goalkeeper to dislocate his shoulder. The celebrations too were dislocated.

There was only a day to prepare for the game with Wolverhampton that would decide the League, with authority unfeelingly insistent that the match be played on the Monday. All Leeds needed was a draw for the double on which Revie had set his heart. They lost and the players returned to the coach as disconsolate as if they had been relegated. Revie had to stand up in the front and say, 'What's the matter. We've won the Cup and finished runners-up in the Championship.' But there was no joy for him that night and it was heartache again as listless Leeds went down to Sunderland when the underdog had its day.

The Manager is seen by the followers as the central figure in the staff of any football club. Though the structures vary, this is a shrewd enough estimate. The club's destiny depends on success on the field and that is his responsibility.

When Bob Stokoe was appointed to Sunderland, attendance was averaging 12,000, and for years there had been an echoing emptiness in the Roker Park Stadium, once the focal point for Wearside. The Geordies have a special attachment to football, with the North-East the great nursery of soccer. But past traditions and present potential had ceased to have any appeal even to this breed of spectator. Success and excitement *now* was the one way to attract them back. Before Stokoe came, ten successive games had been lost. The next ten were won and within six months Sunderland against all the odds had taken the Cup, the first Second Division team to win at Wembley for forty-two years. The crowds had trebled for League games, and to see Manchester City tumbled from the Cup 53,000 came packing in. It had needed Bob Stokoe, the former Newcastle player, to come home and rediscover the old enchantment. The Chairman, the Directors, the Secretary, the staff had kept the club going, but it only came alive again when the Manager inspired a new enthusiasm, an improved technique in the players.

Ultimate authority and the final power of decision always rests with the Chairman and to a lesser degree his Board. The Manager is dependent on them for his job and for the money to achieve results. Yet there are few clubs now where the Directors interfere with selection, or with the increasingly technical problems of training and tactics. One of the past Sunderland heroes, Len Shackleton, known on Tyneside as the clown prince of soccer, once recorded his view of football club Boards. In his book there was a chapter heading 'A Director's Knowledge of Football' followed by a blank page. That was in the fifties when interference by the Directors in team affairs was common in English and Scottish clubs and was much resented by the players. Now the Manager is given his head and answers with it if the results are not good enough.

But his day-to-day powers are shared with others. All English League clubs except Nottingham Forest are Limited Companies and the considerable legal and administrative responsibilities are the Secretary's. For the Football Association he is the Chief Executive Officer and held responsible for the club's behaviour.

When Derby were heavily fined after Ian Storey Moore had been paraded before the crowd at the Baseball Ground without his transfer being complete, the blame was for Secretaries rather than Brian Clough. The one should not have permitted the premature display without the third signature required on the transfer form; the other might have realised that the deal had been allowed to go so far that Nottingham Forest's consent was being taken for granted.

Soccer has made its own financial problems in the struggle for glory. With transfer fees soaring over £200,000 and top wages over £10,000 per annum only the box office of the successful clubs can sustain the extravagant show-business air. The others have to pay more than they can afford to stay in the race as the First Division inexorably puts up the wages and costs of the smaller clubs. Survival on gates alone becomes increasingly difficult and the Commercial Manager, raising money by other ventures, has a growing importance.

The new structure can best be seen by looking at the Third Division club with aspiration to reach the First and with the monetary backing of a wealthy Chairman. Bournemouth's staffing shows the emphasis on money-raising schemes and on developing the club as an entertainment centre for the town, rather than a place where football is played on Saturdays. John Bond, the Manager, is first among four equals, but the club's plans can only develop if he can push the playing staff to achieve the promotion that so narrowly eludes them.

In some clubs an experienced Secretary is promoted to overall control. Arsenal are the most often cited and studied for the strength of their organisation. A fundamental feature has been the balance between Manager and Secretary. Bob Wall and Bertie Mee were powerful enough personalities to keep their independence, cooperative enough to run their departments in harmony. The playing staff and the football is Bertie Mee's concern, finance and administration the Secretary's. Transfers best show the relationship. Bertie Mee decides the players he wants to retain or buy, the Secretary confirms whether the money is available and the timing appropriate. The transfer of Sammels to Leicester for £100,000 was delayed some weeks for accounting and tax advantages.

Bob Wall's experience with Arsenal goes back to the Chapman regime in the thirties, and for his final years he has been promoted General Manager. That is pleasant recognition of his achievements and a sensible use of his knowledge for the shaping of policy.

A.F.C. BOURNEMOUTH STAFF TREE (NOVEMBER 1972)

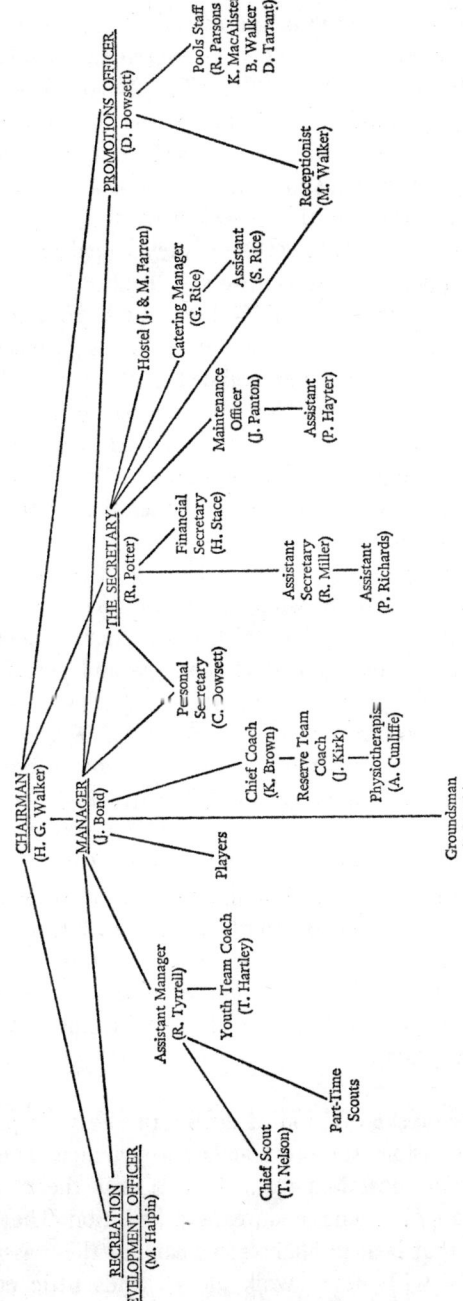

N.B. (1) The Chairman has 4 main people responsible to him – John Bond, Ray Potter, Mike Halpin, Dickie Dowsett.
(2) The Manager has overall responsibility for Ray Potter, Mike Halpin and Dickie Dowsett in day-to-day affairs at Dean Court.
(3) In matters concerning the new development Mike Halpin is answerable directly to the Chairman as is Dickie Dowsett on matters concerning the Pools.
(4) Mr Pardy, Vice-Chairman, is responsible to the Chairman for the financial control of the Club.

Another General Manager with a secretarial background is Eric Taylor at Sheffield Wednesday, who has covered the whole range of duties in his forty years with the club. Although he never played football to any standard, he has at periods in the past been fully responsible for the team, for its selection, training and tactics. It was so when the side contained Derek Dooley, that most exciting of centre-forwards with the red hair, the fiery courage and the instinct for goals. 'Thunderboots' they called him, and as his tally mounted opponents were apt to say, 'Right, Dooley, you'll get no bloody goals today, lad, or I'll break both your legs.' He went on scoring, but when one leg was broken it was pure accident, as he chased a through pass and collided with the goalkeeper. Gangrene set in and the leg was lost, but never the addiction to football. Now he is in full charge of the play as Team Manager. A reflective pipe-smoking man, the only reminder of the eager energy of his youth is his communicated belief that football is a game of adventure and attack.

A happy partnership is the Coventry pairing of Joe Mercer as General Manager and Gordon Milne as Team Manager. Mercer, that kindly avuncular man replete with experience, concentrates on policy, on the shape of team and club. Age and past football injuries deny him any opportunity of being a track-suit Manager in the modern idiom. So the fresh-faced Gordon Milne, whose playing days are only a season or two behind him, is given more than the usual responsibilities for determining the training, developing the tactics.

There was the same relationship at Manchester City as Mercer and Allison revived the club, combining an attractive style of play with sustained success. Their strength as a pair was the more apparent after Allison challenged for and won the whole job. There was no cool judgement now to temper his driving determination to achieve the impossible, and his close involvement with the players became a handicap.

Whatever the titles or the division of duties, the heaviest pressure is on the man responsible for the team's performance. The game has few winners. For most Managers there is only the reality of hard graft, the disappointment of unrealised ambition. The 'glory, glory, Hallelujahs' that beat in Nicholson's ears, or the reassurance to Shankly that he will 'never walk alone', finds little echo in

THE WINNERS AND THE WORKERS 19

lesser Boardrooms. Bob Stokoe, at forty-two could relish the sudden magical transformation at Sunderland after the long apprenticeship which took him painstakingly forward from Bury to Charlton, to Rochdale, to Carlisle, to Blackpool. But that is the exception. Take a look at the course of a more normal season through the eyes of Ron Tindall at Portsmouth, another club with some of Sunderland's traditions and Second Division problems.

1971/2 was Tindall's first as Manager. He is a thoughtful, serious man without any of the spontaneity of the extrovert games player. The reserve gives an impression of diffidence, but masks a quiet confidence in his own judgement. County cricketer with Surrey, First Division footballer with Chelsea, he was reliable and industrious without the brilliance that catches the headlines. When he played for Portsmouth George Smith, the Manager, noted his leadership qualities, and trained him for two years before putting him in charge of the team.

Tindall was one of the group of sixteen who took part in the Football Association's first course for Managers and potential Managers. This was run at Loughborough for two weeks each year, spread over three summers. As his special project Tindall kept a detailed record of his objectives and his degree of success in achieving his targets.

The Manager's job at Portsmouth is as wide-ranging as at any club, more general in scope than most. His five objectives for 1971/2 illustrate this well enough: to improve performance of the present team; to organise and control Waterlooville F.C. and develop them as a nursery club for Portsmouth; to develop a youth policy through Waterlooville F.C.; to make Portsmouth a more integral part of the community so that the town look on it as 'our' club; to improve the financial position and clear the way for future development.

The long-term objective was the standard one of getting into the First Division and staying there. For Portsmouth the past made this a necessary aim, an unlikely achievement.

The town still cherishes the days when the Pompey chimes echoed round Wembley's twin towers as the Cup passed to their keeping for six long years of war. Pride in the team reached its surging climax as they took the League championship in the successive seasons of 1949 and 1950. Against the champagne sparkle of those years, Second Division football at Fratton Park is as insipid as distilled water. But the club's slide at the end of the fifties was due in part to financial problems and that hangover is still with them. To balance the accounts the reserve and youth teams were eliminated, promising players dispersed, transfer money sparingly given. To achieve his targets Tindall was limited to a staff of only nineteen players, hampered by a deficit of £28,000 and a tight limit on transfers. To help him he had an active Board, a development officer, Alan Sefton, trained at Loughborough University with a degree in recreational management, and Jimmy Dickinson.

Dickinson has an unusual background for a Secretary. Most have qualifications in Law or Accountancy, or have learnt the job by long service in the club's office. Dickinson is one of the very few to convert from career football. And what a fine attacking wing-half he was. His 746 appearances is a League record, his 48 International Caps for England a Portsmouth record.

Jimmy started playing in the war under Jack Tinn, famous for his white spats. This lucky symbol flaunted on match days was about all the average player saw of his Manager. Jimmy Dickinson still recalls the awe and the remoteness – the God in the office whom players approached at their peril.

The style of Management then was still authoritarian as it had remained throughout the inter-war period. That was the atmosphere when Dickinson started, with the Manager a distant figure down the long chain of command, the young player having to keep his distance and his station even with the old hands in the team. No consensus football then!

As always, objectives are easier put on paper than achieved. Waterlooville, on the outskirts of the town and in the lower reaches of the Southern League reserve section, was to be the catalyst for the inexpensive revival of a Portsmouth reserve and nursery side.

Pat Wright, a blunt and boisterous Black Countryman, was appointed Manager to their team, coach to Portsmouth. Under his guidance Waterlooville went swiftly to the top and won promotion to the Premier League. There the project foundered, for Southern League rules permit only a club's first team to take part and Waterlooville was not acceptable if linked to Portsmouth. In the wrangle over rules much work ran to waste – an aid to solvency was lost.

The redevelopment of a youth policy was no easier. Coaching sessions at Waterlooville attracted large numbers, but only twelve of the permitted thirty schoolboys were signed on Associate forms. Standards were lower than expected, with lack of enthusiasm for learning basic skills. Whereas once all schoolboys wanted to be a Matthews or a Finney, now they all saw themselves as a midfield player.

The new approach to the search for young talent had a fitful start – but at least it had achieved some small gains.

The development of schoolboy football depends on the quality of coaching from teachers. To help this Tindall organised a comprehensive programme of courses for them with seminars and practical sessions, hand-outs, a match analysis of tactics in some home games. Yet only in the special coaching for representative schoolboy sides was there full attendance and cooperation. Tindall, keen to meet the teachers' expressed needs, was disappointed at the relative failure, accepted that the revival of interest would be slow.

There was more enthusiasm from the drive to integrate the club into the community. Five hundred boys came to the holiday football arranged by Alan Sefton, while more than one hundred school teams entered a penalty-kick competition that intrigued the spectators before home matches.

The community project linked in with the target of improved finances. The gymnasium area was converted into a floodlit training ground and hired out to local clubs – the profit £500.

The Pompey hotel at the stadium entrance was taken over to be converted into a club for members on match days, a centre of entertainment for those using the training facilities.

The constant review of fund-raising schemes was no more important than the cost cutting. A thousand pounds was saved by travelling to matches by coach instead of train, a similar sum by restricting the party to travel to fourteen and by cleaning the ground by their own staff, rather than contractors'.

All had their importance, all took their toll of the Manager's time. But inevitably the season would be judged against one overriding objective – improved performance of the team.

There were five special targets: sixteen points for the first fourteen games to give a basis of confidence; a major improvement on last season's dismal home record; a higher level of consistency;

the playing of the transfer market to maintain existing standards, but make money available for further development. The reviews after each fourteen-game period plotted the graph of hope and disappointment. The start was impressive enough, only one point short of the target. The weaknesses identified were worked on in training, the main concerns too many goals conceded (twenty-one) and poor performance away from home.

The one home defeat by Blackpool had taught a lesson that was emphasised to the players – the need to keep playing methodically and not risk all-out attack even when frustrated by defensive play.

There was no urgency yet to revise contracts, or play the transfer market. The one pressing requirement identified was another goalkeeper, but the search was maintained for any possible improvement.

First Division players were likely to be beyond Portsmouth's purse, so the scouting staff's and Tindall's own searches were directed to lower Divisions and reserve teams. Exchange deals were the main aim, with four of his players – Pointer, Storrie, Travers and Standen – judged surplus to requirement. But it became clear that there was a shortage of players available for transfer in the required price and wage range.

Tindall also hoped to cut costs and keep reserve players in form by loaning them out to other clubs. This, however, was not an acceptable arrangement to most of them and no progress was made. Now the financial position improved and the new target was to widen the search into Scotland and to concentrate on making the best deal even if it involved losing a player in part-exchange and reducing Tindall's limited numbers.

Bromley, still troubled with a knee injury, was transferred to Brighton, Wilson bought from Blackpool to strengthen the midfield.

A New Year trip to Scotland had been abortive despite an offer of £8,000 for centre-forward McCormack of Dumbarton. Scottish clubs, much milked by English football, offer no cheap bargains now and the price was put too high. McDonald, Clydebank's goalkeeper, also impressed Tindall, but again the fee was out of his range. Since the overt search for a substitute, Milkins' performances in goal had improved enough for the effort to be switched to finding a young 'keeper to train for the future.

A list of players for transfer was prepared for circulation to clubs – Storrie, Standen, Travers and Trebilcock available without fee, Munks for £10,000.

The early success bred only complacency, not consistency. Two-thirds of the way through the season there was no chance of challenging for promotion, hopes confined to a comfortable place in the middle of the table.

With nine matches left they had already reached thirty-two points, a not unpromising position for an improved record. Instead they slid to the edge of relegation before a draw at Charlton and a win at Blackpool gave security. Amid these worries Tindall had to concentrate on building for next season. It seemed likely that the bonus system had proved a hindrance rather than a help. The main element was a £500 payment if thirty-five points were achieved and relegation avoided. At the start of the season this was too remote an incentive to be effective. At thirty-two points it was too easy to be stimulating. Then, as the games slipped away pointless, the large amount of money hanging on one win was an unnerving backdrop for some players. So the new wage system became a priority for the future. The £500 bonus and the crowd bonus were both abandoned. In their place for next season came a pounds-per-point incentive starting at £5 for a home point, £10 for an away point. This was stepped up after each ten points and applied only to those playing in the match. In addition there was a consistency bonus related to five-match periods and available to all the players on the staff.

The new contracts offered were based on a summer wage, winter wage, and appearance money, the basic amounts increased to allow for the introduction of First Division players within the structure.

The last is a growing problem for lower Divisions. All players in a First Division 'squad' get the high basic pay and even those not playing regularly have a secure First Division income. The difference between average First Division pay and what a Second Division club can offer may be £1,500 or more.

Tindall had played the transfer market to stiffen the wilting defence that had conceded sixty-eight goals. Alan Stephenson was bought from West Ham for £32,000, less than the asking price, but all Tindall could afford and ultimately satisfactory to Ron Greenwood. Looking at his playing staff Tindall now had:

Goalkeeper: Milkins
Back Defenders: Smith, Hand, Collins, Stephenson
Mid-field: Piper, Wilson, Ley, McCann
Forwards: Lewis, Jennings, Hiron, Reynolds

Blant, Youlden and Munks were also retained, but available for transfer. Ray Pointer had been taken on the staff as Coach, but his registration maintained for emergency.

The strengthening now needed was a goalkeeper, another back-defender and a goal-scoring forward. For the first two Tindall was in touch with Arsenal for the current Youth International goalkeeper Graham Horn and abortively discussing terms with Chelsea for Marvin Hinton's transfer.

The final player on the scouting staff's list was being narrowed down to Price of Peterborough, scorer of twenty-eight goals in the current season. McCormack of Dumbarton had now been eliminated on standard as well as price and Tracy of Charlton judged too dear at £30,000, the figure that Price ultimately cost.

Like so many Managers, Tindall could look back in disappointment, forward in optimism. There had been some progress, some high-quality performances. Portsmouth had reached the fifth round of the Cup, only to lose heavily at home to Birmingham when without three key players.

If the proposed deals went through, if Stephenson strengthened the defence, if the players were more consistent – then there would be an autumn of hope, a spring of fulfilment. And Managers must always believe that the ifs of success are almost accomplished fact, the ifs of failure remote fancy.

His final thoughts were being shared in most clubs in all the Divisions.

We must demand more dedication to their profession from the players. The theme for next season will be work, work and still more work. Those who cannot respond must be replaced, whether among staff or players. The will to win, to succeed in everything they do must be constantly drummed in. There can be no room for complacency or satisfaction of near failure such as our bonus scheme inspired. A new training schedule involving heavy weights is being evolved and the players will be called on to drive themselves to the utmost. A series of personal targets for players will be prepared and laid on the line when they report for pre-season training.

But as everyone strives for excellence the standards of performance rise together. The massive improvement hoped for left Portsmouth standing still last season – not washed back into the Third Division, but barely afloat in the Second.

The Managerial Revolution

It is easy enough to judge a great player, more difficult to define a great Manager. A handful can claim the title on a personality that has deeply affected the game, like Walter Winterbottom who organised the country's coaching scheme, or Jimmy Hill whose sharp intelligence and showman's flair has altered the image of football. As Chairman of the Professional Footballers Association, Hill was the flamboyant figure spotlighted at the centre of the successful fight to end the maximum wage. As Coventry's Manager he brought his team from the depths of the Third Division to a foothold in the First, and with his Chairman, Derrick Robins, introduced the idea of Coventry City as a centre of entertainment, not just a football club. As head of I.T.V's sport he used the action replay as the basis for educating the public in the tactics of the game and for an impartial examination of refereeing which no players or Managers can make. Winterbottom and Hill are exceptions to the rule that you judge Managers on just two counts. How good is their team's playing record over a span of years? Have they made any tactical change that has had a lasting effect on football? Many earn the title for the playing record of their teams. Matt Busby once seemed to have discovered the secret of perpetual success for Manchester United. Don Revie, Bill Shankly and Jock Stein have brought sustained success to Leeds, Liverpool and Celtic. Bill Nicholson and Bertie Mee have both achieved the elusive double.

There are only two to qualify under both headings – Herbert Chapman and Sir Alf Ramsey. That pairing suggests that there is no standard pattern for success. The one courted publicity, the other shuns it. The one was an indifferent player, the other won thirty-two International Caps. Chapman's ingenuity ranged over all the affairs of the club. Ramsey's sharp concentration has been on the game and the players.

We think of football clubs now in terms of the Manager, his personality the talisman of their success. That prominence has been a slow growth and owes much to a few.

The Executive of the Football Association and the Football League shows where the power traditionally lies within clubs. There are many club Chairmen but, Busby apart, no ex-Player/Managers represented on either body. There are many former and present club Secretaries, no former Professional players. Both the League and the F.A. address all the correspondence to the Secretary, never to the Manager.

In the early years the clubs were run by Chairmen like H. H. Morley of Blackburn, famous more for his velvet smoking jackets and his Churchillian cigars than any tactical originality in his echoing shouts of 'play FOOTBALL, Rovers'.

There was Major Sudell, whose determination to buy the best for Preston ended in the legalisation of professionalism. His shrewd judgement of a player produced the Preston Invincibles, who won the Cup without conceding a goal and the League without losing a match.

As often as not the captain was in practice nearest to the modern track-suit Manager. He would work out the formation and the tactics of his team, or organise those training walks which they took in Sunday best with watch-chains in waistcoats and bowlers on heads.

From this grew the idea of the Player/Manager who would run the team and advise on the acquisition of players.

Typical of the shrewder of these before the First World War was J. T. Robertson of Chelsea. Gibson and Pickford comment in their history of the game,

> To speak of the team is primarily to record the characteristic business aptitude of Manager J. T. Robertson. Chelsea are perhaps the 'cheapest' team playing League football today. That is to

say the expenditure of £500 sufficed to bring together a side which includes four Internationals. To think of it, a £50 note obtained the signature of a personality like 'Captain' William Foulke. A football wonder is Willie, the most talked-of player in the world. A Leviathan (22½ stone) with the agility of a bantam. The cheeriest of companions and in repartee is as difficult to score against as when between the posts.

Of Player/Manager Robertson himself they wrote:

> One of the finest half-backs that ever kicked a ball, a football strategist of the reasoning Scottish school. With Glasgow Rangers 'Jock' scored fifteen goals from the left-half position.
> He has also played for Greenock Morton, Southampton and Everton and was much sought after by Plymouth Argyle when the 'Pilgrims' started to become famous. True to his club, Jock refused an inducement which would have made a financier blush.

It was another Scot, John Cameron, who made Tottenham a force in the Southern League and helped them to win the F.A. Cup in 1901. He was even more the player of all work, Secretary/Manager as well as inside-right. Oddly, his duties did not include captaincy on the field, and it was symptomatic of the Manager's lack of status that there he should take his instructions from the Welsh International J. L. Jones.

However, Tottenham recorded that,

> He had much to do with building up the Spurs, many of the players having been obtained by him. Formerly associated with Scotland's world-famous Queen's Park, for whom his consistently fine performance gained him much renown, he is just as happy in his present dual position in shaping and guiding a professional side. When he crossed the border he went to Everton, for whom he played as an amateur. Tottenham in securing him obtained a fine businessman and a player of much subtlety.

He may well have been influenced to organise more intensive training than most Managers of that day by his Everton experience. Their pre-season practices were so unusual that they drew thousands of spectators and the Everton team was noted for the precision of its play. But as late as 1914 a leading authority was commenting,

> It is certainly true that our professionals evince no great anxiety to learn anything of the theory of the sport and in most teams there is no evidence of preconceived tactics or thought-out manœuvres.

Management was concerned mainly with the buying of players, with the finances and administration of the club. The great Newcastle team, the dominant force in football at the start of the century, was in complete control of its fortunes on the field. 1904 was the season of success and at the start the Chairman told the captain and two senior players to lock themselves in a room and select the best team. Soon they were working out the tactics as well, with Veitch, McWilliam and McCracken passing a train journey by devising the off-side trap which they exploited with such deadly and deadening effect.

In these days of highly developed coaching schemes and Management-planned tactics the initiative of players can sometimes be crushed. Those who feel the trend has stifled creative expression can cite Newcastle as the example of what the players can achieve on their own. But while they dominated the game and the headlines, the man who was to make a greater impact on its history was playing in obscure matches for Tottenham reserves. In football's early years the team captains had not been important enough to record in the papers. Until the First War Managers had been of little more account. Now Herbert Chapman was about to change their status and radically alter the structure of football clubs.

Significantly, he was no great player himself, more noted for the peculiar yellow colour of his boots than for his shooting. Yet this was to be his strength. For he based all his thinking on what he himself would have liked to be able to do, how he would have wished to be treated. Lacking football talent, he was the quicker to spot and nurture it in others.

In the long list of successful Managers so many are players of the highest class, like Cullis, Busby, Shankly, Revie, Nicholson or Turnbull. Chapman established the different tradition at Arsenal, where the club thrives most under those whose footballing ability is the least. Allison, Whittaker, Mee maintained the momentum, not Jack Crayston, George Swindin or Billy Wright. All had one characteristic in common with Chapman – the ability to motivate players, the man management that is the first essential in football as in any other business.

Good football is so much a matter of belief in achieving the improbable, and Chapman had this trick of confidence. When he moved Cliff Bastin to the left wing the young player came to see him, anxiously concerned about playing out of position. By the time he left the office he was happily convinced that he could become the best winger in the country. And he did.

On the other wing was Joe Hulme, England cricketer as well as football International, a man of great standing in the game. When out of form he asked for a rest. Instead Chapman made him play centre-half in the reserves. He reasoned that in that position Hulme would be at the heart of the action and that at that level he would regain confidence in his own skill. The cure worked.

Chapman is still unequalled as an all-rounder. Tactical theoriser, shrewd businessman, motivator of players, builder of teams, he had the golden touch through the whole range of a Manager's duties.

His entry was comment enough on the position of the Manager at the start of the century. He had played his last game against Brighton. As he dressed he looked back on the two goals he had just scored, forward to a new career as a Mining Engineer. One of the team, Walter Bull, interrupted the reverie, asking Chapman to take over his recent appointment as Player/Manager to Northampton Town since Bull had decided to have another season with Tottenham.

The switch, casually fixed in the dressing-room, was accepted without argument. It was fortunate for Northampton that they did not object. Within two seasons Chapman had lifted them from the bottom of the Southern League to champions. That was to set the pattern, the subsequent achievement confirming a unique talent.

In 1912 he moved on to Leeds City, struggling at the bottom of the Second Division. This was his one setback. The playing performance quickly improved, but the club closed down after only eight matches of the first post-war season, convicted by the Football Association of making illegal payments. Chapman is said to have burnt the books, but his reputation was unsinged.

Huddersfield, in financial difficulties themselves, thought of leaving a town dedicated to rugby and starting afresh in Leeds. But instead of City's ground, they took over Chapman, and that was a better bargain. Over four seasons Huddersfield won the Cup, then the League twice.

In Chapman's eight years with Arsenal, who had never before won a major honour, there were only two seasons in which they were not either winners or runners-up in League or Cup. The reserves won the London Combination Championship six times in succession.

Much can be attributed to chance at football, but this record needed other explanation. From the start Chapman gave new importance to the Manager, insisting on selecting all his own teams. At the time, as he noted of other clubs, 'Directors join in picking the team and no one seems bold enough to suggest that the system is out-of-date and should be scrapped'.

In handling his players Chapman was a martinet, convinced that disciplined effort and attention to detail was the way to win. 'I will never tolerate slackness. If it enters a team there can be no success that is worthwhile. That, at any rate, is my view, and frankly I cannot be bothered with any man unless he is prepared to give his whole mind to the job.'

But he was the first Manager to realise what could be achieved by players devoting their whole minds to the study of football and by encouraging them to express themselves. He had a table marked out with a diagram of the field to help the more reserved to express ideas they were too reticent to put into words. That is still standard equipment for any club.

From his own experience he was aware that players spent more time discussing snooker or bridge than soccer. So he developed the pre-match tactics talk in which they all joined. Frankness was encouraged, for he was in sympathy with Alex James' comment that the more the old Celtic teams argued with each other on the field the harder they played.

The discussions in a Leeds hotel before home matches were a simple beginning. With Arsenal these were refined until the players contributed a detailed analysis of opponents' style and helped to evolve the plan.

Years later a flamboyant and successful Manager, Helenio Herrera, used to urge his European teams with cries of 'Think of the match, think of next week's match!' as they drove wearily back from away games. It was a technique Chapman exploited long before.

From such pooling of ideas came Chapman's main tactical innovation, the 'stopper' centre-half, still doubly important in the seventies.

The changed off-side law, requiring two not three between attacker and goal, had let centre-forwards run riot as the legislators intended. Chapman was not amused when Newcastle put seven past his goalkeeper. The response of holding the centre-half back to block the middle was not particularly complex. But to make it effective Chapman exercised his other skill, his ability to select men for the job. Jack Butler could not meet his requirement so the burly Roberts was found at Oswestry. He was weak in kicking, particularly with his left foot, but a powerful header of the ball. Chapman told the young man, 'win everything in the air and you will stay in the side'. He did just that.

In one other aspect Chapman was before his time. He recognised that professional football was an entertainment as well as a sport. 'Can it be believed that the Arsenal, in order to produce results, would cultivate a style that did not appeal to the crowd?' he once asked, and answered himself, 'The old idea that a club may sit back and wait for the crowds to come should have died long ago. In these days you have to fetch them by making an irresistible appeal, and in this respect, at least, we do not differ greatly from other entertainment promoters.' Forty years on the old idea is far from dead, despite those like Jimmy Hill or Brian Clough who have understood the importance of entertaining as well as winning.

Chapman's most important legacy was to establish the Manager as the man who mattered in a football club. If the players were to call him 'boss' he must be seen to be so. There was never any doubt of this with Chapman. George Hardy, the Chief Trainer, was sacked in public in the middle of a Cup replay for daring to shout to a player to move up-field, unwittingly interfering with a tactical plan.

Hardy was in the 'magic sponge' tradition of trainers without medical knowledge, who relied on the mystic healing properties of cold water. The players used to comment that if you weren't injured when they ran on the field you were by the time they left. But the Trainer's main role was as companion and confidant of players, and Hardy was also a close friend of Chapman, another

Yorkshireman from Byker-on-Tyne. He was an old servant of the club, but there was no hesitation in the dismissal and no reprieve.

Chapman could be as ruthless with his footballers. When Arsenal in all their fame were humiliated in the Cup by Walsall, that rugged game was finally settled by a penalty. Tommy Black gave it away feuding with a forward. He was sent home by Chapman, ordered to keep away from the ground, and transferred to Plymouth.

This hardness, however masked, is an essential for success in managing so competitive a game. Billy Wright, himself the model of a disciplined club player, was the most easy-going of Chapman's successors at Highbury and the least effective. He was relieved when his resignation was finally requested after a home gate for a May game against Leeds of 4,554. Terry Neill, Player/Manager of Ireland and Hull City, was one who saw the effect of such tolerance: 'We all liked him, but you cannot help taking advantage. Footballers are tough competitors by nature. They are trained to walk over people. If he lets them they'll make a doormat of the Manager as well as of opponents.'

Before Chapman's day the Manager was rarely the dominant figure in the club, his authority with the players all too easily undermined by the Directors or the Secretary in control of the selection and the pay. Thereafter any Manager of character could ensure the proper relationship. This should be like that of the Headmaster and his Board of Governors, with no one in the school in any doubt of who has charge of day-to-day affairs.

The dapper, smiling Herbert Chapman, with his polished phrases, his shrewd publicity, made the point by example. But there was more forceful advice from Harry Storer, the blunt Manager of Coventry, Birmingham, and Derby County whose career spanned twenty-five seasons. He was one who looked for 'brave' players and was known to march a faint-hearted member of his team back on to the pitch to 'look at the hole you've been hiding in all afternoon'. He was as spirited himself in his dealings with his Directors, expressing his philosophy to his colleagues, 'Don't try to keep your job by taking advice on football from the Chairman. Do what he says and you will lose it soon enough on your results.'

By bringing in Tom Whittaker to replace Hardy as Trainer Chapman made yet another change in the management of the game, paving the way for the more scientific treatment of injury.

Perhaps this was a chance development, perhaps unusual foresight. Whittaker's appointment seemed typical reward for a player to whom the club felt some obligation. On an F.A. tour he had broken a leg and Chapman fought to increase the compensation and put him as Assistant to Hardy. Whittaker was a Marine Engineer, able to master quickly the growing range of treatment apparatus installed at Highbury. He had also a natural skill in diagnosis and in handling people. The one made him forerunner of today's qualified physiotherapists, who hasten the walking wounded back into battle. The other won him the Manager's chair and the wide recognition that this quality is central to the job.

Whittaker's belief in shared communication and in frankness with his players was taken to embarrassing extremes. Anything discussed with one should not be kept secret from the others. Bob Wall, the present General Manager, still keeps the office door open. He recalls with amusement the days when Whittaker would converse with one player inside while the others sat outside in the corridor listening.

Too readily accepting an outdated belief that if you wanted a footballer you only had to call down the nearest mineshaft, Whittaker paid little attention to the youth policy. The fifteen lean years that followed his own seasons of plenty can in part be traced to that lack. For the Managers who were shaping the football from the late thirties to the sixties – Buckley, Cullis and Busby – all set out to attract the young.

Major Frank Buckley was a burly, aggressive centre-half, good enough to win a cap against Ireland when with Derby County. His career as Manager started quietly with Norwich and Blackpool, flared into headlines with Wolverhampton. These concentrated on the colourful inessentials, the trivia attracting the attention to Molineux. There was the publicised 'monkey-gland' treatment that led the MP for East Leicester to ask the Minister of Health if 'his attention had been drawn to statements that gland extracts from animals are being administered to football players . . . and whether he will order an investigation into these allegations.' The injections were ordinary inoculations against colds. There was the 'therapeutic diathermy machine' and the visits to the psychologist in the search for that elusive confidence that is so important to footballers. There was the watering of the pitches before home games to take full advantage of his players' stamina, to build the tradition that Wolves revelled in heavy going like mud-fixated hippos. But these were camouflage for the main thrust, the seek-and-develop operation with the young.

Buckley had the same policy then as Burnley today, his large nursery providing a flow of players for the team and money from transfers. When he took over, the overdraft was £115,000. He made £300,000 for the club from the sale of players alone.

Strength through youth was his philosophy. Jimmy Mullen was played in a Cup semi-final, Alan Steen and Ray Goddard in First Division matches, when only sixteen.

Bryn Jones was the most telling example of his ability to detect and mature talent, then make the maximum profit from it. Buckley saw something of the qualities of Alex James in this quiet Welsh boy who was with Aberaman when he watched him. Southend and Glenavon had already rejected Jones, seeing only the frailness, the lack of pace. Buckley saw only his mastery of the telling reverse pass, his ability to control the game without haste.

In Jones' five years at Molineux he developed into the best inside-forward of his day and was sold to Arsenal for a record £14,000. Buckley, so good at publicising the team, the town and himself, never troubled to keep the supporters in sympathy with his methods. This was his one failing as Manager of a club, the one vital communication he ignored. As often before the unexplained sale of a popular performer was resented, the need to keep making openings for the youngsters pressing behind unappreciated. Yet Buckley always had his replacement ready. This time it was Dorset whose enthusiasm helped Wolves come close to the 'double' the following season.

Billy Wright, England's most-capped player, and John Charles, who towered over Welsh football, were both brought on by Buckley. Both were reported on as only a 'slip of a boy' when he became interested in them. Wright, nearly dispensed with as too small, remained short and wiry. His battles at centre-half against John Charles, fourteen stone and six foot two, provided one of the game's most entertaining duels, enthusiastic terrier squaring up to placid bulldog.

It was when Buckley had finally moved on to Leeds United that his Scout, Alf Pickard, sent him the young Charles. In his handling of him Buckley anticipated the theme of modern football, the need for a versatile all-rounder. It was the Major's coaching theory that every player should be equally competent with either foot, ready to play in any position, a novel outlook at the time. Since Charles had been playing regularly at left-half he found himself put down as right-back for his first practice game with Leeds.

For Buckley, Charles was his 'greatest find' and was to become the best expression of his method. Charles was given his chance when seventeen, careful induction substituted for the shocks of training. He was brought in for a game without tension away from home in the season's final match against Blackburn Rovers. This gave him the opportunity to establish himself and gain confidence far from the critical eyes of the home crowd. Buckley, like Matt Busby after him, took as much thought over the launching of his youngsters as over their discovery.

Stan Cullis was another example of how quickly he could mature them. Cullis was in the team at seventeen, captain at nineteen. He had already experienced the iron backing to Buckley's velvet touch. After his first League game he was returned to weeding the ground and cleaning the boots. At the end of the season his summer wage was kept at £2 10s – ten shillings less than Cullis thought he should have. The two were nicely matched in determination, Cullis prepared to leave if he did not get his rights. He had his way and his £3 a week. In many other ways he was to go one better than Buckley.

Cullis was to be totally absorbed in the game as player and as Manager, and as both he is a colourful part of its history.

He was a centre-half imbued with the spirit of attack, neat in his control, bristling with aggression, captain of England at twenty-two.

A weakness in his forehead forced him to give up the game early, the victim of bouts of concussion from heading a heavy ball. The day he announced his retirement Wolves had only to win at home to take the League Championship. But in the tense finish to the 1947 season it was Liverpool who won the match and the title.

Cullis was kept on as Assistant Manager to Ted Vizard, soon taking over from him and imposing his own style on the club. Throughout the fifties it was Cullis and Busby, Wolves and Manchester United who dominated our football. The period was neatly spanned by Wolverhampton's Cup victories in 1949 and 1960. In between they won the League thrice, were runners-up thrice, and scored more than a hundred goals in four successive seasons.

Cullis drove them on with relentless impassioned determination. To be near him at a match was to experience a total involvement, the torrent of words a meaningless chant to ease his tension.

Sitting in front of him once as Wolves overwhelmed Luton in an away Cup-tie was a painful experience as he kicked and tackled his way through the ninety minutes, living every second with his players. Broadbent, the delicate gifted ball-player he had knitted so carefully into a team dedicated to power, was abused for a yellow streak as wide as the pavement. When a Director praised a raking pass to the wing Cullis whipped round on him, 'Good pass? You cannot give a good pass to ruddy Deeley. You want to keep the ball away from a useless player like him.' The Director should have been on safe ground for he was praising the essence of the Cullis style – long passes and little wingers.

Buckley had built the organisation, Cullis refined the tactics. His method suited his temperament, his impatience always to be at his opponent's throat. Mid-field there was to be power with the big broad-shouldered men, Flowers, Clamp and Slater, driving upfield. But the ball was to be moved far and fast down the centre or wide to the touchline.

Hancocks and Deeley were typical of the wingers so important in the Cullis plan. Both were diminutive men, clever dribblers, accurate in their crossing and with a nose for goals. Hancocks, tripping over the field in his tiny size $5\frac{1}{2}$ boots, was the most powerful shot of his day, lancing the ball in from thirty yards or more. He was also an infallible taker of what he always mispronounced as 'pelalties'.

There was another facet to the Wolves play. They were the apostles of the modern gospel of work-rate and constant pressure. Whoever lost the ball fought to get it back. Opposing defenders were put under instant challenge. Indeed the ball was sometimes played to them deliberately, with one forward waiting to tackle, another hovering to shoot if it ran loose.

Fifteen years of achievement was no protection for Cullis when the authoritarian approach, the power play, no longer took the First Division by storm.

No club can sustain success indefinitely, but the greater a Manager's achievements the more is expected of him. Cullis, a hard judge of others, was just as critical of himself. As Wolves slipped down the table he had no complaint when he was dismissed in September 1964. It rankled only that there was no word of appreciation for his thirty years' service at Molineux. There is no sentiment in football Management; success is the only loyalty.

Cullis, with his balding head, his hat with the droopy brim, his thin reedy voice in strange contrast to the belligerent face, had been the most explosive and exciting Manager of his time. The two who challenged him for results were his opposites in manner – quiet, courteous, attracting confidence.

Arthur Rowe had only three successive seasons of impressive performance when Spurs won the Second Division Championship, then the League title and were runners-up the following year. Yet he has a special place in the history of Management, for his ideas have flowed on as smoothly as the Spurs play. So many like Vic Buckingham, Billy Nicholson or Alf Ramsey have drawn on his philsopy, and the style Catterick favoured at Everton echoes his principles.

Football tactics can be made to sound banally simple or confusingly complex. Rowe opted always for a simplicity that players could understand, but a subtlety of application that might confuse opponents. *Push and run; make it simple make it quick* were the catch-phrases to describe his method.

It was the work-study approach to which most modern styles have some affinity. Rowe takes Billy Bremner of Leeds as the example of a man who plays it to perfection. 'When he makes an easy pass he has his hands flung wide, a theatrical intensity. The crowd think he is posturing, call him "big head". In fact, by his balance and his concentration he is ensuring absolute accuracy when so many others are too casual over the undemanding.'

Rowe is not one to claim any credit for himself, ascribing his ideas to the influence of the Tottenham Manager of his playing days, Peter McWilliam. McWilliam had been a member of the great Newcastle team, an expert with Veitch and Lowe in the short-passing triangular game of the period. He had started Rowe thinking with a phrase that caught his imagination: 'Football is a simple game in which positional play is everything.' The movement of the men without the ball was as vital as that of the man in possession.

But Rowe's system built up from the study of one goal Tottenham scored in the last minute of a match at Bradford. After the dash for the train they were still enthusing over this decisive thrust, seven passes without challenge and the ball swept from their goal-line to Bradford's net. 'Let's take it back and see what happened,' said Rowe. It had started with a quick interchange between right-back and right-half which had stranded two Bradford players in the Tottenham area. Thereafter they had always outnumbered the challengers and had only to be quick and accurate to score. From that developed the practice of swift counterpunch, of starting attacks from their own goal, with the last line of defence becoming the first line of attack.

As a Manager, Rowe could never apply his own advice on simplicity to his job. Too willing, too eager to do well, he, like Joe Mercer at Aston Villa, worked himself into a breakdown of health, through involvement with everything from secretarial work to scouting.

At Manchester Matt Busby was building a club well organised at every level, with Jimmy Murphy's development of young players helping United to take over from Wolverhampton. Even Busby's saga of success has its sad ending. But he is still so inseparably linked with the club's present fortunes that he is not yet a part of football Management's past.

Of those we have looked at who shaped the Manager's development only Chapman was unscarred at the end of his career. How many who started with disappointment might still have made good with encouragement? One man's career indicates how close failure is to success in the hard competitive world of football.

The *Guinness Book of Records* lists an Englishman as the most successful Manager of any national team. He is not Sir Alf Ramsey, but the retired and retiring Yorkshireman, George Raynor. The statistics may have been carefully chosen to give him pride of place, but his record is remarkable. Raynor is no forgotten hero, just one we never recognised. His story tells much of past attitudes to footballers and football Management. He took Sweden to an Olympic gold medal in 1948 and a bronze four years later. In the 1950 World Cup when England were defeated by U.S.A., Sweden came third. With Raynor in charge again they were runners-up to Brazil in Stockholm in 1958. The King of Sweden made him a

Knight of the Order of Vasa, Brazil gave him a gold medal, yet English League clubs have given him little but heartache.

He lives now in a bungalow in Armthorpe close to Doncaster. The light wood panelling is Swedish in style, the room full of silver and glass gifts to remind him of his years of success. Each winter scores of Swedes still come to Armthorpe, making the pilgrimage to a soccer prophet without much honour in his own land.

Raynor was born in 1907, son of a miner, one of a large family. He was clever enough to win a scholarship to Barnsley Grammar School, but with his father out of work he had to leave to earn money as a butcher's apprentice, then lorry driver. Football was an early passion and he soon turned professional, earning 15s a match. He was to play for seventeen seasons for clubs such as Sheffield United, Mansfield, Rotherham and Bury. £208 a year was his normal wage, though with Bury he reached the magic six, seven, eight – £6 in summer, £7 in the second team, £8 a week in the first. When he was first put up for transfer by Sheffield United he was without pay or work for the summer, unable to draw unemployment money since the Labour Exchange classed footballers as 'seasonal' workers.

During the war Raynor, like so many leading footballers, became a Sergeant Instructor in the Physical Training Corps. It was then that he developed skills as a Coach which were confirmed when he trained the Iraqi team for its first successful tour of Arab countries. He had developed his own manual, his own theories on physical fitness, and was determined on a career in coaching.

No English clubs were interested, but the Football Association was more helpful. Stanley Rous gave his name to the Swedes, who had asked assistance in finding a National Coach.

Raynor's Manager at Aldershot had been one of the game's great thinkers and the player the crowds enjoyed hating, the Irish International Billy McCracken, whose skill with the off-side trap had reduced forward lines to angry shambles.

McCracken's advice was to remember that a Manager's job is sixty per cent bluff and be confident that he had enough experience for it. 'But don't pretend you know it all, or you will get no help. You are a nice humble fellow and if you keep that way everyone will confide in you.'

Humility came easily to Raynor after watching Birmingham

City play in Stockholm. He was put in the place of honour at the dinner only to be unrecognised by the English players and for their journalists to query persistently how someone of whom they had never heard could be made Manager of the Swedish National Team.

With the bluff called so early Raynor could justify himself only by his originality, by belief in his methods – and by results. The originality was at once apparent when he was told he could only have the team for brief training periods before matches. 'If they are not to be allowed to come to me I will have to go to them' was the response.

Two weeks at a time he would take over the coaching of the leading clubs, getting to know the players and laying down training routines for them. This was as revolutionary as if Alf Ramsey were to relieve Bill Shankly and then Don Revie shortly before Liverpool and Leeds met in the Cup.

Raynor's personality alone made the unthinkable acceptable. From a firm foundation of knowledge he was able to mould the National team, tell them after they had been beaten by Denmark, 'With the players you have in this country you won't lose to them again in the next ten years.'

His great test came with an International against Switzerland. The Swiss had a new defensive system, the left-back moved into the centre, the wing-halves dropping back to mark the wingers, the centre-half free to roam. They had just held England to a draw, and, when Stanley Matthews and George Hardwick came to Stockholm with an R.A.F. side, Raynor pressed them for the details on which he based his plan. He revived an idea with which Bury had experimented – the G plan or deep-lying centre-forward that the Hungarians were later to exploit so successfully. He pushed Gunnar Gren, a skilled mid-field player, into an attacking role beside the right-winger, to exploit the defensive weakness on the left. The Press were invited in to see the training and to hear the plan, Raynor staking his reputation on the result. Gren scored four goals, Sweden won 7–2.

Raynor had appreciated that the Swedes were masterly in their control of the ball, but too delicate in keeping possession. He encouraged the skill and covered the weakness with a few strong players like Bertil Nordahl in the key positions.

His training was designed to supplement the tactics. 'You will make our players hungry for the ball like the English – you will keep it from them,' had been his reception. Instead he was soon shown in cartoons with an immense string bag of balls on his back as he emphasised their importance in practice. The quick reaction, the agility and the hardness he built into the Swedish players was usually done under cover of work with the ball.

The better the Swedish results the more he needed his ingenuity, for the Italians bought up the best of the Swedish amateurs, forcing constant change in the National teams.

Raynor himself was finally attracted to Italy, the money to manage Juventus being prudently invested in a house at Skegness. It was the only time he could save from his earnings in the game.

With Juventus and Lazio he achieved results, but was soon disenchanted with Italian football. He sensed that what the goalkeeper was paid often had more influence on matches than the Manager's tactics. So, with Jesse Carver, another Manager of European reputation, he returned home to Coventry City. There too he found only disillusionment. When Carver went back to Italy, Raynor acted as the Team Manager. As always he was interested in the development of skilful footballers and that was not always the best prescription for the Third Division South. Raynor was given no time to test his theories with Harry Warren brought in over him in the usual search for instant success. He had hoped to settle in England but with no other club offering to take him on he accepted the Swedes' importunate requests to prepare them for the World Cup to be staged in their homeland.

Of the British teams only Ireland and Wales reached the quarter-finals, but Raynor's side went smoothly through to the Final, destroyed at the last by the Brazilians and the brilliance of Garrincha and Pelé.

Later, England at Wembley were to prove no problem, the tall graceful Simonsson confirming Raynor's confident prediction that Sweden would become the second foreign team to beat us at home. Yet when he left Sweden the best position he could command was a job in the stores at Butlin's Camp and to be honorary Manager of Skegness Town.

Two final incidents sum up a career of so much talent, so little exploited at home. Alick Jeffery of Doncaster Rovers was briefly the young prodigy of English football, a powerfully built inside forward with an appetite for goals. A broken leg failed to respond to treatment and he was written off as unfit to play again. The insurance of £15,000 was paid for a career prematurely ended. Jeffery's own share was £4,000, soon dissipated in drink and disillusion as he sought vainly to recapture the vanished glamour.

On impulse he wrote to Raynor to ask if he would help him get fit for football again. Raynor's only condition was that Jeffery must work as hard as he would himself. Out of condition, permanently crippled in the medical view, Jeffery was transformed by Raynor's routine of exercises carefully developed over the years. But when Jeffery was declared fit for League football again the authorities had the unrelished problem of explanations to the Insurance Company, Raynor the criticism, not the congratulations.

In his sixties he was asked by Doncaster, in one of their frequent periods between Managers, to help tide them over. He took them to second in their Division before declaring his job done and his wish to help with the youth development in the club. This too was a reward that escaped him, but his belief in the value of coaching had won a wider acceptance.

The National Interest

The Club Manager achieved power and importance long before the Managers of British International teams were accorded the same status. Alf Ramsey was the first to be made full-time Manager and given control of selection as well as of preparation. Only in 1967 did Scotland appoint a full-time Manager of their National team and not until Tommy Docherty bustled into the job was he to have a reasonably free hand.

Wales and Ireland have more limited playing strength and the part-time Manager is still adequate for them. Terry Neill has coped with being Player/Manager of his country as well as of Hull City, Dave Bowen with the cares of Northampton Town as well as the problems of Wales.

Both Ireland and Wales are in a sense family teams, the circle of players close-knit enough to reduce the Manager's work, the more limited aspirations lessening the pressures. With their past reputation and present resources the English and Scottish teams are always *expected* to win, the supporters accepting victory as a right, defeat as an insult. For Ireland and Wales anticipation is more modest.

Wales had gone twenty years without a win over England. When, after losing at Cardiff, they drew a World Cup qualifying match at Wembley, there was celebration in the Valleys, recrimination in London. England might have three points, Wales only one, but the abuse was for Ramsey, the praise for Bowen.

Walter Winterbottom was the man who in the post-war years brought England in line with developments abroad. As Director of Coaching he shaped the scheme that has given a network of coaching throughout the country and through which so many of today's Managers have been trained as Coaches. A more scientific approach was overdue, with so much of the training then confined to dull repetitive running. Many welcomed the change, but the opposition was vehement. Billy Walker wrote with the authority of a man who had two Cup Winners medals and had managed two teams – Sheffield Wednesday and Nottingham Forest – to Cup victories. 'In my opinion, planned coaching, like any other form of control, gets into a bureaucratic state which not only continues its mistakes, but tends to increase them.' Of Coaches, he commented, 'They are all well-spoken, they are all good-living and all in their different ways deferential to authority.' He had been used to rougher instruction on the field from the great players of his day, Frank Barson and Clem Stephenson. When he saw a coaching demonstration on TV his reaction was, 'Had I been wearing my normal walking shoes they would both have finished up in the works.'

Winterbottom's good-humoured enthusiasm wore down the attacks, laying the foundation for sophisticated schemes from school to International. He can take credit for the raised standards of performance in the country, outweighing the criticism that this has been achieved by coaching out some of the self-expression and flair that make for spectacle.

The organisation of coaching absorbed so much of his time that being England's Team Manager was a secondary job. The Selection Committee then had the governing voice in choosing the team and Winterbottom had none of Alf Ramsey's certainty that he would field the players he wanted. He was advising the Committee, whereas the Committee now are assisting Ramsey.

Winterbottom's international reputation was built on his detailed study of the game, on his ability to chart and analyse. Tall, with a boyish smile and a compelling personality, there is more of the Carnegie College don than the Manchester United centre-half in his appearance. For some of the England team he was too erudite and theoretical. Phrases he used like 'peripheral vision' meant little to a natural player such as Jimmy Greaves, while

Bobby Charlton was put off by the impeccable accent, by the lack of swear words or criticism to which professional football had accustomed him.

Tactically Winterbottom was in advance of his time and the players could not always respond. The only time Club Managers have been called together for a conference was after England had suffered her first home defeat, losing 6–3 to the Hungarians shortly after a 4–4 draw at Wembley with a FIFA side. In both games the defenders had been in confusion against the tactic of a centre-forward who came stealing up from deep positions in mid-field, or wide on the wing. Stanley Cullis was incensed that the centre-half had not been instructed to follow him wherever he roamed.

Winterbottom demolished the argument, reducing it to absurdity by pointing out that the centre-half could hardly go and mark the right-back if the right-back happened to wear a No. 9 shirt. Theoretically he was right, but in practice the players had failed to respond to his instruction and ten goals had come from their indecision.

England's overall record was impressive enough under his leadership, but in four successive World Cups they could find little inspiration.

The final disillusion was in Chile in 1962. England reached the quarter-finals for only the second time, but there was a notable lack of spirit. Jimmy Adamson, the Burnley Manager, was Winterbottom's Assistant there and he is still critical of the players. 'Once they found they were in a small town with limited amenities some could not wait to get home and were hoping for us to be knocked-out. With that attitude it was more surprising we qualified for the quarter-finals than that Brazil beat us.'

The following season Winterbottom became Director of the Central Council of Physical Recreation and Ramsey took over with the brief of winning the World Cup in England.

There is little romance about Ramsey, but a remarkable record of achievement, as International player, as Club and National Manager. Once, travelling back from reporting Stoke's match against Liverpool, I was in Ramsey's compartment. He asked my view of the game and I enthused over the surging attacks, the constant challenge, the five goals. 'But you *cannot* have enjoyed it,' he said. 'There were so many mistakes, so much unprofessional play.' For me that sums up his desire for perfection, his cold analytical approach to the game. 'I am not one to jump over the moon or off a cliff' is his own description of himself.

There was an air of detachment even in his playing days. To the spectator Ramsey was the most poised of full-backs, cool and precise in his use of the ball, an unruffled taker of penalties.

To Ted Bates, who played with him in the Southampton side of the 1940s, he was a man who kept to himself, never offering advice, but ready enough to help if asked.

To Arthur Rowe, who managed him at Tottenham, he was a hard competitor, with strong views of what was right. After one game Arthur asked the team why they had ignored a new free-kick move, diligently rehearsed. Most of them shrugged, and Rowe said, 'So you didn't think it could work. All right we'll forget it.' At that Ramsey flared up, banging the bench and saying, 'We said we would do it, so why the hell didn't we do it?'

Wilf Grant, Manager of Worcester City, was in the Southampton side with Ramsey and was dismissed by him after he had taken over at Ipswich. Scott Duncan, the previous Manager, asked Grant his view before Ramsey was appointed. 'He will be good, but he will be boss,' was an accurate prophecy. Grant had no resentment at being laid off after two seasons. 'We were not much of a side when he took over, but he gave us all a chance. One thing immediately impressed me. We trained hard, tried hard and were still thrashed at home by Torquay. We expected wholesale changes in the team and a dressing down. Ramsey merely analysed the faults, kept the same team for the next match. That started us on a run of success.'

That success was to take Ipswich from Third Division to League Champions in seven seasons.

Ramsey is often seen as a reserved, colourless character, wary, cautious, worrying about the tutored correctness of his diction. But his distinguishing marks are a driving determination to be professionally competent at whatever he does, the strength of character to trust his own judgement.

Any good football Manager has to be a good administrator and his experience at Ipswich, watching the halfpennies, has served him well. His desk at Lancaster Gate is as tidy as the short hair, the blue suit, the Civil Service impeccability of manner. He might be any business executive working on any routine project, using his expertise, the mind committed, but not the heart.

He gives the same earnest attention to the routine queries as to the watching of players, the discussions with Managers. How many balls should be made available for the Common Market Celebration Match? Is £25 too high a price for the contents of doctors' bags at Internationals. How many new track-suits should be ordered for the four international teams? Each question is carefully considered, meticulously answered. But Ramsey is a different man in his own track-suit with the England players grouped round him at Roehampton. Here he is utterly at ease, companionable with the players, glowing with vitality – a fifty-year-old feeling again the enthusiasms of his youth. For him these sessions are all too rare. This is what he missed most in that worrying year after becoming England's first full-time Manager with no outside responsibility. There was a loneliness, a forced isolation from the players he had to manage that was alien to his whole feeling after being with a club. If a match was lost in October he might have until January to worry about the criticisms without the relief of further action.

Criticism has always irked Ramsey, particularly when it stems from imagined ignorance of facts or figures. His feelings about journalists express much about himself. 'If they get in touch with me it's always to ask for something – there's nothing I ever want from them. The people I feel respect for are those whom *I* have to ask for favours, the Club Managers and the players.'

His 100th International was a moment to review the statistics of stewardship. The game at Ninian Park pursued a predictable course, Bell steering home the single goal that won the World Cup qualifier against Wales. An ordered precise victory that stemmed from dominance in mid-field, freedom from error in defence. Only the chances were squandered, only the flamboyance was missing, the centenary match a fair reflection of the strengths and weaknesses of Ramsey's teams. The record read:

P. 100   W. 63   D. 23   L. 14   F. 201   A. 88

In League terms that is an average of nearly 63 points over two-and-a-half seasons, a formidable record to sustain in a country that has such abysmal results in other international sports. It fairly reflects the determination to win and explains the respect of his players. As Bobby Charlton commented, 'He's a good judge and his strength is that he sticks to his opinions. He is always after what makes a team, rather than individuals.'

Ramsey's fires are so carefully banked it is the more revealing when they suddenly blaze up uncontrolled. After the Argentinians had behaved with such ill-grace in that astonishing World Cup match at Wembley, his players were still willing enough to swap jerseys in the traditional gesture of friendship as they walked off the field. But Ramsey would have none of it, rushing out to prevent the exchange. Still fuming, he told the press conference: 'We have yet to produce our best football. It will come against the right type of opposition, a team who come to play football and not act as animals.' Events justified the comment, but he was quick to comply with FIFA's demand for an apology.

The occasional indiscretion makes him more human, hints at the depth of his competitive feeling. The Scottish Internationals most often stir this response. As he came off the plane at Glasgow, a journalist called out 'Welcome to Scotland'. 'You must be joking' was the acid response.

Aware of past antagonisms, he cannot always contain his pleasure in victory. When England won handsomely at Hampden the determination to keep to trite comment on a good and enjoyable game was suddenly forgotten. As the reporters crowded round he grinned at them and said derisively, 'We outplayed you'. But after the crushing 5–0 defeat in their centenary game, the heaviest since 1888, he was generous in victory, reminding Willie Ormond, Scotland's new Manager, that he himself had lost his first International 2–5.

Twice Ramsey has changed the current concept of tactics. The success of his attacking method at Ipswich was ultimately countered by the widespread development of the back four, with its spoiling effect on the game.

As England's Manager he sacrificed the specialist winger in favour of more versatile forwards, higher work-rate, more involvement.

The admirers of flair and the devotees of efficiency can blame or credit him with the scientific soccer of the sixties. But like the laws of gravitation the discovery owed more to an accident acutely observed than to deliberate plan.

In his first season with Ipswich promotion was missed by a point. But in the next the start was dismal and after nine matches change was imperative. Jimmy Leadbetter was switched from inside-forward to the left wing in the hope that a good left foot would cover a lack of speed.

Backs used to a winger who ran at them were confused by one who held back. Uncertain of their positioning they came half-way to meet Leadbetter as he lay deep. Leadbetter had unusual perception, a mid-field player's feel for an opening. He began to slide the ball into the space behind the back, letting the other forwards steal in on it. Once he realised how effective this was, Ramsey steadily reinforced success.

The power so often was down the left as Malcolm, Elsworthy and Leadbetter worked the ball clear for big Ted Phillips, the tall, rangy inside-forward with power in either foot.

As Ipswich moved up to the First Division Ramsey restored the balance by bringing in Stephenson on the right. He was a fast decisive winger, capable of adapting to the cover plan of playing as a thrusting attacker at home, as another Leadbetter in away matches.

With Ray Crawford partnering Phillips the design was nearly complete. These two instinctive goal-scorers took full advantage of the centre-half's lack of cover when his backs were lured up-field, and Moran was added as a third front-runner.

In a friendly against Arsenal before the season started Ramsey was riled to hear the comment, 'What is this team doing in the First Division?' For months we wrote in bafflement of the simplicity of the Ipswich play without recognising its subtlety. But Managers too took a whole season to understand and by then Ipswich had mystified everyone by winning the League. They had isolated the centre-half, helped to destroy the old concept of three defenders.

The seminal change in England's tactics came on the eve of Ramsey's World Cup Year. He had pursued his slow evolutionary way, keeping the same teams even when his first two matches as Manager were lost to France and Scotland. 'I cannot criticise players until I know they understand just what I want from them' remained his philosophy. He soon found he wanted four in defence and was satisfied with the experiment in a drawn match with Brazil. In 1965 there were good results on the summer tour, but Ramsey was concerned over the performance of the wingers. He wanted them to drive behind the defence and pull the ball back to the advancing forwards. Instead they relied on the high centre, or the pass played forward towards the goalkeeper.

From his failure to find any adequate successors to Finney and Matthews came the idea of using the best all-round players, of letting the backs drive through down the wings. The system put a premium on work-rate and stamina, but that was playing to the main strength of the English game. And when he tried it out in the winter sunshine of Madrid the Spanish team were left trailing.

His uncompromising functionalism won a World Cup and set a trend that was copied throughout our national game. Since then Ramsey has been a prisoner of his own success, the emphasis on sweat and versatility inimical to the development of gifted individualism. He can only select as he finds and it is the hard and the fast who abound in English football.

Ramsey's principles of Management are simple and as unchanging as the man. Herbert Chapman once commented on a supporter who wrote requesting four replacements in the Arsenal side: 'Drop four players. I hate to have to make changes at all and when they are necessary I try to arrange they cause as little disturbance as possible. If I were to make four alterations I would regard it as a confession that I had been seriously at fault before in judging the merits of the men.'

Ramsey echoes that thought. He also regards the response of the players as all-important, their respect as the only basis of achievement. So none is discarded lightly. Any may discuss with him anything from tactics to personal problems. No dissatisfied player was kept with club or country.

At Ipswich he let anyone move who wanted to. When Hudson and Todd refused the chance to play with the England under-23 team he rejected them to emphasise his own standards.

He requires complete commitment, absolute acceptance of his authority. In return he gives unstinted support to his players. One incident in itself explains why he has appealed to them so much more than to the public.

Before the World Cup the European press had begun to brand Stiles that jaunty abrasive little man with a tackle like the snap of a steel snare. To Ramsey this represented perfection of timing, a rare skill. To European journalists it was the essence of the destructive English style, a rare menace. And they set out to destroy him, the campaign reaching its height after a mistimed tackle had crippled Simon in the match with France. Stiles was caricatured, the cheery toothless grin transformed to a fanged sneer.

Referees were warned to watch him. As the pressures mounted Ramsey broke his inflexible rule never to comment on individuals.

Instead of the stylised remarks there was fulsome tribute to Stiles, to his ability, to his fairness, to his part in the England plan.

Had it been Stiles not Rattin who was sent off in the next match, Argentine not England who scored the only goal, that might well have ended Ramsey's career. But when his player needed help he was prepared to risk his own reputation to give it.

Until then Stiles had given a muted, stuttering display. In the remaining matches his influence was decisive, his response giving Ramsey that moment of emotion as he kissed the golden trophy and the crowd chanted his name. He was not often to be in tune with them again. But his players have never been out of sympathy with him.

Alf Ramsey has given the same hard gloss to English football as Ray Illingworth to its cricket – aim for the result and let the entertainment take care of itself.

Dave Bowen, of Wales, is by nature softer, more expressive, at his happiest when the phrases or the football are flowing free.

He has the essential quality that Joe Mercer predicates for all successful Managers – eternal optimism. He has need of it. For the Welsh side has so small a pool of talent on which to draw, such difficulties in getting the team together to train. Even the scouting is by remote advice, though the players to be reported on are few enough. The cares of running Northampton Town leave Bowen little time to watch those in higher Divisions. Struggle for survival in the Fourth is an absorbing and depressing task. The financial problem hangs heavy, and, as Bowen comments, 'Here the Manager has to do everything even to tying up the players' bootlaces.'

His own role as Secretary/Manager of Northampton involves him more in public relations and fund-raising than in team preparation.

> I leave all that work to Bill Baxter. Players get used to you and after a few years you have nothing more to teach them. In my view a League Club needs a new Manager or six new players every few seasons. Otherwise the team gets stale.

The reports from the Selection Committee keep Bowen informed of any new talent worth considering or any loss of form of established players. If they point the need he will try to make time to watch particular players before deciding on his squad. The final selection is discussed with the Committee, but they never force any changes on him.

The team gather on the Monday night for a Wednesday International. In Cardiff they train briefly at the Sports Centre but there is no time for any but minor adjustments.

> It's a question of sorting out the marking system. We mark by zones, but some have been marking man-to-man with their clubs. At International level players adjust easily enough but they need to be told who is taking the responsibility for decisions in various parts of the field.

Unlike full-time Managers, Bowen can rarely research the opposition himself. Even for so important a game as the World Cup qualifier against Poland he had to rely on reports and on information from Ramsey.

He puts no faith in tactical changes at half-time:

> There is no point changing in a couple of minutes what you have been planning for a couple of days, and I have already said all I can to inspire them. Once the game starts it's up to them. I might as well go home and read the result in the newspaper.

There is some exaggeration in that, for in the Poland game Bowen did make changes in the interval. Toshack was told to work more in the centre, to keep out of the way of wingers who had the beating of the Polish backs. Within a minute he had a part in the goal that put Wales on the way to winning.

My memory of Bowen as a player is of the Solna Stadium in Stockholm on 17 June 1958. This was the match that qualified Wales for the quarter-finals of the World Cup – the only time they have got so far. Bowen was their captain in that play-off victory against Hungary – the finest achievement of any Welsh side. That day he expressed in his own game the poetic imagination, the fiery enthusiasm that the mind still associates with Welsh football against all the evidence of the eye.

There were less than three thousand spectators, but an unusual intensity of atmosphere. The day before, Imre Nagy, leader of the Hungarian insurrection, had been executed. To demonstrate against the ruthlessness of Russian Communism a group of Free Hungarians marched round the ground, their banners draped in black, their sad slow songs echoing round the near-empty Stadium.

By half-time the Hungarians were a goal up and had crippled the great John Charles. But in the tactics of those days the wing-half could still be king of the field, with enough space to be creative, the sufficiency of forwards to respond to his prompting. Bowen, unflinching in the tackle, unruffled in his passing, drove his team to a ceaseless, surging assault that brought the decisive goals from Allchurch and Medwin.

Nostalgia can be an appropriate mood for Bowen, the past holding none of the repressions of the present. In his early days as Manager, Northampton surged into the First Division. That heady run of success unsustained by reserves of talent was the surprise of the sixties. Bowen still cannot find a rational explanation for it nor for the swift slide back to the Fourth.

> There is so much luck in football. Going up, everything ran for us. When we reached the First Division we had eight cartilages in the season. And we were relegated with 33 points – usually a safe total.

'All Managers are frustrated players' is a wise comment of Joe Mercer's and very applicable to Bowen.

The names roll easily off as he reflects on the world-class footballers in the teams with him – John and Mel Charles, Walley Barnes, Jack Kelsey, Cliff Jones, and that most graceful of inside-forwards, Ivor Allchurch. The contrast is as bitter at National as at club level. His current World Cup squad of 16 included only 7 regular First Division players.

Even the optimist has to come to terms with drear reality. Bowen's approach has been conditioned by the insecurity of football, the fear of defeat and its consequences. Preparing for that centenary contest he recognised the derivative nature of Wales' style, saying:

> Of course we've all followed Ramsey. The winger was dead once you played four defenders. Alf saw that in 1966 and it just took the rest of us a little longer to understand. With only three defenders it was different. The back on the far side was always covering behind the centre-half so the winger always had space from the crossfield pass. With four defenders the backs can play tight on the winger and he's lost his acceleration space.
>
> Without that a winger's finished. He's just got to keep looking

for an opening. So it's better to opt for work-rate, for a player who will go again, show his courage and not be confined to the touchline.

We cannot pretend we have the same quality players as England so we have to adjust to that

The modern game is about possession. If England have more skill, they may need an average of 40 possessions to score, while we may need 60. So tactics will be about possession.

Mid-field is where that is resolved. You have choice in there of playing the possession winners or the creators. We shall have to opt for the ones who win the ball. We're all cautious. We can't afford to lose. If you've got a team like the Brazilians or the West Germans, then your strength is in attack, and you've got to use that. Otherwise the first priority is defence.

That was the priority in the two World Cup qualifying games against England. After losing tamely at Cardiff there was a resurgence of Welsh spirit at Wembley as the team battled fiercely for a point. Roberts and England were unshakable at the heart of a defiant defence, while Rodrigues, Mahoney and Hockey won the possession Bowen demanded. Then Toshack flicked home Leighton James' pass. So far plan and execution were perfect. Wales had found a rich vein of form. But once Hunter's surprise shot had levelled the score all was careworn caution, as the team wasted time playing for the draw. The mood had changed, a sad contrast to that sunny afternoon at Solna. 'There is always fear of England. You never *expect* to win.' Fear is the dominant note of so much of modern football.

Scotland were always a step behind England in their Management appointments and again it was the World Cup that motivated them. They took no part in 1950, declining the offered place in the Finals once England had beaten them in the Home Championship. Four years later they competed in Switzerland and Beattie was made their first Manager. It was a part-time, short-lived appointment, for Beattie resigned within months, claiming he had neither direction nor support. Arguments about a successor were unresolved in the next three years. With the World Cup looming again, Matt Busby was put in charge, only for the Munich air disaster to hit Scotland as hard as Manchester United. With Busby seriously injured it was the team trainer, Dawson Walker, who presided over Scotland's early elimination.

The demands of clubs often take precedence over country, but this was carried to extremes when Andy Beattie was surprisingly re-appointed. With a brief note of apology he slipped off to watch his new club, Nottingham Forest, play at Blackpool, rather than Scotland at Cardiff. That terminated the appointment, but still did not impress any need for a full-time Manager without other interests.

The needed spur was the humiliation of failure to qualify for the Finals which England won. Again, all had been confusion, with Ian McColl of Rangers sacked as he was preparing the team for the initial matches and the temporary appointment of Celtic's Jock Stein failing to retrieve the day. 'Most roads are paved with good intentions, but this was littered with obstacles,' was Stein's comment, which nearly every Scottish Manager must have echoed.

Certainly when the job was advertised as one which 'might suit those with other business interests' the men they wanted, Willie Waddell and Eddie Turnbull, found the terms unsuitable. John Prentice, Manager of Clyde, accepted the post but was sacked the month after his contract was at last negotiated. Bobby Brown was the brave man who took over in February 1967, but in his four years Scotland won only 9 of 27 matches, a bright start fading to the bitter end amid the catcalls of Wembley. He was replaced by the irrepressible nationalist Tommy Docherty.

You have to be a Scotsman to appreciate Docherty's impact, to share the excitement that he inspired as Scotland's Manager.

English reporters could admire the bubbling enthusiasm, the quotable comment. We enjoyed the quip about one centre-half, that you couldn't get a newspaper under his feet when he jumped to head the ball; and about another that he could win possession all right, but could not pass the time of day.

Yet there was some distrust of Docherty's record at club level. There was a memory of Chelsea relegated, then brought to a Cup Final and the verge of greater success, only to be torn apart by impetuous action against the players. There was a memory of Aston Villa slipping expensively back into the Third Division, of Rotherham burdened with debt and with no compensating success on the field, of Queen's Park Rangers abandoned after 28 days. The 'Doc', it seemed, was as likely to kill off his patients as to cure them. Certainly, the record of achievement at club level was slim, the tactical invention suspect, signs of stability unobserved. In Portugal he had fared no better with Oporto. Returning home he hoped for work, saying he had never had to apply for a Manager's job in his life, and asking:

> Will they look at my record and say I did a great job at Chelsea and a sound one at Rotheram? Or will they harp on the QPR incidents and say I failed at Villa Park in a job I never had time to complete?

He had to be content with a second-string job, so it was clear that QPR and Villa Park were nagging at the mind. Even his ebullience was momentarily muted.

As Assistant Manager at Hull, Docherty's career seemed to have drifted into the backwaters of the game. Then came the unexpected appointment as Scotland's Manager, the hard challenge others had cautiously declined. Courage at least was a quality unquestioned in Docherty and this time his boundless belief in himself was to be fully justified. Ian Archer of the *Glasgow Herald* watched him revive belief in the glory of Scottish football:

> A few days after Tommy Docherty had become manager of Manchester United, he sought out a handful of Scottish journalists who were at Wembley for the match that marked Britain's entry into the Common Market. He avoided the usual group of well-wishers who always surround this gregarious man, took the reporters on one side, and said: 'I want you to know that I realise who helped me to get this job. It was you lads.'
>
> In the fourteen months of Docherty's reign as Scottish team manager, he had stirred a publicity campaign that had brightened that country's football after a series of International failures. His words were rarely off the back pages of the papers, his face was seen every week on television.
>
> Scotland had wanted Docherty and he rather needed the £7,500 a year job after his fluctuating experiences at club level. An opinion poll held shortly before his arrival had made him overwhelming favourite in the eyes of the fans, especially among the Glaswegians who recognised in his bravado and impulsiveness an attitude fundamentally their own. Only those who have known and lived in some of Europe's worst housing conditions

can truly understand the affection they felt for one of their neighbours who had succeeded in life – and still stayed the same man.

Docherty is aggressively Scottish. On the day he was appointed – as second choice after Willie Cunningham, the Falkirk Manager, had turned the post down – he said quite bluntly, 'We must succeed. No country in the world possesses as much talent as we do. Possibly Brazil, but that's all.' After one goal in ten previous internationals under Bobby Brown, it was the kind of outrageous statement that the fans wanted to hear.

Docherty's earlier career suggested that he was best over a short distance. He did not stay long enough at the offices of the Scottish Football Association to find out whether that would have been the case with this job. But certainly he gained quick returns from two players.

For his first two internationals against Belgium and Portugal in the European Nations Cup, he brought Celtic's Jimmy Johnstone back into the Scotland pool. This tiny winger once jumped a train on his way to a Wembley match and caused his Club Manager Jock Stein more trouble than any other man at Parkhead. Johnstone was captivated by Docherty, walking around hotel corridors muttering, 'He's some man, the Doc, some man.' After two successful games, he was out of the Scottish side.

Docherty worked the same trick with Denis Law, then nearing the end of his International career. He returned to score the winning goal in a friendly match against Peru and he too insisted that while Docherty was in charge he would always want to play for his country.

He gained a kind of devotion from highly professional players. The task was made easier by having no need to haggle over the day-to-day contracts that cause dissension at club level, but it was an impressive achievement. He was, during the same period, Scotland's most-sought-after speaker at Rotary Club lunches and sporting dinners. His energies were immense and often he travelled more than 1,000 miles a week checking on the current form of Scots playing in the English League. For a year he was the most easily recognised man in Scotland.

In football terms his record was good. Although the country did not in his term of office win an International of outstanding merit, they avoided those crippling defeats by lesser nations that have always scarred the record. He lost his only match against England, a brawl at Hampden that suggested that some over-patriotic and highly charged words had been spoken among the players before the start.

He fought and won a successful battle with the S.F.A. to take Scotland to play in Brazil in the mini World Cup competition in the summer of 1972 and they lost only by a late goal to the World Champions. Despite the fact that clubs were reluctant to release players, the side there formed the nucleus of the team that won its first two World Cup qualifying matches in the autumn of that year. These were the last of Docherty's games before he doubled his salary by going to Manchester United.

It was left to his successor, the quieter but equally intense Willie Ormond, to build on this inheritance and no one will ever know if Docherty himself could have taken Scotland to its first World Cup Final since 1958.

That was what he had been appointed to do, and he had restored the pride and the will to the team to make it possible. For him too there was pride of achievement, for he got on with the job of Management without rows and with the rapturous backing of his own fellow Scots. He had enthused the players and widened the selection to include the best of the Anglo-Scots. Yet in his going there was an echo of Andy Beattie, of the priority of club over country. His contract had been drawn with the aim of making Scotland World Champions. Saving Manchester United from relegation proved more important.

There is a beguiling charm in the unpredictability of the Irish. They will beat England at Wembley, then lose to Cyprus. They will be inventive and adventurous one match, doggedly defensive the next. When so much of the modern game is played to a formal pattern, such inconstancy is a refreshing change.

At their best there has been a lilting beauty in their football, subtle and spontaneous. This freedom of expression flourished best with Blanchflower as captain and Peter Doherty as Manager, the two deriving inspiration from each other.

The Irish team then had more than its share of outstanding players, with Blanchflower, McIlroy, Peacock and Gregg all of

World class. The Swedish crowds revelled in their play as victories over the Czechs and a draw with Germany took them to the quarter-finals of the World Cup. The wins were too well-earned to be attributed to the luck of the Irish. Blanchflower was asked to reveal the secret of success. 'It is our new tactics. We equalise before the others have scored.'

The same light-hearted approach and sharp wit was to be seen in the flowing moves on the field. Doherty's ability was to infect the players with his own bounding enthusiasm and a little of the perception he had himself shown as a player. Selection was not his concern. Motivating the team was. In training, Blanchflower marvelled at his example.

> I could run for ever, but even though he was nearly forty Doherty would pass me three times on the way. He was so fit we used to tell him he should be back in the team. We enjoyed working out set pieces with him, drawing on his ingenuity in devising new moves for free-kicks and throw-ins. But mainly we reacted to his sheer enjoyment of the game. The sides he managed at Bristol City and Doncaster had not the wit to respond to him but he could lift an International team above itself.

Danny Blanchflower shared his impassioned belief in the need for change and improvement.

> Doherty had been a great player and most of us idolised him. He had a tremendous competitive spirit, so bold that it dismissed outrageous odds against it. Doherty had brought a wind of change into the Irish dressing-room. He showed us how quickly the outlook could alter once a team became united in its desire to improve things. Anybody can become better once they set their minds and energies to that end.

In the playing season National teams can never get their players together for more than a couple of days' preparation, so reluctant are clubs to release them. Only on summer tours or in World Cup preparations does the Manager have the opportunity to develop team plays or complicated moves. For the rest he must use the style drilled into the individual at the club and adjust his tactics to the strengths of the chosen players.

In this sense the part-time Managers of Ireland or Wales are at no disadvantage.

With the small number of competent players available they have few difficulties in integrating new men into the team. As Northern Ireland's Manager, Terry Neill had the added advantage of playing himself in the centre-back position with the opportunity that gives of controlling and organising on the field. His main problem as Player/Manager was to exert authority when he himself was off his game. But Neill was backed by the prestige of being Northern Ireland's most capped player. That is a slightly surprising statistic for there have been many more gifted footballers in Irish teams. A strong resolute tackler, Neill had always been slow on the turn, vulnerable to the man with quick acceleration. At club level he was at full stretch to hold his place in the Arsenal side, before the transfer to Hull. His record is like Billy Wright's for England. Both won their string of caps for consistency and competence rather than unusual flair. Neill could be quick-tempered and had his share of bookings. But there was a natural optimism in his philosophy that left him unworried by his own performance. 'There are no action replays in Heaven so you might as well enjoy playing and managing while you can. Football has let me live in style, but I should still have savoured it if the rewards had been a Mini rather than a Jaguar.'

Neill fits the Jaguar image, with his elegant clothes, handsome good looks and former model as a wife. But he has the social poise that eluded his more tempestuous countryman who was for so long the talking-point of the team. No sooner did George Best stay moping in Spain than the Irish achieved their most notable victory of recent years by defeating England at Wembley. His absence, it seemed, was what players call the 'X' factor, the stimulant that made the others play harder to prove themselves. Neill did not see it that way. 'So long as George was in the team all the publicity and interest centred on him. Whatever others did was unnoticed until they began to feel inferior. Without him they had more confidence, but that was not George's fault.' Neill scored the only goal of that game and that surely should have been the most joyous moment of his career. It left him unmoved. 'They gave me a copy of the film of the game, but I never run it through. I watched it once and was disappointed at how untidy the match and the goal looked.'

That is the phlegmatic approach which enabled Neill to survive the fierce pressures on the Player/Manager, particularly when he himself was struggling to keep his place as player. He has played his last game, taking Ireland to second place in the Home Championship before giving up.

But he never faced the problem that confronted Charlie Hurley when he was Player/Manager of Eire. It is hard to make a careful assessment in the heat of a game, but at half-time in a match with Czechoslovakia Hurley realised some drastic change was needed. 'I am having a rotten game,' he said, 'bring on the substitute.'

The Magnificent Seven

The Highbury career booklet for aspiring footballers begins: 'Arsenal . . . Benfica . . . Ajax . . . Inter . . . Santos . . . throughout World soccer perhaps twelve clubs are truly international names recognised by every fan everywhere.' Arsenal naturally will not confuse their own success story by mentioning other British clubs in the top dozen. Yet there are six more who could compete for inclusion in that list together with teams like Real Madrid. Liverpool, Leeds, Manchester United, Tottenham, Celtic and Rangers are of this stature. What in their Management accounts for achievements so widely recognised?

'Football is a simple game made unnecessarily complicated by Managers. . . . A Manager's success depends on how he motivates his playing staff.' Both sayings come close to truth, and the best Managers are uncomplicated in approach to the game, expert in their handling of men. Shankly is the elemental expression of these qualities. Liverpool's tactics are as straightforward as any in the English League. The basic rules are few. Give the pass to the nearest man. Get behind the ball when you've lost it; move into attack when you have possession; use your skill and your speed; give them no respite; chase, challenge and run at them all the time, but keeping to a zone that does not overwork you.

As so often, the style of the team reflects the strong points of the Manager's own play. Shankly ran with his palms turned out like a sailing ship striving for extra help from the wind. Tireless and determined he quartered the field for Preston, a right-half unfettered by conventional position. When Joe Mercer was playing against him, a colleague whispered, 'Shanks is lazy today. He's letting the left-half take his own throw-ins!'

Running on his toes like a ballet dancer he needed great strength in his calves. 'I've got it still' is his proud boast, and at sixty he is able to show his players his fitness. He demands nothing of them that he did not give himself. Long before the expression 'total' football was in vogue he was the totally committed footballer.

One of Liverpool's early heroes was Alexander Raisbeck, described as 'an intelligent automaton fully wound up and guaranteed to last through the longest game on record. To watch him play is to see a man pulsating to his finger-tips with the joy of life. Swift, rapid movement, fierce electric rushes are to him an everlasting delight.' That could just as well have been written of Shankly and that is the Liverpool tradition he embodies and communicates.

With this outlook his tactical talks are always positive, based on what Liverpool will do to exploit weakness in the opponents. Only once was he known to pay undue respect to the opposition. As the team gathered round his tactics table one Friday Shankly's admiration for Matt Busby and Manchester United led him to emphasise their abilities. 'Denis Law, now, there's a player. Verra good with his head, and quicksilver on his feet. The man can dance on egg-shells. Watch Bobby Charlton – let him surge through from behind and ye will na' stop his shot. Ye canna' give Best an inch either. He's clever and strong. Ye can hurrt him and hurrt him, but he will keep coming.' There was an anxious silence as Shankly stared at the heavy metal discs on the simulated field, red for Liverpool, white for United. Suddenly his arm sent the white spinning off the table. 'That to Manchester United,' he shouted joyously, 'We'll sweep them off the field.'

It is rare for him to so delay the punch line. One of his ways of building morale is a humorous catalogue of opponents' frailties, deliberately deriding their talent. Having seen them off their coach, he and Albert Shelley, the late Trainer, would solemnly recount the depressed looks, limited abilities and unusual antecedents of the visiting team. The routine was designed to amuse, to relax and to build confidence.

Typical of his style was a conversation with Peter Thompson

and Roger Hunt, his International forwards, sitting together on the bench before a match. 'Dinna be soft-hearted, Peter. Yon back's so scared after the fool ye made of him last time he's asked to be dropped. He's trembling in the dressing-room. But show him no pity. I'll ask a favour of you, Roger. The goalkeeper's mother is a relation of mine. She's worrit you'll break the puir lad's wrist with your powerful shooting. I've promised her you'll no' hit him, but put the ba' in the corners of the net out of his reach.'

Thompson knew the back had been his master before, Hunt that the goalkeeper's mother had probably never heard of Shankly, but both felt lifted by the familiar patter.

Shankly's ability to enthuse players is obvious enough from the response. Toshack was hardly a worker with Cardiff or Cormack with Notts Forest, but they run themselves breathless for Liverpool. Six scouts from other major clubs rejected Kevin Keegan in his Scunthorpe days as lacking strength and heart. Shankly built this modest, likeable man into the most exciting of players.

Shankly is simple too in his loyalties. In his playing days he was single-minded in his belief in Preston. Tom Finney recalls in the first game he played with Shankly being driven on by shouts of 'Keep fighting. We can do it yet.' They were four goals down with two minutes to play.

After his managerial apprenticeship with Carlisle, Grimsby, Workington and Huddersfield, Shankly has devoted himself to Liverpool with a fervour that came to express a city's feeling. In the final stages of one League Championship Arsenal, Derby and Manchester City were all in close competition with Liverpool. Before a critical game between Manchester City and Derby, Shankly rang his old friend Joe Mercer at Manchester: 'I'll be coming to your match with Derby. I hope you both lose.'

There is only one club for Shankly and only one Manager who can satisfy Liverpool.

Towns react to certain types of Manager, certain styles of football. Liverpool and Shankly are in tune, sharing the same boisterous whole-hearted approach to life, the same passionate feeling which accepts as natural that two fans should ask for their ashes to be scattered in the goalmouth.

Shankly has no sympathy with paperwork, but types all his own letters himself. He has no love of theoretical coaching, but is the epitome of the track-suit Manager, passing on his knowledge to his players. His feel for the game and for people is instinctive and practical. Yet his and Liverpool's success stems from a thoroughness of organisation. Shankly was one of the first to have the Third and Fourth Divisions researched in depth when other Managers were somewhat scornful of their quality. Before he buys a player he will consider every aspect of his game and his personality. The approach will be oblique, but many people will be sounded out to build up the picture. And if the team has to stay in an hotel Shankly will probably have slept there before to make sure it is not too noisy or too luxurious.

One good team may make a Manager's reputation for years. But it is continuity of achievement that proves his powers. While Liverpool were winning the League twice and the Cup once in those three seasons of soaring success in the sixties he was planning the succession.

With few injuries and no failures there was little chance to experiment. No good First Division player would transfer to Liverpool to adorn the reserves. It was then that Shankly built his youth teams and bought from lower divisions. Lloyd was happy to come from Bristol in the hope of taking over in time from Yeats, Clemence to wait until he could replace Lawrence.

That policy and an unsentimental appreciation of the moment great players began to decline has kept Liverpool in the forefront for a decade.

The same judgement runs through the club. The highest transfer fee Liverpool had paid by the end of 1972 was £115,000 for Cormack. A million pounds had been spent to give modern comfort to a ground surrounded, like so many soccer stadia, by those rows of dingy redbrick houses, and the blackened walls with their scrawled graffiti. Now the contrast ideally expresses the therapeutic value of soccer, of the liberation it can bring from the dreary constraints of city life.

A professional economy of effort, a husbanding of resources for the decisive thrust, these proved profitable tactics in their accounts as well as in their play. Not one in a thousand of those crowding into Anfield on a match day would recognise or notice Eric Sawyer, the Financial Director. He is as unobtrusive as Shankly is gregarious, as in love with figures as Shankly with football. This partnership of opposites has given the club its strength. In the Second Division days it was Shankly who knew he needed players of the calibre of

Yeats and St John to win the elusive promotion. It was Sawyer who recognised this was sound investment and found the £80,000 in transfer fees for them when this stretched the club resources. When Lloyd was bought, the price of £50,000 was known to be higher than hard bargaining could achieve. But to save tax it was desirable that the deal be completed before the end of the financial year.

The Secretary holds the balance between finance and football, match performance and the administration demanded of a club that has won its way to Europe for ten successive seasons.

Peter Robinson is prototype of the majority of League Secretaries in the shape of his career. Handicapped by rheumatic fever, he was watcher rather than player, but interested enough to win a job as office boy of Stockport County. Since their Secretary had no other assistance, though crowds averaged over twelve thousand, he had perforce to learn quickly the full scope of the job. Evening study took him through half the finals of the Corporation of Secretaries examinations, but a move cost him his chance to complete the qualification. After his grounding at Stockport he went as Secretary to Crewe Alexandra. There he was blooded by that hectic Cup-tie when Crewe, at the bottom of the Fourth Division, so nearly beat Tottenham Hotspur on the way to winning the trophy for the second successive year. Robinson's memory is not of Brown's fingertip save that kept Spurs from humiliation, gave them the chance to show the difference in quality by winning the replay 13–2. It is of the overwhelming pressure of administration when a near-empty ground is suddenly flooded by a capacity crowd without the staff to cope. His education was completed by spells at Scunthorpe and Brighton. In the eight years since he was selected for Liverpool from some 250 applicants there has been no relief from the pressures of success. Yet with an Assistant Secretary, five full-time staff and extra help for Cup-ties, it is all smooth routine after that experience at Crewe. And that smooth routine, the financial commonsense with which Liverpool runs, allows Shankly to concentrate on maintaining a team that keeps the supporter on the Kop in good heart and voice.

Lancashire has usually been the dominant voice in English soccer but Yorkshire have a worthy champion to maintain the traditional rivalry.

Leeds is a club of strange contrasts. Relentlessly consistent, their record better even than Arsenal's in the thirties, they have so often failed in the crucial match. Relishing hardness, with Don Revie scoffing at the soft southerners, they have welcomed players of Eddie Gray's gazelle-like grace.

Their results were built on a steely defence yet they score goals in profusion, play with style and subtlety. Organisation and teamwork is their strength yet the club's performance centres on one man, Don Revie.

A Manager is only as good as his players. That is an over-used phrase, a half-truth at best. Certainly it is the players who win the games. But the Managers with the feel of success select the right ones, train them properly, enthuse them totally. Revie is such a Manager. Before he took over Leeds had bounced restlessly in and out of the First Division. When he was appointed in March 1961 they were near to relegation to the Third. A season later they came even closer, with only twenty-six points scored with but six games left, four of them away from home. They saved themselves with ten points from those last desperate matches, their relief indulged by wild celebration on return from the final victory over Newcastle at St James's Park.

For the last three months Revie had slept little, worried continually. He would stay up late brewing tea, running over in his mind new combinations of players or tactics. Then he would lie awake brooding on how much simpler it had been as a player. It seemed inevitable to him that his career at Elland Road must be summarily ended, that he would be written off as another failed Manager. Like Shankly, he needed time, needed someone with belief in his ability. That was when the Chairman's support was vital.

Harry Reynolds, a millionaire businessman, had backed his own judgement of men in making the appointment. Revie had come to Leeds two years earlier, signed from Sunderland for £12,000. This was his fourth transfer in twelve seasons, the lower price reflecting that his International career was behind him, his playing days nearly done. Within six weeks he was made captain, the unanimous vote of the players reflecting the impact of his personality. He took over from Wilbur Cush, the little Irish inside-forward, who had found the responsibility affecting his game. Within eight months Revie too asked to be relieved of the duty, concerned at his loss of form, feeling himself an unlucky leader. Yet he still had the resilience to apply a few months later for the Manager's job advertised at Bournemouth. His request to Harry Reynolds to send the letter of recommendation brought unexpected profit. As the Chairman considered the strong points of character and experience he would underwrite he found himself thinking that these were the qualities Leeds needed in a Team Manager. 'If Don is good enough to manage Bournemouth, he's good enough to take charge of our side,' he told his Board. The Chairman had chosen him, so the Chairman backed him when it mattered – and with money as well as faith. For as they struggled to avoid relegation Revie was able to make the decisive purchase – acquiring Bobby Collins from Everton for £25,000. Collins, much capped for Scotland, was small and chunky, with laughing eyes, an angelic smile and the temper of a tiger. He was that mixture of aggression and cunning that Revie looked for in a footballer. At thirty-one he found new appetite for the game, began to organise Leeds in midfield until his carbon copy, Johnny Giles, took over from him.

Revie had already shown his willingness to experiment, his feel for attack, by converting Jack Charlton to centre-forward. Now in one game against Swansea he went against tradition by introducing four untried youngsters to the side – Sprake, Reaney, Hunter and Johnson. No other example better illustrates the shrewdness of his method. This was the season 1962/3 when Leeds had started to climb the Second Division, to challenge for promotion. He was free to experiment without fear. He brought them in away from home to avoid pressures if they failed. His judgement of players was proved by their performance, in that game and in the years of continuous achievement. 'This is a crazy way of running the side,' he told the Chairman before the match. That was no reflection of self-doubt, just a recognition that he was consciously ignoring a basic principle.

With Revie it is never change for its own sake. He prefers to build a stable side, to back it with a stable organisation, to evolve slowly once the foundation is firm. Thoroughness of organisation is the special characteristic of Leeds, devotion to detail almost an obsession.

Even in Scotland they tell a story to point the legend. For their European Cup semi-final at Elland Road Celtic needed to change stockings to avoid a colour clash. They were offered two alternatives – orange or blue. That disturbing reminder of Protestants and Rangers was taken as planned, since nothing ever happens by *accident* at Leeds.

But there is a final contradiction. In that club of hard realism there is a reverence for superstition. Revie had this feeling as a player, keeping fit on a diet of sherry and eggs for a Final in which no one else expected him to play – until Spurdle's boils confirmed his hunch. The first major trophy that Leeds won after many a near-miss was the League Cup. They were heartened when Terry Cooper dreamed he would score the winning goal against Arsenal, not even mildly surprised when he did. The players all have their good luck charms and their rituals, a whimsical preparation for their coldly calculated football. Revie himself always supervises the soap massage that is the Thursday routine, rubbing down his players as if to communicate to them something of his own personality.

Final success has so often eluded, and that is when this close relationship is most valuable, 'when you have worked hard all season and have nothing to show for it at the end there is a terrible flatness. It is difficult to regenerate enthusiasm for the next match, the next season.' As the dejected Leeds team trailed off behind Sunderland Revie was already telling them to forget the match and look forward to the Final of the European Cup Winners' Cup. Their consistent endeavour is a reflection of his own driving determination.

The stability of the Leeds side is matched by the backing organisation, this contribution publicly acknowledged when Don Revie made long-service presentations to five of his staff in front of the Elland Road crowd. But there is no doubt who has built up Leeds as a club, just as there is no doubt who has built up Manchester United.

Matt Busby is synonymous with the club, the immense prestige of both suddenly shadowed by the frustrations of the past three seasons, the panic of coming face-to-face with relegation. Others might fight their way out of trouble with flailing boot, but surely not United. Other clubs might have little faith in football as a contest of skill, an expression of personality, but United surely would live or die with style. When the pressure came they behaved like just another club in trouble.

The Manager sacrificed, the lack of faith, the lavish spending, these were standard responses in a struggle for survival. The appointment of Tommy Docherty was understandable in the light of his popularity with the press and the need for a dominant character who was seen to be in charge. But the combination of Docherty, Cavanagh and Crerand clearly signalled the end of an era, the death of a tradition. There would be more emphasis on the hardness, less on the free expression and the skill that had overlaid it in the past. It took only a few weeks for that improbable headline to appear after a match at Coventry, ' "We are not animals," says Busby'.

Next it was Malcolm MacDonald complaining after the Newcastle match that Holton received the strident instruction 'You've done one. Now do another.' Before United had fought their way to safety the recurrent theme from press, Managers and players was of a hardness that did little credit to the club. Opinion was too uniform to be shrugged off as prejudice, especially when the past had prejudiced so many in Manchester's favour.

Arthur Hopcraft was one of those who had rejoiced in the magic of Busby's teams and written of them with sensitive perception. Saddened by the change, he can still see it in the perspective of all that Busby achieved over a quarter of a century as Manager.

> The events at Old Trafford between the summer of 1969 and the close of 1972 had a distressing shabbiness. Wilf McGuinness, a product of the famous Busby nursery of the 1950s, was callously given the responsibility of managing the players while denied convincing authority because Sir Matt stayed on in his old office, an intimidating grey eminence called 'General Manager'. When McGuinness failed, inevitably, he was humiliated by being returned to the reserve team as Trainer (he left the club later), and Sir Matt took the reins again. A new Manager, Frank O'Farrell, lasted eighteen months before the cumulative hindrances of acrimony in the dressing-room, disfavour in the newspapers and the defection of George Best to the Never Never Land unfitted him for the job in the eyes of the Directors, of whom Sir Matt was now one. It was a sorry tale of equivocation and disavowal.
>
> The sense of disappointment, of betrayal, was evident in the acres of newsprint used to report, and comment on, the dismissal of O'Farrell and the accompanying exit of Best – off to Los

Angeles, and Acapulco, and Spanish sun, and nowhere. It was present, too, in all the conversation one heard on the subject in pubs, in the street, in the newsagent's. Manchester United gets a different kind of attention from that paid to any other football club in Britain. More is expected of it than from any other: more excitement on the field, more praiseworthiness, more 'character'. The reason for this goes back to the vision by which Sir Matt Busby began to create a team twenty-five years ago, and it is tied up with the personality of this man, who became the most famous and most respected of all British Managers. And it is because Busby had made his reputation – his life, in fact – inseparable from Manchester United's that there was such bitter regret when the club was seen to be as fallible as any other. National heroes come and go; but Busby had dominated English football from a pedestal for two generations of players.

Sir Matt's personal contribution to the game has been immense. As important as the record of success United achieved under his management is the fact that he broke new ground in extending the range of the Manager. I believe that the single quality which is common to all successful Managers, and which lifts them above others who may be indefatigably conscientious or exceptionally shrewd, is to possess a dominant will – to possess it naturally, not to assume it. Busby always had this, and it has been of lasting significance to English football that he chose to use it not merely in composing and tutoring his teams but in aspiring in the game in a much broader sense.

His decision to build *a supply of players, not just one new side*, which would be drawn principally – *entirely*, was the ideal – from boys acquired directly from school and developed as a unit, was a daring thought 25 years ago. He was looking a long way ahead, trying to establish a plan that would give him not just his next team but one after that. Such a nursery *system*, as against looking for a gifted youngster when a Manager thought he might soon have to plug a hole in his team, is now a commonplace in the League.

He set out deliberately to break down the barriers of status in the club. He had been a wing-half with Manchester City and Liverpool (and also Scotland's captain) before he became United's Manager in 1945, and he wanted to engender a different atmosphere from what was common in League clubs. He remembered the dispiriting effect a young player suffered by being 'just left on his own – no-one taking any interest'. He saw the dangers in a situation where 'the First Team hardly recognised the lads underneath . . . and the Manager was a man sitting at his desk, and you saw him once a week.'

That seemed more than likely to discourage young players; and always in Busby's mind was the essentiality of encouraging talent, of urging promise into flower. He was one of the first to realise the importance of the Manager's sheer presence among his players, being involved in their ambitions and doubts so that every hint of discontent or concealed fear or unsuspected ability comes to the man in inflections of voices, flickers of expressions.

Busby was prepared to insist on backing his own judgement against Directors' views at a time when a football Manager was regarded very much as a servant of the Board – and as even a smaller minion in the eyes of the executive of the Football League. He defied the League in 1956 to lead the first English challenge for the European Cup.

It was that competition which determined Busby, and Manchester United, would give the British public surely the most emotional of all memories of football: the destruction of a brilliant young team, the fruit of Busby's youth policy, when the plane bringing the group home from Belgrade crashed at Munich airport, killing eight players; then, ten years later at Wembley in 1968, the pictures of the ageing Busby and his captain, Bobby Charlton, who survived the crash with him, embracing in the tearful triumph of winning that trophy at last.

Between 1945 and 1968 Busby saw his teams win also the League Championship five times (seven times taking second place), the F.A. Cup twice (and twice being the beaten Finalists), and saw them consistently attract huge attendances when the public was fickle elsewhere. He was made a Freeman of Manchester and a Knight. Probably he will eventually be Chairman of Manchester United, and he has at last opened the executive of the League to the voice of a professional in the game, even if a retired professional. It is never going to be possible to dissociate Busby from the tawdry episode that injured McGuinness, O'Farrell and football itself; but his achievements stand, and they were reached by a man who aimed very high when few thought to.

C*

Another who has aimed as high is Bill Nicholson. He has none of Busby's bland persuasive personality but in his gritty way an even greater dedication.

Tottenham's record under Bill Nicholson has a remarkable consistency. Since he took over in 1958 the F.A. Cup has been won three times, the League Cup twice, the 'double' achieved in 1961, the European Cup Winners' Cup won in 1963 and the UEFA Cup nine years later. In his first season Tottenham finished eighteenth, but in the next thirteen years only once were they out of the top ten. Seven major Finals were won, none lost.

That argues a meticulous preparation and a care for detail which is the characteristic of his success. Nicholson has no life outside Spurs; his time and thought are wholly devoted to the club. There is still a nostalgic feeling for that remarkable side which not only won the 'double' but won it with such elegance and ease. At the heart of that early triumph was the relationship between captain and Manager, between Blanchflower and Nicholson. For both it was something special and its development tells much of Nicholson the Manager. This was how Blanchflower developed his ideas of captaincy finding understanding only from two Managers, Peter Doherty and Bill Nicholson.

I grew up with fancy ideas of captaincy. I suppose I got them from the boys' magazines. In those boyhood stories the Captain was always larger than life. He was a figure of authority and responsibility. He made decisions and changes out there on the field that dramatically altered the course of the game. And in those fantasy games that took place in my own imagination this was the kind of central figure I imagined myself to be.

On reflection, this grand fellow doesn't have much chance in reality. Perhaps he had more chance in the early days when the game began in the schools and universities. They didn't need managers and directors and all sorts of other officialdom to play the game.

Then came a competition and prizes and recognition of success. To win you had to get better. That demanded organisation. Somebody had to lead. As soon as they got paid to do the job there was more competition for it. So the original seat of power became dissected. The grand old Captain became a Limited Company – with Directors, a Secretary, a Manager and all. They even had a guy to carry the strip and apprentice kids to stud the boots and clean up the dressing-rooms.

It was thus when I came into the business as a professional. The Captain was just another player. He carried out the ball and tossed up the coin in the middle of the pitch and swore at you occasionally during play, but other than that he never seemed to have a lot of authority. At least the ones around me didn't. They were usually older players. I respected them for their age and experience and if any of them had asked me to do something I'd have been glad to do it. But they didn't.

But as I grew older in the game and became much better at it I started to become more critical of the lack of activity around me. I wanted to get better. To get better means you must change your habits in some way. You cannot get better while keeping to the same routine. I found that to do this in a personal sense was not enough. I could change some of my own habits and improve but to continue the improvement meant that others in the team must change some of their habits too.

I tried to bring about some of these changes at Aston Villa. The Manager encouraged me. But he had no great authority at the club and as he had no clear idea of what I really wanted to do he had no passionate belief in the experiments. He just wanted things to get better without any trouble from anybody. And what I was asking others to do was change their own habits – ones they felt safe and comfortable with – and some of them were unwilling to do that. I had no authority to enforce change and no desire to upset other players. We tried the experiments with those players that were willing to change and let the others train in their old-fashioned way.

Even though the team was split and the new movements restricted I found them encouraging. By trying to tackle our problems in a different way we found a new zest and belief in ourselves. By doing something different we surprised the opposition. A sequence of good results followed but we soon found it wasn't as easy as all that. The more we developed the new movements the wider we made the split in our own team. We surprised our own unwilling team-mates with the new moves as well as the opposition. This led to confusion and argument and to a growing lack of confidence among some of the willing players. Old habits that don't succeed are more acceptable. The players had lived with them for years. But new habits are expected to bring instant and constant success. If not, then why change? So the new ideas were destroyed because they had not been tried by a whole-hearted team and by a growing resentment fostered by old habits. Old habits die hard.

This led to some frustration on my part. I could not quell my natural ambitions to improve. If I could not change and improve at my club then I would just have to change my club.

This desire for change was encouraged by my fortunate experience in playing for Northern Ireland under Peter Doherty as Team-Manager.

Our sympathetic understanding made my feelings towards Villa all the more frustrating. I felt I was wasting time. I was twenty-eight. It was time to change clubs.

I joined Spurs in 1954. I had been Captain of Northern Ireland for a couple of seasons. I'd had a good grounding in First Division football with Villa. I was ready for the challenge at Spurs.

Tottenham had that great 'push and run' team at their peak in the early 1950s. They were beginning to slow down and Arthur Rowe was building again. He wanted me as the new Captain. We talked about it a good deal during the transfer negotiations. I told him of my experience with the Villa players. That had taught me I must have authority on the field if I was to accept the responsibility of doing the job properly. He said he would be glad to give it to me. He wanted players and Captains who would accept responsibility.

It did not work out. By the time I had succeeded Alf Ramsey as Captain of Spurs Arthur Rowe had left the club because of a breakdown in health. Jimmy Anderson became the Manager. He had been the Assistant Manager. The job had come to him rather than him going out to look for it. He had the problem of building a new team on his hands. He knew nothing of the promises Arthur and I had made to one another during the transfer deal.

So, in time, when I found it necessary to make changes on the field of play, Jimmy Anderson and I found ourselves on opposite sides of the fence. I said I could not accept the responsibility of captaincy without the authority to act on the field. Otherwise it was just a fraud.

The changes I had made were in Cup-ties. We had been losing 3–1 to West Ham at home in the 6th round. Half-way through the second-half I changed our centre-half Maurice Norman up to inside-forward so that he could frighten Hammers in the air. I figured that if the orthodox was not working we should try something different. It worked. We scored two goals and won the replay in orthodox fashion.

In the Cup semi-final I faced a similar problem. We were losing 1–0 to Manchester City at Villa Park. With thirty minutes to go I sent Norman up again. We went close a couple of times but we failed to score. That's when the trouble started with Jimmy Anderson.

The disappointment of losing a semi-final had something to do with it. So had the Press. Having little in the game to write about they chose the obvious controversy. Should the Captain make changes? It was alright when I had done it against West Ham. It had worked. But it had not worked against City. I was back to old habits dying hard.

I saw it in a different light. If the normal process was not working I reasoned that one must try something else – not something complicated that would be confusing, but something simple that every player in the team could recognise as a call for emergency stations.

I was dropped from the Spurs team. It was a convenient way of changing the captaincy without making an issue of it. Three or four different Captains were tried in my place. Then Anderson asked me to be Captain again. I'm sure it was a genuine approach on his part. I insisted that we should announce I had authority on the field. I would not accept the job without that. Jimmy was reluctant to make the announcement. He said I could have the authority but there was no need to make a fuss about it. I could understand his feelings and had no wish to make life difficult for him. But what if others did not understand I had the authority? What if Jimmy left as manager? What if I tried changes and the Press or public did not accept my authority? It was a public sort of job, open to wide criticism. I was not afraid of that but I wanted it clearly understood where I stood on the matter.

Jimmy Anderson retired and Bill Nicholson succeeded him as Manager. The team was inconsistent but Bill gave most of the players on the staff a chance to justify themselves. But as the team sunk lower in the table and the fight to avoid relegation grew more frantic he eventually brought me back one night at Wolverhampton. He told me he was reinstating me as Captain. He did not have to say anything else. He had thought a great deal about it and he had made his decision that he wanted a Captain who would accept responsibility. At last the Manager and Captain were united and this had an immediate effect on the morale of the other players. We got a hard-earned point at Molineux that night and soon climbed the table to safety. Meanwhile Bill Nicholson was buying the other players who would help turn the team into a great one – Dave MacKay, Bill Brown and John White. Jimmy Greaves came later.

The paradox was that having fought so hard for the right to make changes on the field as Captain I never really had much of that to do with a great team. What need is there to make changes when things are going right? But because the authority had been fought for and generally accepted I never had any real trouble with the other players when I asked them to do something different. That did not happen often because it was rarely that an emergency happened on the field that we had not thought about and prepared for in training. If the 'keeper was hurt we knew who would take his place. If the first choice as substitute in goal was not playing we knew who was second choice. Yet, in such circumstances, if I thought someone else would have been a better substitute I could have changed this.

Only once were we caught out that I can remember. At Ipswich we lost a couple of quick goals and our defence was confused by Alf Ramsey's formation. The Ipswich wingers were lying deep and playing like inside-forwards on the wing. Their three inside-forwards were well up-field as a striking unit. Dave MacKay and I were out of touch with the men we should have been marking because we had an attacking job to do as well. Our two full-backs were in the habit of facing wingers further up-field and the confusion was too great to solve while the game was in play.

At half-time I said that Dave and I should mark the wingers because in a true sense they were playing like inside-forwards. Our full-backs could come inside and deal with the two inside-forwards.

MacKay said he would prefer to mark his own man and the full-backs thought the same. I think their pride was hurt by the confusion and they each wanted to handle their own man. Bill Nicholson suggested I should mark the winger on my side and Dave could mark his own man. We settled for this compromise but lost the match in the end by the half-time score – 3–1.

I was injured when we played Ipswich at home and they caused the same confusion. In the end they won the League title that season and we had to play them in the Charity Shield. I insisted in training that we should prepare ourselves to play them as I had suggested in the first place. Bill Nicholson agreed and that was that. We beat them 5–1. Surprise had been their greatest asset and we had robbed them of that. By training specially for it we had erased the fears of our own full-backs who had to change their habits slightly.

I go through all this detail to explain that so much depends on habit in football. That the better habits a team has the better it will be. And yet the more flexible it can be in changing its habits when the demand arises the greater that team will be.

There is no simple explanation to the relationship between the Manager and his Captain. It is like a marriage. Most of these marriages are nothing out of the ordinary. More often than not the Manager finds it difficult to pick his Captain from the players he has. He has to choose one because fashion dictates that somebody should lead the team out and carry the ball and toss the coin. And if there was one player in the bunch who had ideas of his own about authority and responsibility then most Managers would be suspicious of him. I'm sure that is how many Managers looked upon me.

One Manager of another club with whom I was friendly called me into his office one Saturday before the match. 'If I came to Tottenham as Manager,' he said, 'the first thing I would do is call you into my office and tell you that I am the boss here.'

'That's OK,' I replied. 'Then I would ask you: "What am I?"'

'I would tell you,' he said, 'that *you* are nothing.'

'Then I would have to say that *you* are the boss over nothing.'

So I appreciate the part that Peter Doherty played in my development as a Captain. He did much more than accept my ambitions. He encouraged them beyond question. Thus I had great experience and confidence when I first faced Bill Nicholson as Manager.

I think Bill was suspicious of me at first. Then I think he realised that we both had the same thing at heart although we were different by nature. We both wanted the team to get better no matter how good it was. The understanding that grew between us started slowly and became very deep through the years. And as the years pass on I think we both realise on reflection that it was so much better than we realised at the time. When it was happening we were too busy to appreciate it properly.

The Manager's is a very lonely job. It is difficult for him to confide in his players because in a sense he is the master of their destiny. The Captain is one of the players but if he wants to be a great Captain he must in some way be slightly apart from them. You cannot lead them from the middle of the pack. By instinct I always tried to find a place to stand somewhere between the interests of the players and those of the Manager. I would talk about other players with Bill but I would never suggest that he pick one instead of another. I would have felt disloyal. But if he asked me which of two I thought was better I would be honest and tell him why I thought as I did.

I tried to be an example to the others in training. This was no hardship because I liked training. But this must have helped the respect grow between Bill and me. Nor did I drink or smoke. Not that these are crimes but abstinence was another common link between us. Nor was I emotional about our achievements. I did not enjoy dancing around waving trophies in the air. I accepted I had to do it for the enjoyment of our fans but I did not like doing it. I'm sure he did not like it either. His comments regarding success were always cold, much colder than mine. I was embarrassed by the boasting around us but I escaped it with humour. He gruffed his way out of it. Our satisfaction was in doing the job. We both wanted to get on with the next one.

I believe that is the reason for Bill's continued success. He sees no reason why anyone should want to rest from the job at hand. Go into his office and ask for a day off and he'll be gruff about it. He'll give you a hard time. He might not even say anything but he'll look grim. He might even give you the day off but you will leave his office feeling uneasy about it as if you'd taken the bread from his mouth. You might complain about his attitude to the others, but there is no way you could ever justify that complaint in your own mind because you know that no matter how hard you might work or how many hours you put in that he's doing a lot more than you. You know that he is straight and honest and not making a profit behind your back.

I used to say to him: 'I'm here to do the work. You are here to see that I do it.' It was my way of saying that if I was going to play the game and perform the tactics then it would be better if I worked out ones nearer to my own understanding. If they proved not to be good enough then that was the time for him to interfere. If others couldn't think for themselves then he ought to be on their backs.

He did not need telling. He knew all that himself. But by keeping at everyone he kept them going much better than he would have done by easing up and expecting them to do it themselves.

We had a very special relationship. I know it. He knows it. And that's all that matters.

Bill Nicholson sees it that way too. 'I gave him authority on the field, but told him always to remember two things. I had been responsible for the money paid out on the players and I took the responsibility for the results. So he must not knowingly go against my policy. It was a question of trust.' Nicholson is a man you can trust.

The English League is with some reason characterised as the hardest in the world, the depth of talent making every one of the forty-two games a challenging contest in a long, wearing season. But it cannot be claimed as the best while English clubs have made such intermittent impact on the main European competition.

In the first seventeen years of the European Cup only Manchester United reached the final in that triumphant spring of 1968.

The record is much better for the European Cup Winners' Cup with Tottenham, West Ham, Manchester City and Chelsea all winning in its first twelve seasons and Leeds making their impact this year.

But no English club can rival the record of Celtic and Rangers in these two competitions. The concentrated League programme may provide part of the explanation, since the two Scottish clubs have no such relentless pressure in their season. Yet part must be in the style and confidence of Scottish football, in the encouragement of talent and the rejection of negative tactics.

Rangers won the European Cup Winners' Cup in 1972 and have twice been runners-up. But Celtic were the European Champions of 1967, the runners-up three years later. That makes them our prime team in Europe as they have been in Scotland over so many seasons.

Jock Stein is known as 'the Big Man' and he towers over Celtic's achievements, as dominant in personality as he is in physique. Yet for an Englishman the main impression is not the craggy, formidable figure, but the kindliness, the absorption in the club.

The Scots have a reputation for hospitality and Managers like Stein give this feel to a club, which is often so lacking in England. Anyone who phones the ground is as likely to get Stein himself as any other official and to have his query dealt with in person by the Manager.

Stein still has a sense of wonder at the strange reversal of fortune that transformed an unknown player into a football legend. He had been a centre-half with Albion Rovers, impressing his Manager, Webber Lees, more by his readiness to talk about the game than his ability on the field. After only three seasons he drifted out of Scottish football and into obscurity with the non-League Welsh side, Llanelli. Stein had been a pit-worker and he settled happily enough into that mining community until the house he kept back in Hamilton was twice burgled.

Waiting until Llanelli was beaten in the English Cup he went to tell the Manager that he would return home, give up the game and go back to the pits. Instead he was informed that Celtic wished to engage him to give experience and solidity to a team of young reserves. He left at once for Glasgow, but never played for that reserve side. Before the season started both regular centre-halves were injured and Stein had to deputise in the First Team. The good players round him and the challenge of top-class football brought a new dimension to his game. He went on to captain Celtic and lead them to the Cup and League double.

His first managerial appointment was to Dunfermline, on the verge of relegation. They had not won a match for months, but they won the next five and the following season beat Celtic in the Final of the Scottish Cup. Stein had solved the difficulty of 'making a provincial team think they were as good as a big City one'. But once he himself went back to the big City the gulf opened wider than ever.

His career is unmatched in the history of Scottish football, yet his simple start has kept him in sympathy with the ordinary player and supporter. Typically, when a party of Welsh miners on their way to the rugby International came to look at the closed Parkhead ground it was Stein who showed them round for two hours. And when recently an away game was cancelled late it was Stein who stood by the main junction outside Glasgow flagging down supporters' coaches to prevent a wasted journey.

Stein has a great affinity for 'football people', but is as happy discussing history or politics, his interests wide-ranging, but his time dedicated to Celtic. He is as open with the press as with Celtic supporters and John Rafferty has seen him work himself to exhaustion for the club.

On a March morning in 1965 the late Sir Robert Kelly announced that Jock Stein was to be the new Manager of the Celtic Football Club. Stein was but the fourth Manager of the club since it was instituted as a charitable organisation in the East End of Glasgow in 1888. Sir Robert, Chairman and son of the first Captain of the club, James Kelly, concluded an emotional occasion with the charge, 'It's all yours now, Jock.' Stein was to take him literally and become totally committed to the club and its players.

Not only was Stein to work himself to the point of exhaustion, travelling to keep himself abreast of what was happening in football, imparting what he had learned to his players, worrying and scheming and planning, but he became involved in their private lives, in their homes and their families: 'Of course I like to win matches and win competitions but nothing gives me more pleasure than to see one of my players do well, to marry, to buy a house and to have a nice family. That's what makes it all worth while.'

That was no light talk. Some were astonished recently before the club's annual Christmas party, a family affair, when Stein took charge of the gifts and labelled them, writing the names of all the players' wives and their children without using a list. He knew them all.

Stein has an astonishing memory. In Lisbon, three years after Celtic had won the European Champions' Cup there, I bought an ordinary picture postcard which showed the National Stadium in which Celtic had won that cup. It was a wide view of the ground and the players were but specks on the card. There was no indication of who the contestants might be, but Stein, after a glance, said, 'That's the cup final against Inter Milan.' I asked him how he could know and he looked astonished. 'That's the play leading up to the penalty kick,' he said. 'That will be right,' I told him scornfully and then with some irritation he began to give names to the dots and explained that the ball went from there to there and to there and Jim Craig made the tackle which was punished with a penalty kick there. And it all happened three years before and he was surprised we lesser mortals had not been able to see that.

Stein worked extraordinary hours for the club. He took the training every morning, stayed on for special coaching of individuals, was interminably on the telephone at the ground and in his home, talking to football people, to Managers, to contacts, becoming satiated with the current news in the game.

He was ever available to the press, providing the routine news of the team, arguing, trying to influence opinion, putting the club's case and at times winning press friends by helping with a story on a dull day. He was up-to-the-second in newspaper office gossip, taking a delight in stirring up argument among the travelling band of reporters.

There has been recurring talk among those who do not know him well that he is a tough man. He says, 'I know people think that I am hard but maybe I'm the softest of them all here.' He could be right. He has never been one to dismiss the troublesome player but instead has tried to understand him. He told me once when discussing such a player, 'What would he do if I threw him out, and he has a wife and family.'

There was a long troublesome relationship between Stein and Jimmy Johnstone; there were quarrels and suspensions, and Stein said once in exasperation, 'No player has ever given me such trouble.' Johnstone in a chastened mood agreed that no player could have. Stein was often advised to rid himself of the troublesome winger but he would say, 'What a player he is when he plays.' Johnstone was tolerated and matured under Stein's patience and settled to become a good professional and the only reward Stein wanted was to see his trickery and maybe watch him resist provocation.

This total involvement in the affairs of the club and all in it inevitably placed a heavy strain on the man. He never did sleep well. On trips abroad it was noticed that he was always last in bed and nobody was ever down before him in the morning. One player said of him, 'He sleeps with his eyes open thinking about football.'

There was the strain of long fast journeys to watch football. If there was a mid-week match in England, when Celtic were not playing, in Manchester, Liverpool, or Leeds he would motor down after the afternoon's work was done in Celtic Park, talk a bit, watch the football then motor back immediately afterwards and be first man in Celtic Park in the morning.

Such exertions were more than any man could bear and at the start of 1973 he became ill and was taken to the coronary ward of a Glasgow Infirmary for observation. He was ordered to take things easier. That was a terrible sentence to pronounce on Jock Stein.

Rangers in recent seasons have trailed behind Celtic. Their triumph in the European Cup Winners' Cup would have been all the sweeter for that had it not been marred by the unruly behaviour of some supporters. Ian Archer has observed their Manager closely.

Willie Waddell, speaking strongly into a microphone erected in the centre-circle of the Ibrox pitch, addressed 20,000 Rangers fans before the start of the 1972–73 season. It was an unusual step for any Manager to take but it was his personal contribution to football's continuing fight against the hooligan problem.

Waddell delivered in strong terms a ten-point plan – including the prohibition of drink inside the ground and a ban on all the songs of religious bigotry that can be heard whenever this club plays – and he was applauded as he left the field. This cameo illustrated graphically the difference between his job and that of any other Manager in Britain.

Rangers hold a unique position in world football and the man in charge has always been expected to concern himself as much with the club's image as with the tactical motivation of the team. Waddell, an uncompromising personality, rather typified the

Rangers tradition. His singlemindedness matches that of two famous predecessors, Willie Struth and Scot Symon, who between them brought the club 25 League titles and 15 Scottish Cup victories in less than half a century.

It is doubtful whether any English Manager would seek or be given the role that fell to Waddell during that same year. When Rangers, after a decade of annual continental journeys, eventually won the European Cup Winners' Cup with a victory over Moscow Dynamo in Barcelona, that triumph was obscured by the rioting during and after the final which led to a two-year EUFA ban on the club. It fell to Waddell and not a member of the Board to fight that decision.

He did so in Brussels and the result of his impassioned plea that the players must not be penalised for the acts and indiscretions of the fans led to the suspension being halved. That was probably as important a victory as any Manager could win, for a good European season probably brings about £100,000 of gate receipts.

Shortly after this battle Waddell decided that running both the Ibrox club and the team was too much work for one man and he assumed the position of General Manager, with Coach Jock Wallace gaining promotion to the title of Team Manager. Increasingly, he saw his job stretching beyond the boundaries of the club, and he concerned himself with the politics of the Scottish game.

In February 1973, Rangers invited every other club in the country to hear their proposals for fighting the decline in gates. A hall was hired in Glasgow and again Waddell, rather than a Board member, expounded plans, which included a change in rule to deprive sides of any points from goalless draws and a series of cash prizes for the country's leading goalscorers.

It is unlikely that any other Manager would be given as wide a brief as Waddell, but few have his all round qualifications. He was a famous winger in the Rangers side that won the Scottish 'double' in 1949 and 1953 and that ensures him of the affection of the fans and the respect of the players. But between serving his managerial apprenticeship at Kilmarnock, whom he took to a surprising Championship victory in 1965, he also worked as a full-time sportswriter on Scotland's best-selling daily newspaper – and not a single word was ghost written. That experience allowed him to take a wider view of the game than many Managers whose whole adult life has been spent in the closed world of football and whose attitudes are often restricted by its sheltered nature.

Those are the six other clubs who could most appropriately be added to Arsenal's list of the Internationally famous. What of Arsenal itself? The club has won the Fairs Cup, but not so far achieved the success in International competition of Celtic, Manchester United, or Tottenham. Yet it is still true that Arsenal is the English club that comes first to the mind of the foreigner. In the 1930s its name echoed round Europe and the memory lingered on even in its years of depression.

Now there is justification once more for Arsenal's reputation. The present vein of success is backed by a record no other club can match (four F.A. Cup victories and four times losing Finalists, eight times League Champions, the 'double' in 1971, and all achieved in the last forty-five years).

Recalling his time as an Arsenal player, Joe Mercer puts high value on the tradition 'You always expected to win. Even in an away game there was no satisfaction in a draw.'

Its strength is not in fading memories, but in the power of organisation, in a name that attracts the young to the club and the supporters to the terraces, in a reputation to inspire pride in the players, in a bank balance to satisfy aspirations.

These were little comfort to Bertie Mee when he took over as Manager in 1966. Three predecessors had been worried into resignation by the poor results, the falling gates, the burden of only the best being acceptable. Mee agreed to manage for a trial year, already clear of his priorities. Morale was his first consideration then as it remains today. He had seen a collection of talented players lack the will to knit into a talented team. There must be no more failure in the mind.

> I had been impressed by the difference between the professional footballer and the professional golfer. The golfer will always produce a highly competent performance no matter whether he has just had a bad night's sleep, or flown a thousand miles, or has to play on a strange course. He knows no-one else is responsible for the figures he produces. Players are not so constant in football where one can always excuse one's own

failure by blaming it on others. To win the League you need a squad of footballers who will give you forty-five top-class performances out of fifty. Occasional brilliance is no good over a long season. That was what I set out to impress on my playing staff, that was the response I sought. We kept and recruited those who had that attitude, the others could go.

Mee is quiet, precise, a little formal in manner, very neat in mind and appearance, not given to excessive enthusiasm. He had been one of those small nippy wingers who abounded in pre-war days when forward lines swept up five strong. Mee had been just good enough to satisfy Derby County, never good enough to satisfy his own ambition to be at the top. He was realist enough to see that he had no great career as a player even before a back injury put him out of the game. His was not a personality or a background to appeal to those who believe that footballers, coming mainly from poor homes, are more at ease with rough language and wisecracks, only respect those who have themselves been outstanding in the game. But it has been Mee's handling of men, his ability to communicate his own passion for order and excellence that has revived Arsenal.

Charlie George is the most striking example of his method. Here is a player with flashes of George Best's talent and temperament, who was as much the centre of adulation and as liable to be destroyed by it. His temper is quick to flare on the field, his comment 'if they knee me, I butt them' a reflection of attitude.

Mee has integrated him into a team of workers, made him accept long periods as reserve, dealt firmly with his exuberant estimate of his own ability. That goal which won the 'double' tempted George to demand special treatment. In his firm decisive way Mee made it clear that there would be no special treatment, that the club was always more important than the individual and if George knew a better one he was welcome to go there.

Always polite with the press, Mee protects the players from publicity, never revealing a private interview, never encouraging the sensational story.

When Arsenal won the 'double' it was only on the Monday night before the Cup Final that they made sure of the League. Mee was quick to exploit the advantage. With one title safe there was less tension. Concentration on the League had kept them free from worry over the Final, aloof from its preliminary pressures. Liverpool had had it on their minds for three weeks and were still involved in interviews on the morning of the match. Mee made his players unapproachable for forty-eight hours, was not surprised that the quiet preparation gave them the strength in extra time to outrun a team noted for its fitness.

Fitness is no fetish for Mee, just the expression of his technical competence as physiotherapist. He was in the Army at twenty, his football maintained by guest matches for Southampton and in a representative Wanderers side in the Middle East. At his own request he went to the Army physiotherapy school and learnt enough to complete his civilian qualification. Out of the game at twenty-seven, he made a new career in the Health Service, running remedial centres, one of them at Camden Town.

Organising the F.A. Treatment of Injury courses at Carnegie College and Lilleshall kept him in touch with the game and in 1960 he came to Arsenal as their physiotherapist. That gave him six years to note what he would do if he was Manager. His second priority was to get the best Coach in the country. The choice was Dave Sexton for his technical knowledge, his ability to be inventive and sustain interest in routine training, for the respect in which he was held by his players.

Safeguarding the future was the next consideration, unusually expressed by cutting out one of Arsenal's four teams, their Metropolitan League side. This was no cost-saving measure. The aim was to give all young players the chance to come through quicker to high-class football, to make more rapid decisions on whether they had the necessary potential for Arsenal. Good organisation, quick decisions are the essence of Mee's style and nowhere was this more important than in the scouting system. He took on Gordon Clark as Chief Scout, a former Manchester City player, who had later established a reputation at West Bromwich Albion for his ability to unearth young talent. Clark was out of a job at the time, but had the qualities Mee appreciates. His mind is a filing cabinet of players' statistics, his enthusiasm takes him to seven or more games a week, his judgement of ability has other clubs consistently phoning him for his opinion.

Mee, the organisation man, has built a highly successful method team within the disciplined framework of a club whose standards are rather special. I once asked him if he regretted letting go

Forsythe, the Scottish full-back who was with Arsenal as a youngster. He looked surprised: 'It doesn't follow that because you are an International you are good enough for our squad.' There was no more to be said about Arsenal.

The Supporting Cast

Such is the strength of British League football that those seven clubs and Managers are backed by at least another ten who have made their mark on European football. West Ham and Ron Greenwood, Manchester City with Joe Mercer, Chelsea and Dave Sexton have all carried off the European Cup Winners' Cup. Newcastle and Joe Harvey have won the UEFA Cup and under Bill McGarry's firm leadership Wolves reached the final of that competition only for Tottenham to beat them by the narrowest of margins.

Although Celtic and Rangers so dominate Scottish football, other clubs have had their moments in European competition. Bob Shankly, Bill's brother, built a Dundee team that came close to being the first British side to win the European Cup. When this competition was first organised by Gabriel Hanot, a former French International, and the Paris sports paper *L'Equipe* for which he worked, Hibs were one of the sixteen clubs invited to compete. Under Eddie Turnbull they have again made their mark in European competition.

There are two more clubs who command wide attention. Everton have had a couple of lean seasons since winning the League Championship. For them such failure is the more bitter while Liverpool keep up their winning ways. But over the years they have made as great a contribution to the City of Liverpool's unique football record.

Merseyside has never had a footballing occasion to match the Charity Shield game at Goodison Park in 1967 with Liverpool as League Champions against Everton, the Cup-Holders. As the two trophies were paraded round the ground one player from each team, Roger Hunt and Ray Wilson, waved aloft a third – the golden Jules Rimet Cup which they had helped England to win. Then the clubs could share each other's triumph and forget, however briefly, their own intense rivalry.

Everton are not such regulars of European competition as Liverpool, but only a surprise home defeat by Panathinaikos prevented them reaching the Final of the European Cup in 1971. And though they have lacked Liverpool's consistency Everton have had a full measure of achievement in the twelve years since Harry Catterick joined them in April 1961. Twice they have won the League Championship and twice reached the Final of the Cup, winning the trophy after trailing two goals behind Sheffield Wednesday. That was a day for Catterick to savour, for Sheffield Wednesday provides the other main strand of his career. He came to Everton at seventeen as an apprentice from Stockport and he was their centre-forward when they were relegated in the 1950s. Their final game was against Sheffield Wednesday and a draw would have kept them in the First Division. They lost by six clear goals and the two teams went down together.

Like Bill Shankly, Catterick learnt his trade in the hard proving ground of the lower Divisions, as Player/Manager at Crewe Alexandra, then for three years as Manager of Rochdale where he built a successful team from free-transfer players. But it was at Sheffield Wednesday that he established his reputation, winning them promotion, taking them to runners-up in the First Division and to a Semi-Final in the Cup.

But at Wednesday Catterick did not have the free hand he desired, resigning rather than accept any interference. He was only out of work for ten days before Everton approached him, with the offer of the job as Carey's successor. His first match as Manager was an away game at Sheffield Wednesday with Everton soundly defeating his former club.

Catterick had always been a keen student of football. As a player he took the trouble to learn all he could of administration from the Secretary, Theo Kelly. While others played cards on their way to and from games Catterick read books on the laws, the organisation and the control of the game.

He has much in common with Ramsey, shunning publicity, hoarding his words, never publicly criticising his players, his opponents, or the referee. This has earned him the title of the silent gentleman of football.

While Shankly, Clough, Revie or Docherty caught the headlines with their repartee, Catterick worked with quiet dedication. Transfers best express his style. Whereas most moves are reported before they are fact, when Catterick pounced the press were taken by surprise. There was no hint before he signed Alan Ball from Blackpool for £110,000 or when he sold him to Arsenal for £225,000. When Howard Kendall transferred from Preston the only speculation had been about other clubs signing him.

Harper came to Everton while an edition of *Scottish Football* was just coming out with this quote: 'Behind many of these goals, of course, has been the ever-sharp reflexes of the most exciting striker in the country, Joe Harper – and it looks as if wee Joe will go on thrilling Pittodrie crowds for some time to come as Manager Bonthrone recently made it clear he has no intention of selling him. Dons, of course, are in the happy position of not needing the money. They've put a lot of cash in the bank from transfers in recent times and they have spent shrewdly too.'

Harper's swift signing was an indication of the unusual freedom that Catterick enjoyed and of the confidence accorded him by Everton's Board. Within the agreed spending limits Catterick bought or sold without consulting further and not even the Directors knew that Harper was coming until the £180,000 deal was complete.

Catterick enjoyed the stealthy approach. The cloth cap in the back of his Rover car was a symbol of his method. Most of his afternoons and evenings have been spent watching football, but anonymously on the terraces. His flair has been in finding young players and developing them through the junior teams. The supply has been constant with Colin Harvey, Joe Royle, Jimmy Husband, Roger Kenyon, Mike Lyons, Tommy Wright, and John Hurst, or those like Dave Johnson or Alan Whittle who each brought £100,000 in transfer fees.

Two illnesses, a hernia operation and a mild heart attack reduced Catterick's ability to be the track-suit Manager training his team. This led first to the promotion of Tommy Eggleston as Assistant Manager. Eggleston was Catterick's Coach at Sheffield, following him to Everton before himself managing Mansfield. Then came Catterick's appointment as General Manager, as reward for past service and a dignified end to his career with Everton. But the responsibility had passed to the new Manager, Billy Bingham.

The essence of a good Manager is his ability to re-shape a side as it falters. Catterick had done that often enough in the past and he looked to have achieved it again when the transfer of Bernard brought an infusion of spirit to the team at the start of last season. Then injuries to Bernard and Royle cut short the revival. Some accidents a Manager must expect, but the crippling of Royle just as he was proving himself the best centre-forward in England was particularly bitter. His back was wrenched by a colleague jumping on him in over-enthusiastic congratulation for a goal and the damage aggravated in training. On such an incident can a team's future and a Manager's reputation be hazarded. Everton at least have the resources in money and men to recover quickly from such set-backs.

When Derby won promotion to the First Division their effective playing squad was only twelve, which gave them no margin for such mishaps.

Derby and Brian Clough have made an immediate impact on Europe while successfully ignoring some of the established principles. Though he went himself to look at Benfica and Juventus, opposition teams in the European Cup were not always researched in depth and there was no special training. Before the quarter-final match against Spartak Trnava in Czechoslovakia the Derby players were encouraged to relax, to drink in moderation, to enjoy themselves, rather than adhere to a Spartan discipline. Yet in other ways the preparations were more thorough than most. Before playing Juventus his squad was given four days in Italy to acclimatise. Despite a commanding lead over Benfica, Bill Wainwright, a Sheffield Hotel manager, was sent in advance to Portugal to check the accommodation before the return match. The beds had to be comfortable, the rooms quiet, the food carefully chosen. 'What would Mr Clough say if the players had upset stomachs?' was Wainwright's comment.

What Mr Clough says has been known to upset a stomach or two, notably at a dinner organised by Yorkshire Television and disorganised by his publicly announced departure to the toilet and his criticism of Peter Lorimer. The incident revealed much about Brian Clough. The desire to shock seemed deliberate, the cushioning comment on Lorimer's skill following, not preceding, the punch line on his readiness to feign injury. In being frank enough to point to a sickness of the modern game, he was perverse enough to fuel a feud by picking his example from Leeds. Outspokenly critical of others, he is unreasonably upset by those, like Revie, who are as outspokenly critical in return. Clough and contradiction are inseparably paired.

He mixes politics and sport, socialism and a silver Mercedes, a creed of equality and a high-paid career in the most cut-throat competitive business of a capitalist society.

His record as a goal-scorer (251 goals in 271 League matches) is formidable, yet he gained but two England caps. When he was made captain of Middlesbrough the team demanded his removal, yet at twenty-nine he had become the youngest Manager in the game at Hartlepool. In dealing with players he regards the Manager's greatest crime as going back on his word, yet he let Coventry down minutes before a Press Conference called to announce that he was succeeding Cantwell as Manager.

On a football panel he refused to allow Bob Wilson to express views on a Manager's job since he had not been one himself, yet Clough holds forth on any subject that catches his fancy. He attacks fellow Managers with gay abandon yet many of them are very protective about him. 'Don't say anything unkind about Cloughy' is common advice. For they accept that, though his manner and his statements are as provocative as his bristling hair and wide belligerent eyes, his thought and action is mainly for the good of the game.

He has slated sterile tactics, deliberate hardness, and the play-acting that wins a free-kick or gets a man unfairly booked. With him that is no vain talk. Clough's convictions are given practical expression in a team with flair as well as courage, attractive to watch and hard to beat. There is no hesitation in disciplining players, even those that are most essential to success. McFarland was fined for a bad offence, publicly lectured for a stupid one.

Confidence and courage were the hallmarks of Clough the centre-forward. As a Manager he is just as daring. When Derby won promotion to the First Division he recorded an interview before the season started, confidently predicting what they would achieve and agreeing to its screening after the results were known. He risked looking foolish and was proved right.

A natural rebel as a player, Clough finds it hard to be Authority. Unable to rebel against himself, he lashes out at others, or finds refuge in fancies of going into politics, or out to the West Indies.

No one has an easy passage working with him and Derby's strength is in the support he gets at his most moody. Sam Longson, the Chairman, knows that Clough spells success and was ready to match Coventry's bid when Derrick Robins made the same shrewd appreciation. This has put Clough in the £20,000 a year class and kept the spotlight on Derby, for a club is never short of publicity when he is Manager.

Yet it is the quiet man of the trio whose backing gives steel and strength to the club and to Clough. His Assistant, Peter Taylor, first recognised his talent when he was Middlesbrough's goalkeeper and Clough was still in the reserves. Theirs has been one of those fruitful partnerships of opposites, like Mercer and Allison at Manchester City, in which each enhances the other's ability. If they stay together Derby may be a name as respected in Europe as any of the others.

The Tactics of Success

The study of tactics is an absorbing interest to Managers, evolving the game into new patterns. The year before the League was formed in 1888 the accepted formation was six forwards, two half-backs, two backs and the goalkeeper. The main attacks were down the wings with two players wide on each touchline.

The authoritative handbook of the day gave these simple instructions on tactics:

> The object of goalkeeper and backs is to get rid of the ball immediately; no delay is permissible to them: 'Away with it' is their motto; so long as it goes, where matters little.
>
> The object of half-backs is to get rid of it, but with discretion. The half-back must restrain himself and be content with skilfully passing the ball on. He is on the debatable ground in possession of the strategic point. Behind him are the backs, whose endeavour is to get rid of the ball; before him are the forwards whose object is never to leave the ball until it is through the posts.
>
> In playing the game it is as well to bear in mind that the foot was made for kicking, the head for thinking. However pretty the performance may look when half-a-dozen men are hitting up the ball like so many goats you may rest assured the goalkeeper would rather have the ball butted than kicked. It will be found sound play never to head in front of goal.

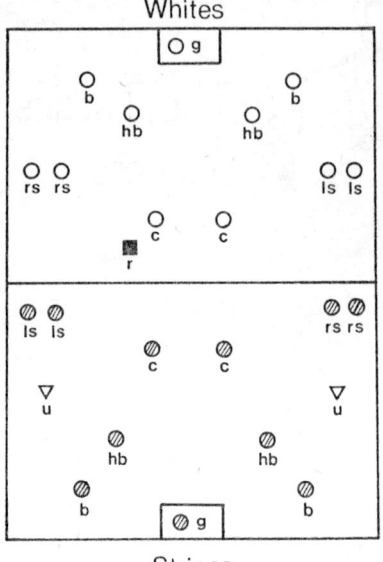

g g, Goals; *b b*, Backs; *h b h b*, Half-backs; *l s ls*, Left side; *r s r s*, Right side; *c c*, Centres; *u u*, Umpires; *r*, Referee.

The line-up in 1887

The contrast with the modern game indicates how far skills and tactics have been refined – not all defensively.

The formations with four or more at the back aim first at preventing goals; but any player in possession of the ball, even the goalkeeper, is an attacker looking for an opening.

The pressures of competitive football, the fear of losing the match or the job, have concentrated too much attention on spoiling play. Herbert Chapman's dictum, 'each time you go on the field you have already been given one point. You cannot lose that unless you throw it away by conceding a goal', has conditioned the mental approaches of most Managers, certainly to away games.

But defensive philosophies are the reaction to successful attacking method. The point is well illustrated by the final paragraph of those nineteenth-century instructions.

> In the newest arrangement of the field three half-backs are provided for instead of two. This is in answer to the tactics of keeping wing players in reserve, leaving eight men to do the

rough work and two to 'confer the artistic merit' by coming with a rush when least expected.

Surprise, superiority of numbers at the decisive point, these are tactics of football as well as of war. And in football too the balance is more easily tilted in favour of defence, the maginot line an easier concept than the blitzkrieg. But a main attraction of football is that its tactics, like its rules, remain essentially simple. Jock Stein cuts through the technical jargon to say, 'Football is a simple game. All you need is four at the back who can tackle, three in the middle who can pass, three in front who can run and shoot.'

Fashions in tactics are as fickle as in clothes. The Wolves' long ball to the winger, Arsenal's retreating defence, Manchester City's deep-lying centre-forward, Ramsey's withdrawn wingers, all set their problems and had their imitators for a few seasons. Yet the fundamental change in system that alters the whole strategy of the game comes once in a quarter of a century.

In the last fifty years there have only been two that have changed the character of football. In the twenties the greater freedom for forwards from the new off-side rule was countered by chaining back the attacking centre-half into a purely defensive role. The sixties saw the further reinforcement of defence with the second centre-back.

Abroad this concept had been accepted for years in Italy, with its negative football, its 'bolt' defences. Once it spread to Britain goals inevitably became scarcer. With four at the back, however you perm the other six you are short of an attacking player.

There is a nostalgic picture that hangs in Boardrooms or Managers' offices. The prints, sent out to commemorate the F.A. Centenary, catch one fleeting moment in the Cup Final between Burnley and Tottenham Hotspur, only a dozen years distant. Burnley are attacking down the left, two in support of the man with the ball, seven clustered round the penalty area. For the artist and for those of us who watched, this typified the creative movement of a match in which such as John White, Danny Blanchflower and Jimmy McIlroy were free to express their fancies. Now it looks sadly dated, a glimpse of pre-back four, pre-numerical systems, pre-strait-jacket organisation. Those days are gone, but even the programmes are still printed in the old formations as if no one wants to recognise the changed reality.

The mental approach has changed too. Leeds' relentless will to win began to harden attitudes and encourage the gamesmanship that angers Brian Clough. Leeds have refined and developed their style but when they first applied the pressure other teams soon matched them.

Lou Macari made candid comment shortly after joining Manchester. 'We are staying in the First Division and I can warn you it won't be a pretty sight. Managers who applauded the "Reds" for letting the opposition play will discover that suddenly we are a team of spoilsports. Now the skills which have embroidered Old Trafford must be sacrificed for the sake of sheer hard graft, guts and determination.' It was an epitaph for a decade, an obituary for the old Manchester.

After that conversion only one top team can be counted on to 'let the opposition play' – West Ham. Faith is the word that comes easily to their Manager Ron Greenwood and there is nothing self-conscious when he says it. His belief in the encouragement of skill is absolute, proof even against threats of relegation.

While other Managers demand longer contracts, Greenwood has none. In Spring 1971 West Ham had a wearing fight to stay in the First Division. The banners appeared 'Greenwood must go', the automatic response, the unthinking, uncaring demand for success. 'Doesn't the lack of a contract worry you now?' he was asked. 'I would be worried if I had one,' was Greenwood's reply. He felt it unnecessary to explain his conviction that a contract is no protection for a football Manager in trouble – as O'Farrell and a hundred others have found; that all a contract can secure you is money and all he is interested in is football; that to have no contract expressed a faith, a confidence between Manager and Chairman that was worth more than any scrap of paper.

Greenwood studies the game in depth, discusses it endlessly, the ideas spilling out in a gentle flow. 'When I was a player I was bored by being told the same thing over and over again. Anything I say is original because that taught me never to repeat myself.' This is unusual enough for him to be regarded with suspicion as an involved tactician too theoretical for the players to follow. But he is the only Manager in the First Division not to have a tactics table, not to rely on diagrammed instruction. His tactics are more a matter of the types of players he selects, how he trains them, what he requires of them.

When the defence needed strengthening he went into the market, not for a destroyer, but for Tommy Taylor, whose control is as delicate as any forward's. Even the strong ball-winners like Bonds are creative, alert to opportunity.

West Ham have limited money for transfers, are not prepared to offer unusual inducements outside the ordinary wage scale. At the start of each season Greenwood will look at the list of his two dozen players and think, 'I am dependent on these for success or failure. My contribution is to get the best out of them.'

He finds it helpful not to have been a great player himself. So many Managers are old Internationals who 'only used to look at the team sheet to see when the coach was leaving. I always had to look to see if I was playing, so I appreciate better the feelings of the average player.'

West Ham's aim is to give expression to the natural talent of the players. In mid-field there is the choice of putting the emphasis on winning the ball or on the use of it. Greenwood chooses those who are primarily creative, like Brooking and Robson, backs them with the strong tackling of Bonds. Forward, West Ham give width to their attack by playing a traditional winger even when they have none of oustanding class. The tactics are the implementation of what has been preached and practised in training. Give support to the man with the ball, move to make angles and space for passing.

Greenwood's style has much in common with the Scottish tradition and Eddie Turnbull is one Manager in sympathy with his ideas. He is a man who likes to win, but to win with style.

Talk to Eddie Turnbull about football and you get no impression of a tough competitor. The voice is soft, the smile ready. But he was the hard driver in that greatest of Hibernian forward lines. While Gordon Smith and Willie Ormond danced down the wings and Lawrie Reilly snatched the goals, Turnbull was the one who fought for every ball. The last time Scotland qualified for the World Cup finals in Sweden it was Turnbull who won Tommy Docherty's place at wing-half. He was near the end of his playing career then after twelve years on Hibernian's staff, but in three gruelling games over eight days he brought some fire to a listless team performance.

That Scottish team was without a Manager and their solitary point reflected a lack of discipline, a lack of will. When Turnbull is running a side there's no danger of that. He demands dedication, the same absolute loyalty to Hibs that he has himself. The road back to the club was a winding one for him. First he coached at Queen's Park, coming to terms with the more casual amateur approach. He found it a useful lesson to have always to persuade players and still drives only by kindling enthusiasm. As Manager at Aberdeen he found challenge and success. He ignored other offers, turning down the Scotland job, declining to be Assistant Manager of Rangers, waiting until his old friend Tom Hart was able to recall him to Hibernian. His ambition for the club is limitless. It was not enough that Hibs should beat Celtic in the Final of the Scottish Cup. Striding out from the celebrations in the dressing-room he dared any reporter to say his Hibs had been lucky. Stabbing his finger at them he said, 'What did you think of the match? And you? And you?' No one would accept the challenge, provoke the argument he sought. All recognised that he had already made Hibs worthy rivals for Celtic and Rangers. And only half of the three years had gone in which he had promised to mould Hibs to a championship side.

It is his conviction that all worthwhile players want to work, want to learn, want to succeed in their profession. 'They ask from a Manager that he shows them how to improve, that he is able to help them when things go wrong. If he can do that they'll not stint themselves. But if he cannot, shouting and shaking his fist won't help for long.'

During the game he will watch from the stand, a telephone at hand to the Coach on the touchline. And at half-time he will coolly analyse the faults. On a New Year's Day Hibernian scored seven against Hearts in a bewildering display that blended the best of old-time craftsmanship with the searing speed of the modern game. By the interval Hibs were five up and Turnbull stilled the rejoicing in the dressing-room. 'Sit down, relax, and I'll tell you how you can win this one.'

There was no hint of humour, just the conviction that the easier a game seems the more difficult it is for a Manager to sustain performance.

The crowds at Easter Road had dwindled to a few thousand when Turnbull took over. He is attracting them back by the flourish of the play as well as the results.

The tactical emphasis is on the swift switch from defence to attack. The speed with which the back four move up when they anticipate possession can leave forwards stranded, creating the illusion of an off-side trap. Turnbull gives free range to backs who have the ability to thrust forward. Brownlie, so full of promise before he broke his leg, was confined to his own half playing for Scotland, encouraged to drive up-field for Hibs.

The dearth of wingers has contributed to the sterility of forward play in England, but they still flourish in Scotland. And Turnbull makes use of them. He pounded the field behind some of Scotland's best and his teams are never short of a talented winger.

Dave Sexton, the quiet man of soccer, is in the group of Managers whose tactical approach is most flexible, governed by players available and the desire to be creative. He is friendly and responsive with his players, most relaxed when he is taking part in a practice game with them. But his shy reserve of manner keeps him remote from the public, the antithesis of Brian Clough. The clothes are as unassertive as the man. In grey suit, formal shirt and club tie he is the traditional image of the staid Manager. The elderly leather belt round his waist is more expressive of his feeling that clothes do not make the man.

Like many who commute long distances he has little time for the social round. But living in Brighton is a welcome excuse for avoiding London parties. For he is another of the Managers whose enjoyment centres on football and the family, absorbing all his interest. Normally he travels by train, rather than in his red Scimitar car, to get a chance to think. Four children leave little opportunity for quiet reflection at home.

And Sexton has always been eager to experiment. As a player he was forever trying out the latest in cut-away boots or shorter shorts, any new development that might give him the edge over the more conventional. That is reflected in his tactics and in Chelsea's. Take set-piece moves like corners and free-kicks. These can be most carefully rehearsed, most ingeniously planned. Like that one by Coventry's Willie Carr endlessly replayed on television. Standing astride the ball he flicked it in the air with his heels for Ernie Hunt to volley over the defensive wall into the corner of the net. This donkey kick even took the referee by surprise, the goal allowed to stand but the method later ruled illegal.

The principle was simple enough. If you hit the ball from the ground the angle needed to clear the defensive wall will also take it over the bar. But volley it from a few feet in the air and a flatter trajectory will take it over and under. Sexton had worked on a legal variant long before. He and Summers were taking their coaching certificate together when Winterbottom instructed the course to pair off, work out a novel free kick and demonstrate at the day's end. Sexton's proposal was perfected in an hour's practice. When their turn came he stood in the defensive wall and Summers chipped the free-kick to him chest high. Sexton swept it on with an overhead bicycle kick that sent the ball dipping into the corner. Winterbottom laughed, 'That's it for the day. No one can cap that.'

When Chelsea played Leeds in the Cup Final both teams were expert in these dead-ball plays. Jack Charlton's gambit of standing on the goal-line at corners unsettled all goalkeepers, but it was the more effective for not being constantly repeated. This time he stood deeper in the area when he beat Bonetti to open the scoring. With Leeds ahead and only six minutes to play Chelsea saved themselves with a rehearsed free-kick. The ball was pulled back to Harris, with Hutchinson already boring in to meet and head home his lob to the near post. And it was Hutchinson's long throw that finally settled the replay as Webb forced the ball in.

Each year Sexton finds a new tactic to practise in training for the surprise of opponents, the mental stimulation of his players. Watching the Hungarians in the Olympic semi-final he was struck by the way one of their back four moved up when they were in possession, allowing a mid-field man to thrust forward as an extra attacker. So that was Chelsea's practice for the start of the season.

Sexton's early experience taught him that the other tactical essential is good fortune. On the F.A. coaching course he had caught the eye of Tommy Docherty and been brought to Chelsea as his Assistant. Outwardly it was a lion and lamb combination, the forceful Scotsman and the mild Londoner. But Docherty respected his original thinking as much as Sexton admired Docherty's drive and ebullience. It was an ideal partnership until Sexton set out on his own to manage Leyton Orient. The first season relegation was barely avoided, the second he resigned when it seemed inevitable. 'I was saying the same things, trying the same thing's as I say and try now. But with the O's they just didn't work.' That was a daunting start for one who inevitably blamed himself, a harsh reminder that the game itself makes Management a lottery.

But the reason perhaps was not unrelated to size. Alec Stock had achieved remarkable success at Leyton Orient when deeply involved in every detail of the club. Moving to Arsenal he was ill-at-ease with the larger organisation, the delegated duties, the less demanding work. For Sexton it was the reverse. As Manager of Chelsea he can exploit his special flair for coaching and for tactical innovation, knowing that he has support for the rest of his job.

Tactics have to fit the players, not the players the tactics. To alter a style means changing a team. Manchester United can spend a million and start again. That's the gambler's way, but it would never suit Joe Mercer, who prefers slow evolution. He is used to instant miracles being expected of new Managers. His first appointment was to Sheffield United in the 1950s, inheriting a deficit of £18,000 and a playing staff without a centre-forward. He had been out of the game since breaking a leg with Arsenal, working for some months at his grocery business.

Always a man who needs to know all details of his trade, he was busily boning bacon when a newspaperman came in to suggest he applied for the Sheffield vacancy left by Reg Freeman's death. It was the Thursday before the season started and at once he rang the Chairman, who was acting as Caretaker Manager. The interview with the Board of fifteen was arranged that day and after a brief discussion the Chairman said, 'I hope you are going to be our Manager. I know damn all about the game and this lot know even less.'

The first match was lost at Newcastle, the second drawn at home against Charlton, whereupon one of the Directors remarked to him, 'You've made bloody little difference.'

Joe knows better than most just how long it takes to change a pattern of play and fortune.

It was at Manchester City that he built a reputation for free-flowing attack when the game was beginning to be dominated by defensive thoughts. But there was nothing adventurous about the play his first year as City fought to get back to the First Division. It was the defence he strengthened with the crude but effective George Heslop from Everton. And it was O'Dowd's remarkable goalkeeping that was the main prop of promotion.

The next reaction was defensive too. Tony Book was converted

D*

to a sweeper after Chelsea had run riot against them. But as Young, Summerbee, Bell and Lee were brought on together the tactics changed. 'With such forwards you had to be a lunatic not to play attacking football,' was Mercer's verdict. For a season it took other clubs by surprise. Then they realised that as City stretched forward they could drive wedges behind them. It is never easy for long.

At Coventry Mercer inherited a team with a dreary defensive image and a desperate struggle for First Division survival. Change was quicker there, the most obvious cause one shrewd transfer deal. The sale of Jeff Blockley and the acquisition of Stein and Hutchison was for Mercer a single operation, though it involved three players and three clubs. Blockley was not sold to Arsenal until Mercer was sure the £200,000 would get him the two forwards he wanted.

Coventry's defence was strong enough even without Blockley, and he had not been effective as a young captain. The combination of Manager and captain is always vital in any football success story – Ramsey and Moore, Revie and Bremner, Shankly and Smith, Mee and McLintock all reinforced each other's strengths.

Stein and Hutchison were surprisingly quick to settle into the forward line. Stein, physically hard and aggressive, is a dominant leader for any attack. Hutchison's delicate footwork baffles and bewitches, his style not unlike Leed's Eddie Gray.

Mercer gives Milne full responsibiity for developing the training and tactics, unworried by any thought that it was this delegation to Allison that finally undermined his own position at Manchester City. Milne still bears marks of playing for Liverpool and Shankly, with all that means in dedication.

> Liverpool is the most uncomplicated side in the League [says Mercer]. Gordon is imbued with their method and he coaches our players to go and get the ball quick, to pressurise all the time.
>
> I was brought up on a different tactical method, the Arsenal method of let them come, then go in collectively. Instinctively, I still believe that to be best. But it's his responsibility and it's working well.

Mercer was once a player who quartered the field much in the Shankly style. But at the end of his career he tucked in behind the

Arsenal centre-half, using his head and saving his energy in the role perfected by Bobby Moore.

If the Coventry tactics smack of Liverpool, that transfer deal was in the Arsenal tradition. Both Milne and Mercer were wing-halves with a feeling for driving up-field like an inside-forward. But it was not the middle of the field that they strengthened. Mercer was in tune with an old saying of Herbert Chapman's: 'If I've got a good goalkeeper and a good stopper centre-half, all I need is the two best wingers and the best centre-forward there is. It doesn't matter what the rest are like.' Hardly a compliment to all those mid-field men who are supposed to win matches, but it is the goal-scorers who can transform a side.

Mercer leaves most of the dressing-room talking to Milne, who has watched the detail of play from the touchline. Higher up in the stand he has had a clearer view of the pattern of play and adds his comments on this. This will be a cool tactical evaluation. During the unsuccessful start to the season, before Stein and Hutchison came, he was once moved to a rare burst of emotion. 'If we are going to lose,' he said, after a particularly depressing first-half display, 'then let's lose like a First Division side.' That, win or lose, is the way Coventry play for him.

Southampton have had a somewhat different reputation in the past few seasons. Survival in the First Division was hard for a team with a limited following and they fought hard to survive. When the average age of the side was 28 they had players like Gabriel whose tackling was not always angelic, Hollywood as tough as teak and McGrath who was in the tradition of rugged centre-halves.

The team was nicknamed the 'dirty old men' with rather more wit than justice. For Southampton has always encouraged the gifted ball-player and that is a truer reflection of Bates' intent to score goals.

Tactics, as we have seen, must always fit the players, so the Manager's outlook is best expressed in the ones he buys or develops. Think of Southampton and you think of forwards – powerful strikers like Davies, Chivers and Channon, or clever wingers like Paine in his prime.

Terry Paine, with more than 150 goals and 650 League appearances, typifies the club and the skills that Bates admires. Born in

Winchester he was picked out by the local scouting network to be the most durable of the club's players. Even when he was in the England side and Southampton in the Third Division Paine remained a one-club man because of the encouragement given to express himself as he wished. And if the expression is sometimes violent it is more often clever and sophisticated.

How you use a player is also vital. So many Managers try to mould them to their own image to develop skills they haven't got. Bates has the right method. 'I buy a player or give him a team place for his special ability, not his weaknesses. I tell him "This is the strong point of your game and that's what I want exploited. We'll cover your weaknesses." That does not mean just doing his own thing for in modern "total" football no one is excused the chase and the challenge.'

This is the main change Bates has seen over thirty-five years. Every player now has to take his responsibility for getting the ball, for using his fitness to help the team. Bates looks on this as a part of attacking tactics, of getting the ball back quickly or moving up swifty in support. His two main maxims are: 'In possession move forward collectively; when you've lost the ball put instant pressure on the man and the space.' To explain the pressure on space he darts to the tactics table, moving the red discs to cover the players to whom the opponent with the ball might easily give a pass.

The two other maxims are aimed at keeping the team organised and playing collectively. If you lose possession get behind the ball and start again. Do not sell yourself in mid-field. Again there is the quick illustration on the tactics table of the ill-judged tackle near the half-way line leaving the defenders exposed, the man with the ball under no pressure.

Any football Manager who can keep his job and his good humour for nearly twenty years has some special assets apart from a level-headed Chairman. Ted Bates' enthusiasm, his total absorption in one game and one club have made him synonymous with Southampton. Characteristically he never mentions his age, only his *football* age. For him life started in 1937 when he came to Southampton as an apprentice, brought down from his mother's home in Norwich by 'Gentleman' Tom Parker. There could be no better mentor than Parker, captain of Arsenal at the height of Chapman's era before he returned to his old club. Parker's sportsmanship was unblemished and he never countenanced a protest to the referee by any of his players – not even after the famous ball-over-the-line incident that cost Arsenal the 1932 Cup Final. To be coached by him was total fulfilment for a man like Ted Bates, born to sport. His grandfather, Billy Bates, had played cricket for Yorkshire and England, his fifteen Test appearances, all in Australia, an oddity never repeated.

Ted Bates was a front runner, not one of the fetch-and-carry type furrowing up and down the field. But in more than 400 games for the club he played in every position – even goalkeeper. He took over in goal once when Hugh Kelly was injured in a game against Leeds. 'I'll protect you,' said the referee as Bates recalls it, 'and he saw to that all right. But I let in a near-post goal – the great crime for a goalkeeper.'

Having experienced every position on the field he tried most in the club, from running the youth team, to Coach to Team Manager: indeed a man who can talk from experience. His work has always been confined to football and the players. Finance and administration are the Secretary's and the Board's worry. That is appropriate for a man with no interests outside football and talking football. His wife at least can understand this since she was Assistant Secretary of the club when he married her. What spare time he has he spends at home, though his teenage daughters complain he's never there when they want him.

Inevitably Bates is a well-known figure, hailed in street or pub, invited to Rotary lunches. But the social engagements are limited by the work, the desire to spend some time with his family. His winter routine involves him in watching matches on the first three evenings of the week; Thursday is the meeting with the Board, Friday the day of preparation, Saturday of revelation, Sunday morning he is always back at the ground. And if Campbell Forsyth, his Scottish Scout, tells him of a likely prospect, he is apt any day to rush to London after the morning's training, fly to Scotland, catch the late plane back and be home at three in the morning, back at the ground by nine.

His office is more footballer's than Manager's, with the piles of boots stuffed behind the cabinet, the towel and playing shorts dumped on the radiators, the picture of the Tottenham-Burnley Cup Final on the wall.

The tactics table is the focal point of the room, rather than the desk in its centre. On this miniature field the red and blue discs line up in modern formation, but marked with old names as if nothing has changed from the days of five forwards and three defenders.

Bates still hankers for two wingers of the old kind whose burning pace or deft dribbling took them to the goal-line to cut the ball back. But he accepts this is no longer possible. 'In the modern game you must have depth as well as width. Two wingers give you the width, but leave you too exposed. One is essential, two a luxury you cannot afford.'

Bill Shankly is another still fascinated by the old-fashioned winger. His model player is Tom Finney.

> No one ever got to the bye-line as often as Tom and he made goal-scoring simple for others. He had everything – good with both feet, good in the air, a deadly shot, precise in his passing. Many skills have improved but he had one that is a lost art today – the accurate cross when running at speed. There were several wingers who could do that when I was playing, but none now.

Pace is Shankly's main requirement of forwards and his faith in wingers is expressed in Liverpool's tactics. He can only afford Heighway out wide most of the game, but another forward or an overlapping back will work the other touchline, stretching the defence across the whole field instead of allowing it to concentrate.

The study of the opposition, the small adjustments of style to exploit their weakness or eliminate their strength, these are the essence of tactics on which Managers concentrate before a match.

Shrewd preparation played as significant a part in Queen's Park Rangers' promotion to the First Division as the purchase of three exciting forwards in Don Givens, Stan Bowles and Dave Thomas. Both showed the enterprise of Gordon Jago, one of the most impressive of the younger Managers.

He describes himself as a Londoner who never willingly goes north of Wembley. Coaching the Baltimore Bays in America has somewhat confused the accent and the expression, startled apprentices being jollied along with 'Jeesy Beeze, that was a little bit of magic'. The bustle of America is in tune with his own personality as he challenges the detail of the architect's work at the stadium, prepares plans for pop concerts or for the holding of fashion shows to attract women to the ground. The priorities never get lost in the enthusiasms: 'Yes, gentlemen, we will be improving the press accommodation, but bear with us as we have a lot on our hands.'

Like so many of the more intelligent Managers he analyses his own unfilled needs as a player to guide his handling of his staff. 'I was looked after well enough at Charlton when in the team. But once you were dropped you were treated as an outcast and that was when you most needed encouragement. Training was by the watch – the quality of the work less important than filling in the time. I would loiter round the café at the end of a run, rather than arrive back early.'

Jago always involves the players in planning the tactics. In the achievement of promotion to the First Division the most crucial game was the home match with Burnley, unbeaten that season in an away fixture. This was the tactical preparation.

> We've studied them closely away from home and our assessment is that we are too strong for them down the middle. Don Givens and Stan Bowles are too clever for Waldron and Dobson. If it is two-against-two Don and Stan will win out often enough. So we've got to give them the chance. That means pulling the rest of the Burnley cover out of the way and leaving the two in the centre isolated.
>
> Young Docherty likes to stay with his man so Dave Thomas will keep him wide on the wing. Keith Newton is not so quick to recover these days so we can make him stay near the touchline by threatening down the right wing with Gerry Francis working out that way.
>
> But that's too simple. We must have another move to confuse them, the one we'll practise now. Nulty and Collins are not strong enough to tie us up in mid-field. So once in a while Stan Bowles will move wide on the right and Mick Leach or Gerry Francis will slip through in his place.

In the game both moves bring a goal, Givens turning past Dobson to score, Leach moving up to head in a deep cross.

The plan to keep Burnley from scoring also worked well.

> Defensively we have much the same problems as against Aston Villa. You'll remember we researched their most dangerous move as Andy Lochhead heading the ball back for Bruce Rioch to shoot. So we always challenged Lochhead in the air and when-

ever he went up had someone close mark Rioch. That kept them from scoring. Fletcher is a centre-forward nearly as good as Lochhead in the air. He's going to beat Mancini often enough. But Terry, you must always challenge him. When he wins the ball, Fletcher will try and glance it in for Casper. So as he goes up Hazell must stay close to Casper. And the rest of you defenders must watch for anyone else making a run and pick them up.

The other danger is Leighton James. He likes to turn back at the end of a run, go inside and centre. Don't let him turn in, keep him out on the line and make him run for the corner flag.

Such studies and adjustments do not necessarily decide matches, are often less important than the form of individuals or the run of the ball. But they give the team the best chance of winning. It was an assessment like this that could well have cost Millwall the point they needed for promotion the previous season. Bridges and Possee were Millwall's two effective strikers, both deadly when they could run on to a through pass, less skilled in controlling the ball and turning with it. So Jago asked his back four to stay deep, never move up even when Rangers attacked. Bridges and Possee, with a man always at their backs and one covering the space between, had a profitless afternoon.

The Cup can bring its own tactical problems, with the little clubs exploiting the peculiarities of their grounds. Yeovil is the only non-League club whose Cup defeats of League sides run into double figures. The illustrious have been tripped up on its sloping surface, including in 1949 Second Division Bury and First Division Sunderland. Now the preparations are more careful, the dangers better researched, the chances of upset lessened. Tony Waiters faced the problem when preparing Plymouth Argyle for their Cup encounter with Yeovil.

In the main it's a matter of confidence. The pitch has a reputation which the Press and the Club build up into a formidable obstacle before a Cup game. But I told our players that this was a perfectly good ground, the merits of which Yeovil emphasise when they are applying to join the League. The slope is not particularly disturbing if you understand the small technical problem it presents. For most attacks the ball needs to be worked up the slope with the final centres coming down it. The winger at the top should stay right out on the touchline with the other ready to close in for the cross. The pace of passes has to be adjusted, but not significantly.

We practised three days before on a pitch with much the same gradient. But that was more to make the players feel at ease than for necessity.

Margate is another Southern League side with a record of success in the Cup and sharp slope in the ground. The drop is nine feet from corner flag to corner flag, but diagonally across the pitch. Margate is an unusual club in that its Committee is elected by a membership composed of anyone interested in the town's football and ready to pay a subscription of 25 pence a year.

From the Boardroom you can see the top of the Big Dipper in Margate's Dreamland, a fruitful source of humorous allusion in the ups and downs of the Cup. The sickening sensation of the plunge into heavy defeat came when Ted MacDougall scored a record nine goals against them in Bournemouth's 11-0 win. That was the depressing start for Les Riggs who had just taken over as part-time Manager of part-time players. Next season he took Margate to the Third Round without conceding a goal, only to be drawn against Tottenham. Realistically Margate tried to change a home match into an away game at Tottenham, preferring the extra cash to the faint prospects of success. But a change of ground is not permitted for money alone.

For Les Riggs the tactical problem was simple.

We know all about Tottenham's style because Eddie Clayton, our Captain, played with them for many seasons. But with part-time players we can only train twice in the week and there is no chance of evolving complicated tactics. We will keep four up in attack as usual and hope that our enthusiasm will offset the difference in skill. The obvious dangermen like Chivers will be closely marked, but I will stress to our mid-field players that the main threat will be from the sneaky ones like Peters who slip through unnoticed.

Six goals still slipped past his 'keeper noticed by the capacity crowd that was Margate's reward for previous success.

Gordon Milne's approach was similar when Wigan Athletic took on Manchester City, playing away at Maine Road.

> You have one tactical advantage as a little club. The occasion is going to make your players run until they drop whereas the First Division team cannot get excited about the game. That is your strength. Complicated tactics would only confuse and weaken that tremendous drive. We set out to play our normal game, but as Player/Manager I could adjust and advise as the match developed. There was only a goal in it and we chased them hard to the end. We all enjoyed it, but they could not.
>
> When Coventry met Grimsby in the Cup I spent the week drumming into our players the need to get excited and urgent about the game even though they were up against a lesser side. Having experienced it as the underdog I could appreciate their advantage in a game meaning so much more to their players than to ours.

Surprising defeats are often attributed to the small grounds, but this should be nothing new for League teams. Many of theirs are cramped. Arsenal's ground is only 110 yards by 71 – one of the smallest in the League and identical with Margate's, which was once their nursery pitch. More disturbing than the size and surface of the ground can be the small club's supporters crowded closer to the pitch than in the large stadia and with the players much more aware of their presence.

The Manager's influence on tactics is in part his ability to influence his players. Their outlook, their response to the opposition, to the referee, to the pressures of the game are his first concern. Terry O'Neill recorded Allison's attempt to lift Manchester City before an away game against Crystal Palace, his reaction to their fifth defeat in six matches. The scene sums up for every Saturday on every ground the Manager's emotional commitment, the players' enjoyment of humorous repartee, their quick-tempered reaction to imagined injustice:

REFEREE: 'You know you have to wear armbands tonight lads and there'll be one minute's silence.'
BELL: 'God, we're not playing that badly are we?'
LEE: 'This must be their latest tactics, this dressing-room is worse than a Sauna.'

SUMMERBEE: 'Come on, lads, let's stop playing about at the bottom of the table, there's nothing a little effort won't put right. Who's taking the corners tonight? Me?'

Malcolm Allison enters the dressing-room. 'We've got a Cockney referee tonight so we must have a good chance.' He laughed. He turned to Doyle, 'I want you to mark Kellard out of the game. He's tricky. But don't let him upset you, just walk away. I don't want to see any bookings tonight, and I mean *any*.

'Mike, this fellow McCormick is going to come right up tight on your back. Take him back to our goal first, check him out, then run him. He'll be frightened of your pace, so go wide and then come back inside. He'll get sick. If you don't you'll look like Quasimodo with him on your back all night!'

He squatted down in front of Bell, quietly pleading, 'Col, use your power, use it, please. Rodney, make things happen tonight, don't let them happen, make 'em happen.'

The bell goes, they file out. 'Now any wrong decisions leave it out, or they'll get on to you, forget it, take no notice. Let's get them into the back of the net, then we won't need to argue. I want to see plenty of shots tonight, plenty of shots.'

HALF-TIME 0–0

'You all right, Mike? What happened, did he kick you? Have a rest the first 10 minutes, it'll be OK. Tom, don't leave anything in the air around the box, you were looking at Derek looking at Willie. Get rid of it whack! You've got to chase it, you were a bit casual there once or twice. I had to shout at you before you started looking for things. I think we can beat that full-back on the right, try and get him on his chinstrap early on.'

The bell went for the second half.

DIRECTOR'S BOX

Throughout the match Allison sat with a face as black as thunder. 'Look at that, another bloody penalty, diabolical. He got hold of Rodney's foot in the goalmouth.' He shouted and shook his fist violently at Towers.

City were at last awarded a penalty. Allison leaned back, hands on hips, grinning. 'He had to give one didn't he? There should have been three already.' Lee missed it. The crowd went crazy, applauding, then booing and jeering towards Allison.

He leapt up and left the box, and there was an uneasy silence. People started looking around, whispering, staring and shifting awkwardly in their seats. A general feeling of guilt hung in the air. Later he said: 'I only went to the toilet, I like to get back at 'em occasionally.' He became absorbed in the match again.

FULL-TIME
They have lost one-nil. There was silence in the dressing-room until Doyle exploded, uncharacteristically, 'That goalkeeper's come out, missed the *** ball, punched me straight in the face, I went up to a cross from Mike and McCormick kicks me *** legs from under me, I went up for another cross and Kellard bends his *** back and he never said a *** word to the three of them. And then he goes and *** books me!'
ALLISON: 'You were fighting on the pitch.'
DOYLE: Fighting? He kicked the legs from under me and I fell on top of him.'
ALLISON: 'Look, you've got no chance, *no* chance, I told you. You can't beat them, I've told you.'
DOYLE: 'But I didn't do anything, I just stood there and he hit me.'
ALLISON: 'You were fighting him on the floor. You should have been sent off.'
DOYLE: 'What about when the goalkeeper punched me, then?'
ALLISON: 'He should have been sent off. Two wrongs don't make a right.'
DOYLE: 'Yeah, but we got beat didn't we?'
'Yeah, we got beat,' Allison mimicked. 'But two wrongs don't make a right. You've *got* to accept it. Until you do you'll just get into trouble, more trouble and then more trouble.'
SUMMERBEE (shaking with anger): 'Let me get out of here before I hit somebody. You know what I'd do if I was Manager? I'd stop all our wages, including mine.'
On the coach back from London, Allison asked where Lee was. 'He's hiding in case you give him a right-hander for missing that penalty,' said Marsh.
Allison was in a pensive mood. 'I never tear them off a strip when they've lost. I've done it before and it's led to bad feelings that take too long to heal.' He became absorbed in his cigar. 'You know this game is like being in love, you've got to suffer to enjoy it.'

Training for Victory

Edwin Moscrop, who helped Burnley beat Liverpool in the 1914 Cup Final, recalls the training he did for his club and when picked for England. 'They expected me to keep fit. I am afraid I didn't do a great deal because I'd nowhere to go. My training consisted of skipping in the back garden and kicking a ball in the entry of my house in Southport.' That echoed my own introduction to First Division football. But Managers ensure it is a little different today.

The professional footballer, like the soldier, spends most of his time training rather than battling with opponents. His normal working week, as advised for the old S.E.T. return, is nineteen hours, making him a part-timer by industrial standards. Three-quarters of that is devoted to training and it is there that the Managers have the best chance to influence him. This realisation has accounted for their changed role from office organiser to practical instructor, deeply involved with their players. The need is oddly recognised in the acceptance by the Inland Revenue that football Managers, like deep-sea divers and pilots, qualify for an early pension and that fifty-five is the proper retiring age for them. It is not the harrassing mental pressures or the insecurity that has set them apart from the rest of us, but the need to be active enough to set an example.

Bill Shankly is at his happiest setting off in his orange Ford for the training ground, but most Managers will have lost the relish by sixty. For if the training is short, it is increasingly sharp.

Films of football in the 1950s can be mistaken for a slow-motion replay when compared with today's restless running and instant challenge. Strength, stamina, and the competitive spirit are the characteristics foreigners associate with the British game. These are the qualities that intensive training has further developed. Sleight of foot, conjuring with the ball, such subtleties come more naturally to the South Americans or the Portuguese. Yet within British football there have always been two strains. The English are fast and physical, their traditions rooted in the public school origins that saw the game as a character-building exercise, a test of courage. The Scots have a greater love of style, a flair for attack, a desire to express their individuality.

A hundred years ago C. W. Alcock, Secretary of the F.A., was writing, 'if you want to see the perfection of play it would be advisable to watch for an opportunity when a really first-class Scotch eleven is in the field'. Sixty years later Herbert Chapman made a more penetrating analysis:

> The difference in the game in the two countries is most noticeable in the matter of defence. English defenders are more stubborn, there is more bite to their play. The Scots are more given to spectacular attacking movements. They have greater regard to style in attack, than soundness in defence. In 'watching' a forward in Scotland it is essential to decide how he will fare in the face of the sterner English defenders. With us it is a case of goals and points. At times one is persuaded nothing else matters. To get results we have speeded up the play, and craftsmanship and ball control have, compared with the best Scottish style, been crowded out.

Another forty years on nothing has changed, the differences still reflected in training as well as play. 'Make the players hungry for the ball – by concealing it from them' is no longer the English method of practice, but there is still no great emphasis on ball work and basic skills. Most Managers take it for granted that these have been mastered by intensive practice at the schoolboy or apprentice stage. So the concentration is on fitness, on team plays and set pieces, on the functional drills that knit together a defence or a forward line.

A top-class cricketer like Geoff Boycott will spend hours at the nets perfecting one stroke. Stanley Matthews had the same approach in improving his soccer skills. But this attitude is rare for English footballers, as teamwork is exalted at the expense of individual flair.

There are exceptions. Malcolm Allison would keep the Manchester City players training individually for more than an hour each week in a constant repetition of one aspect of control, or of heading. Ron Greenwood will emphasise skill with the ball as will John Bond at Bournemouth and other former West Ham players who have absorbed and enjoyed Greenwood's methods.

Even in stamina training there are differences of view, particularly over the use of weights. Terry Neill was quick to intoduce weight-training at Hull from his own experience with Arsenal that this builds physique and confidence. Rippling muscles give a feeling of power, a sense of achievement that conditions the right mental approach to the game. Others, like John Bond and Eddie Turnbull, see the body as providing its own weight training when it has to be shifted through the sprints and turns that the game demands.

Most Managers relax the training on the day before a match, easing off to leave the appetite keen for the hard work of the game. But at Hibernian Eddie Turnbull maintains the intensity of effort, reasoning that any relaxation carries over into the mental approach on the day that matters. In his view the body adapts better to an unchanging rhythm and the recovery time of a trained athlete is measured in minutes, not days.

When Jimmy Hill regenerated Coventry this was the theory that underlay one of his unusual training techniques. Having read of the need to sustain the body's rhythm he thought it odd that footballers should always train in the morning when their matches were in the afternoon. At the time when the real physical effort was to be demanded of them they were usually idling in front of the television set on training days. So twice a week he started his sessions to coincide with kick-off time. The results were good enough to mollify the players' dislike of losing a free afternoon, but strangely the method has rarely been copied.

The training and play of a team must mirror a Manager's aims and is usually moulded in his own image, his own style as a footballer.

Bill Slater, who played as an amateur for Blackpool when they lost the 1951 Cup Final, was to captain Wolves to a win at Wembley nine years later. His experience illustrates how a Manager's personality can have a more powerful effect than any practice.

The Blackpool team were always apprehensive of the game against Wolves, who had an earned reputation for hardness, for unrivalled physical fitness. Later, when Slater asked Cullis to take him on at Wolverhampton, he had doubts about standing up to the pressure of the training that produced such formidable fitness. It turned out to be less demanding than Blackpool's.

The difference was Cullis' own aggressive outlook, so drilled into his team that it had become habit. You might be drained with exhaustion but if you lost the ball you still chased back. It was not just a case of better the present pain than the wrath to come in the dressing-room. The team philosophy required it and no one stayed who did not accept that requirement. It is the same now at Anfield. They fight for Liverpool with that dedication which Shankly is able to communicate.

Training breeds habits into Managers as well as players. Cullis was brought up on a tradition of attack, of driving forward using long passes to the wing. It was a simple and effective method in his day, but he was impervious to change. After an away game against Leeds he produced a diagram he had kept of the team's play and criticised the number of square and back passes.

Slater, as captain, defended his side: 'But those passes helped us win 4–0 away from home.' 'That,' said Cullis firmly, 'is irrelevant. There were too many side and back passes.'

Differences in method reflect the differing outlook of Managers. The footballers' routine cycle of training endlessly repeated over forty weeks can stale and bore. Its freshness depends on the enthusiasm and invention of Manager or Coach, their personalities reflected in the intensity of the work, the depth of tactical planning, the attraction of the special games designed to stimulate interest.

Gerry Summers prowls into the Oxford United offices with the suppressed energy of a wing-half denied the opportunity to tackle. That was the position on the field to which he settled from his early days as an apprentice at West Bromwich Albion. It was there that he found the fascination of coaching both from his own involvement in training schoolboys and from his reaction to an unusual Manager, Jesse Carver.

Carver, so highly regarded on the continent where he made his name in Italy, so little used in England, had that one season of soaring success with Albion.

After all that dreary lapping and routine training Carver gave us something fresh and exciting that stirred my enthusiasm. There was a lot of ball work, a lot of emphasis on skill and he had time to talk to us all – even though there were 50 or more players on the staff in those days. Jesse brought interest and innovation into the training and that kept us eager, helped us be imaginative ourselves.

After Carver had returned to Italy, Summers was pleased to transfer to Sheffield United, brought there by Joe Mercer.

I thought to myself, if *he* cannot show me whether I can play in the middle of the field no one can. He was one of the great players and personalities of the day. I recognised that and was ready to learn from him. Looking back I could be critical of some of the methods and tactics as ordinary or outdated. But at the time he had the same impact on me as Carver. You respond to a man you respect.

The respect was mutual. The memory of Summers' transfer still prompts Mercer's slow, happy smile. 'I only spent £3,500 on him. Which would have rated him a best buy – and it enabled me to sell Iley for £23,000 so I got a handsome profit and a handsome player.'

As a player Summers was a little like Mercer in his young days, all tireless running and following his feet wherever they took him. He still has the light step, alert eye and spare hard body of the athlete in full training, the functional physical man untouched by an ennervating elegance. That is reflected in his small trim office with its light wooden pannelling, its tidy desk. On the wall is the large date-list of fixtures and the names of the twenty-four playing staff. In the corner are the essential files, a single grey three-drawer cabinet to keep the contracts and general information. On top is a smaller one with details of Associated Schoolboys, Amateurs, Professional Apprentices and Players, Staff and Directors' addresses and Scouts. A box file with club circulars completes the ready-to-hand information.

The only ornament is a china bull, gift of Hereford United when they were seeking to break into the League and reminder that it is only a dozen years since Oxford were themselves non-League Headington United.

On the wall was just one picture – a colour spread from a magazine. It was headlined 'Hemery's Hell' and showed David Hemery struggling up the Boston sand dunes as his trainer forced him through the endurance barriers. The final caption was 'Hemery Shattered', with the athlete doubled up at the top retching for breath.

It was a Monday morning and Oxford had lost 0–2 to Bristol City on the Saturday. Summers laughed when asked if the picture was significant.

> Yes. Its dedication day. They played bloody awful and they are expecting a right rocket from me, followed by practice to put right what went wrong. That would be normal. But I never decide what training to do until the Sunday and I will surprise them.
>
> Dave Sexton is the man I admire most for his coaching ideas and he believes you must always keep the same routine, the same rhythm in training so that everyone knows what to expect, come success, come disaster. That's the only fundamental in which I disagree with him. I think a surprise or two is stimulating.
>
> Everyone's frustrated today. The boys started well then gave away a penalty. After that they went from bad to worse. The referee was so niggling that play went on until five-to-five because of all the stoppages and that added to the irritation. The Directors have taken it out on me and now the players expect me to take it out on them. But I'm not going to say a word. And I am not going to have a tactical practice because two key players are injured and it wouldn't add up to much without them. Instead we are going running. Sometimes they call it punishment running and sometimes they are right. But it will work the annoyance out of our systems. Later in the week we'll work on the tactics. We are good at two-touch and the wall pass so we've been concentrating more on holding the ball

and taking on a man to widen our range. And that was all they could think of when Bristol City put the pressure on us and split us into man-to-man situations. They forgot how to play themselves out of trouble with the close passing – so I'll have to remind them later in the week.

When Summers followed Ron Saunders to Oxford, one of his immediate priorities was to find more grounds for training, in the belief that change of scene stimulates interest. His club can never compete with the big city teams in wages, in the fervour of crowds, in the ability to build a player into a national figure. But the charm of the surroundings, the more relaxed tempo of life, can be an important asset in taking pressure off the players, in helping them enjoy their football. And this Summers uses. Even this hard physical session is softened by the beauty of the downs above Cowley as they follow the paths that dip and rise like a roller-coaster.

After the switch-back running along these tracks comes the inevitable explosive effort up the steepest slope. To add keenness it is competitive, pairs sprinting against each other. The cries of encouragement are common to training grounds the country over. 'Push, Push, Push! Drive Kevin, Drive. *You* can beat him. That's good Dave, you've got the better of him again.'

As the last pair is started the first is back again, recovered for the next short burst. For the final run Gerry Summers goes a hundred yards or so from trainer Ken Fish.

This is the effort that recalls the picture of Hemery as the driving finish leaves each pair doubled up and fighting for breath. 'Back to the cars, keep moving, run, run.' Most fight their own battle against the momentary nausea, but one relieves his feelings with a muttered 'bastard training' and another with 'bastard trainer'. Goalkeeper Burton is too shattered to follow the others, stumbling a few steps, then hanging motionless in the fight for air. As his breathing quietens he straightens up and says with philosophical acceptance, 'That was good for us. We needed that.' He is running easily again when he reaches the group at the cars and starts a discussion with Summers. 'A pity about that penalty. I got my fingers to it.'

'You could have saved it. It was well placed, but if you had really gone you'd have got it. I told you Gow would put it that side of you because I've watched him taking penalties. You only half believed me so you didn't go without thinking. And that was the fractional difference between touching it and stopping it.'

Oxford had faltered after a good start to the season, but next Friday they win away at Hull, that single goal restoring confidence, rewarding the effort.

The requirement for strength and stamina training is perhaps the most difficult for a Manager to judge. There is no exact knowledge of limits of physical endurance, of when improvement ends and damage begins, of how fitness degenerates into staleness. The work is harder at the beginning of the season or at the end of rehabilitation after injury as the players build to their peak. Maintaining that peak from August to May is the real problem. At least the lengthening season has lessened the early training need.

> They look after themselves better in the close season than we used to. I tell the Oxford players they will be fined £5 if they are 4lbs over-weight when they report back and another £1 per pound. No one's been fined yet; and no one smokes now in the way we did in my playing days. In many ways they are better disciplined now that the rewards are greater. Outsiders get misled by the long hair or loud language, but most of them are more dedicated now to a profession that offers them so much – if they keep fit. That discipline helps training.

Whether it is the hills above Oxford, or the running track around the Arsenal ground, the stamina training is much the same – though somewhat more exact and scientific at Highbury.

On an untypical day there Bertie Mee is supervising the work, which he more often watches from the sidelines. Mee is not the man to delegate responsibility to a Coach, then to take the job away. But it adds an extra edge when the Manager takes the training and they want to raise performance today.

Blockley, Ball and Storey have been called up by England to prepare for the International against Yugoslavia next evening. The training schedule has been adjusted from the original plan of practices to acclimatise Blockley into Arsenal's back four, England's prior need accepted without rancour.

Mee's aim is always quality work in a short concentrated session, no spinning out, no wasted time.

The exercises are geared not to general athletic fitness, but to the special demands of soccer. The longer running is for the stamina requirement of a ninety-minute game, the shorter sprints for the essential acceleration.

The climax is power work to produce the explosive effort that wins or saves goals. Always there are target times or competition in pairs to add stimulus to routine work.

The stamina running is from one goalpost round the touchlines to the far goal – some 200 yards in all. The pairs compete against each other and the target figure is 25 seconds – not too demanding in itself, but there are seven repeats to come.

The crisp exhortations from Mee and Burtenshaw, the Coach, are calculated, like the competition, to bring urgency to a boring routine.

'Go, Raddy, go,' as Radford surges off with his long rangy stride. 'Looks good, Cat,' as Marinello sprints past the half-way line, his thin concentrated face the only discernible resemblance to Catweazle. From the final corner-flag the runners are urged on to a fast time or chided for slackness.

McLintock and Kelly are the pair slowest to warm up, their first run of 27.5 greeted with a testy, 'Not nearly good enough.' There is little enthusiasm for the long runs, but a clear enjoyment of the 80-yard sprints. Players challenge timings with close interest and comments are more relaxed with a hint of humour.

Ray Kennedy, big-boned and angular, pounds down the track, arms pumping, gym shoes squeakily scuffing the powdered red gravel. 'Look at Ray. He's floating. He's floating,' calls Mee. The unlikely image brings a smile to a hard session.

Footballers are an insular group with their own humour, their own familiar language. McLintock is Frank to the football public, but Francis in training, or 'the Gorbals goon'. George Graham, not the fleetest of movers, is urged on with 'there goes the flying Scotsman'. Little George Armstrong is the 'Tyneside Tyke'.

Mee's brisk confidence rarely relaxes into humour. Ask him about the marble bust of Chapman in the entrance hall and he will look perplexed and say, 'Marble bust? In the Hall? Of Chapman? I don't recall one.'

A dry riposte to the thought that Arsenal's Managers must always walk in Herbert Chapman's long shadow. But the funny story, the wisecrack, is not his way. The nicknames and the familiarity are a conscious effort to relieve the impression of driving determination that is his true self. It was Jimmy Robertson who was the first to voice a warning to him of the dangers of dedication. 'You always put me off, boss,' he said. 'You are too intense.' The lesson has been learnt.

But professional soccer *is* intense and to Mee the will to win *is* vital. Though it cannot show through too nakedly all the time, the final exercise allows its expression. The players race up the concrete steps of the stand, straining ankles, heart and lungs to the limit – 'Explode, up the steps' is the constant theme. 'Explode, explode' – the word is a favourite with Mee. He sees the explosive shot, the explosive burst as giving the decisive advantage on a football field. If your effort is stronger, your recovery time quicker, you have a dominating advantage over your opponent – and all the strength training is geared to give his players this edge.

The physiotherapist in Mee is thinking happily of those improved ventricle muscles, the more efficient heart action. He watches with clinical interest for the signs of muscle fatigue telling of lactic acid build-up, the heavy breathing indicating the depth of the oxygen debt. 'Their pulse rates should be above 180 now. That will have done them good.'

From the players there are no quips or chat as they make slowly for the dressing-room. Even with their swift recovery rates the final exercise has taken its toll.

A straightforward week's training is rare for a top team with the constant interruptions of extra matches or International calls. But if there is only a Saturday game, the Arsenal pattern differs little from the routine of other clubs, except that the emphasis is on method and fitness.

After Sunday's rest, Monday is also a winding-down day. It is a time for getting rid of stiffness with a simple warm-up.

In the Highbury 'college' – that vast indoor training school with its powdered red gravel flooring – the players enjoy one-touch and two-touch passing games and five-a-side matches. Enjoy is the key word, for this is designed to highlight the fun of football, to entertain as well as improve.

Tuesday is the work day with hard stamina-building exercises on the track or circuit and weight-training in the small gym. This is when the players are pushed to their physical limits to maintain the fine peak of condition built up at the season's start. Too much and they go stale, too little and they lose the sheen of fitness. This is the nice judgement made more difficult for Manager and Coach when the training schedules are disrupted. So at Highbury peak performance is carefully charted, all players work to their recorded ability.

Wednesday is the rest day.

Thursday is devoted to team-play activities and preparation for Saturday's match. This is where the inventiveness of the Coach is tested for the special games and the individual practices must both catch players' imagination and make a purposeful contribution to improving their skills. Football is more a game of instinct than intelligence. In the seconds that matter the action must be automatic. Hesitate to think and it's too late. Coaching is based on the assumption that to select the right one of five alternatives can only become automatic over months, or years, of practice.

'Only if you learn the right basic habits will the game come naturally to you,' is the Coach's creed.

Friday is for toning up, for an emphasis on the acceleration, on the short bursts that are a fundamental of good football. Quick sprints and five-a-side games give this sharpness.

Equally important is the pre-match routine on the Saturday. So many games are lost in the first few minutes, so many injuries suffered when the body is cold, the muscles taut and inelastic. Before every game the players go through a regular step-up and sit-up routine to work the groin, hamstring and quadriceps muscles, improving the blood flow to them.

The familiar exercises also ease the tensions, so acute for the highly strung player like Charlie George that he is often sick before a match.

For the team practices Arsenal move out to London Colney, near St Albans. There the under-used grounds of London University provide an ideal training centre, the change from clangorous city to quiet countryside a refreshment in itself. The working groups of juniors and First Team squad are so far distant on this unscarred expanse of playing fields that it is a five-minute walk for Bertie Mee to switch attention from one to the other.

The training starts at ten, with the squad dividing for a practice game across half the pitch, the small five-a-side-type goal placed at either end. On such days there are usually small plays within the play.

For Brian Hornsby, the sturdily built young professional on the fringes of the first team, it is the chance to measure himself with established players, to gain confidence that he can match them for acceleration, for ball control, for power of shot. For Bob Wilson it is another step back to fitness.

The most depressing part of long injury for a footballer is the feeling of isolation, the loss of identity with the team, the lack of excitement. By nature athletes are bad patients, unable to rest, fretting to be active, needing to see the end of idleness. Early inclusion in such a practice is as important to rehabilitation as the stamina-building exercises up the steps of the Highbury stands. Wilson's hesitant dives show him still far from confident. Mee has left him to judge himself when he is fit for a return to match play and the moment clearly is not yet.

Practices are poor substitutes in assessing ability, but can be more revealing of personality than the game itself. The natural competitors cannot refrain from challenge even when the result doesn't matter. McNab, Armstrong, McLintock are all completely absorbed, fighting fiercely for the ball in a light-hearted game aimed at improving the coordination of the forwards.

Charlie George, the complete extrovert, is always calling for the ball, always indulging his whim to try something original. When a new trick works, the exultant gesture, the shout of self-congratulation, are instant expressions of his enjoyment. The peacock players colour the game with their bright skills and even the Manager of a functional side like Arsenal must be attracted by plumage as well as sinew.

The quiet introspective men like Peter Simpson seem lost in their own concentration, never calling for the ball, never so aware of other players.

The switch is swift to another team-game of Burtenshaw's devising aimed to stimulate the players' mental awareness. The rules are briefly explained and have to be quickly assimilated. It is four against four within the rectangle marked out by footballs. Goals are scored by dribbling through to touch one of the markers. The players have to adjust swiftly to an unfamiliar situation.

The final practice centres on two particular goal-scoring skills—the precise centre and the volleyed shot. In rotation one line lobs the ball across, the other volleys for goal. The work is variable, the Coach hard put to maintain quality as repetition dulls performance.

The competitive urge revives the interest. McLintock, driving the ball into the top corner with a 'match that', starts a stream of searing shots. Some final swift sprints and the session is over.

There is no profession in which the experts agree and it is the same with coaching. Greenwood, Turnbull and Allison are all accepted leaders in coaching technique. Greenwood believes in developing ability by playing in confined spaces, Allison always works over the full width of the pitch to avoid distorting judgement of distance. Allison puts great store on weight training, Turnbull thinks it a waste of time unrelated to the physical requirements of football. Turnbull increases the pressure of his training throughout the week, the others ease off before the match.

Turnbull's normal training week has evolved from his experience as a Coach, is personal to himself. The light training on Monday is to refresh. In the clear air of King Arthur's seat high above Edinburgh, the running is interspersed with discussion of the previous game and its lessons. Then the intensity builds, maintained throughout the week with no slackening on Friday. The last two mornings centre on functional work, on developing understanding in defence or forwards.

Two afternoons in the week players may come in for additional training in individual skills to keep practising to eliminate a fault or develop a new trick.

At the start of each session every player is given *his* ball. Even in stamina training he must work the ball during all his recovery periods as he gets his breath back.

That emphasis is echoed by Allison, a dogmatic demanding man with no doubts what he wants from his players. He never accepts the popular idea that basic skills are learnt at the apprentice stage, polished up in the practice games. 'Even in a ninety-minute match each player has the ball for less than two minutes. That's hardly time enough to improve technique.' Strength through dedication, skill through repetition is his code. Each week an hour-and-a-quarter session is given to individual practice of heading, shooting, dribbling, kicking, with Allison himself an unrivalled demonstrator of techniques.

Allison tells the story of early coaching at Cambridge when he was driving to the ground behind the ceaseless stream of bicycles.

Just in front two collided, one of the riders falling almost under his wheels so that he nudged him despite sharp braking. 'I'm so sorry,' said the prostrate cyclist. 'I am terribly sorry,' said the friend who had knocked him off. Allison laughs. 'What a difference. If they'd been from the East End all three of us would have had a punch-up.' You feel he would have relished that more. There is a directness in going after what he wants, an impatience with the limits of the possible or the restraints of rules, which puts him in tune with many of the players. Summerbee, facing suspension for being sent off in a friendly, flared up, to get yet another booking. Asked if he would take action, Allison shrugged, 'If I tame him I change him – and I'll lose something from his play. If I discipline him he will sulk and we'll both be losers.'

The identification with his players is complete, enabling him to drive them in training, but making it hard for him to be objective.

It was impatience that drove him to learn his coaching. At Charlton he was disillusioned with the listless, unimaginative training. Moving to West Ham he found even less variety or method, only dull running in the woods or on the cinder track.

Such poverty of performance sent him to Lilleshall to sample Walter Winterbottom's coaching scheme. He was so enthused that he went back every summer for ten years and began to devote his spare time to coaching.

Training is still his special interest. When he managed the part-timers at Bath City he used to rummage through the drawers, wondering what a Manager could find to do if he could not be out with his players.

Football is no longer a game of free expression. Shades of systems and formations close around the growing schoolboy, his masters as concerned as any Manager with the results rather than the enjoyment. At the apprentice stage he will be further conditioned to respond to certain situations as instinctively as a performing dolphin.

At Arsenal he will be endlessly drilled in certain plays such as 'up, back and through'. Move towards the man with the ball if you are more than fifteen yards distant; move away if you are closer. When he pushes up the pass play it back, then spin away from your marker ready for the through ball. Over and over again until you can do it running in your sleep. Good basic habits are the aim of the repetitions. Initiative and enjoyment can sometimes be the casualties.

The encouragement of self-expression makes West Ham's training unusual. The main exercise on their practice ground at Chadwell Heath is playing in ten-yard squares. At first it is three against three in one small box of the pitch marked out like graph paper. A few yards away the Liverpool Street trains rumble by, the players too absorbed to notice as they keep the ball within the square. In such confined space the man with the ball is always under challenge, developing instant control, delicate touch, swift judgement of angles.

Then the range widens. The game now is seven against seven within nine squares, the thirty-yard pitch still cramped with players. Longer passes can be used, the angles are wider, the pressure less intense. The final game is competitive, the square extended to forty yards. Goals are scored by dribbling the ball between the two lines marked out at either end and stopping it there. At once play reverses, the defenders now attackers, practising a forward's skills.

Tommy Taylor is the neatest, most agile in these small-square games. It is typical of Greenwood's method that his centre-half should have the skills of a forward, should relish dribbling under challenge even in his own area. The training as well as the selection reflects his belief that the game should be a flowering of talent, a contest of personality.

West Ham play the type of football everyone admires in theory. They are attractive and adventurous, competitive but not ruthless, fair in method, never petulant in manner. Acknowledging this the critics still put the *buts* in capital letters. BUT they aren't hard enough; BUT they rarely win major competitions; BUT they haven't the determination of a Leeds or a Liverpool. They should rather emphasise the ands. AND they have played that way for a decade without losing their First Division status; AND they always attract a good crowd to a small ground in an unpromising area; AND every team looks forward to playing them; AND the player of the generation, Bobby Moore, has been happy to spend his whole career there.

How has training affected performance? The Ipswich Manager, Bobby Robson, can compare the standards of play of modern football with his own performance for England in the World Cup of 1958.

If I was only as fit and fast as I was then I could not live with the present game. It has never been played at this pace before and the individual skills are much greater. But there is a tight defensive outlook and the speed at which it's played helps to cancel out the skill. You don't get the time or the space to be clever. So it may not *look* so attractive, but anyone who does not realise the standards are higher, does not understand soccer.

When he was playing for England Robson was influenced by Walter Winterbottom to take up coaching. 'Walter has been the major influence on the English game, bringing our coaching up to standard when we were falling so far behind the continentals. So many of the present Managers were influenced by him.'

Robson is an F.A. Staff Coach and it is still his joy to train with the players. Like many young Managers he is in practice the first-team Coach as well. 'I couldn't give it up even though Cyril Lea is our Coach. I delegate to him whatever I cannot handle on my own and if I am away he takes over. But the daily contact with the players is essential to me.'

Robson developed Ipswich into an attractive side, with Lambert as an old-fashioned left-winger ready to beat his man and cut the ball back from the goal-line. The three strikers were free of defensive duties: 'We keep three men up-field all the time and move the ball quickly to them. I don't believe in the slow build-up that gives time to consolidate. With three genuine strikers there is sufficient choice of aim for the mid-field men. And though Hamilton plays there he will move up on the right when we are in possession so that there is width to our attack.'

In the First Division all players must be fast, but Ipswich had five or more in the team with an extra yard of pace. This is fostered by Robson in training. 'We never do any lapping, but on the heavy training day we concentrate on shuttle-running. The lines are marked at five-yard intervals, the furthest 25 yards from the start line. They sprint to the first mark, turn and race back, turn for the second mark and continue till they have covered them all. That is 150 yards, with nine stops and turns. It has to be done in 30 seconds, and they do at least 17 shuttles in the afternoon, about a mile and a half of sprinting. Some who could only just complete a shuttle in 30 seconds are down to 27 – a decisive gain.'

The physical gains of training are measurable and carefully charted. The developments in skill are not so easy to discern, the higher standards smothered by the improvements in defensive techniques and spoiling tactics. Yet control that was once rare enough to win applause is now common enough to be unremarked.

Thirty years ago 'keep it on the island' was the standard cry as defenders booted the ball high into the stands. Now it is taken for granted that they use it with precision and perception. Twenty years ago the Hungarians revealed a range of talent beyond our capability. Now their side would be unexceptional, for our players have the same delicate control with chest, thigh and foot that then looked so unusual. Ten years ago many forwards made only token tackles. Now they are mostly as destructive as a full-back. Training has made the players increasingly versatile, but Gerry Summers emphasises the present lack.

> We have taught forwards the skills of a defender, but the defenders have not yet mastered the skills of a forward. The backs drive up in attack, but waste the ball when they get there.
>
> Our next task in training is to make them as skilful near their opponents' goal as in their own area. That will bring back the goals and the excitement.

Players and Captains

The Manager is dependent for his success on his players. His main job is to motivate them to win matches. They are full-time professionals yet they may spend only twenty hours a week under his charge. How do they fill in their spare time? And how do captains and Managers now share responsibility for looking after them?

Bob Wilson has this view of the players' life:

> What do players do with all that spare time? Well, what spare time? It's curious how many people outside the game still regard soccer as a ninety-minute-a-week job with a team talk and a couple of laps of the track slotted in somewhere. During the last five years with Arsenal I've spent a lot of time off relaxing at home and recovering from the last bout of travelling. All players with the six or seven successful First Division clubs must have done the same and have needed to.
>
> True, we are free nearly every weekday afternoon and perhaps all day Wednesday on those rare weeks when we're playing only one match. A lot of us stick to the traditional footballing time-fillers: to following horse racing, Alan Ball even owning a horse: to playing golf, with Mee, McLintock, McNab and Radford all low-handicap players: to visiting the cinema, or simply to painting the kitchen. Snooker and billiards aren't

as popular as they were because the halls aren't as numerous these days. Even so, you could raise a good team from most soccer dressing-rooms, just as you could find a lot of people to name you twelve films George C. Scott has appeared in.

Those are the old habits, the ones you associate with the player who was on a maximum wage of £20. Now we're in the show business era and that can be very demanding for those at the top.

A lot of us do ghosted columns, and for those who don't there's a long stream of phone calls demanding articles, or quotes. I wonder how many hours Frank McLintock, Geordie Armstrong or I have spent chatting on the phone! There's broadcasting, too, to be fitted in.

Bob McNab has done a bit of modelling in his time, and this has been more popular than you might think with footballers. Another modish occupation which mainly involves showing your face is to have a tie-up with a garage and drop in occasionally to be photographed among the cars. Peter Osgood and Martin Chivers have done this with profit. But the image of the footballer-tycoon has never stood up. Bobby Moore has had much criticism for having too many outside interests and it's probably true that he spends more time on business than ninety-nine per cent of players. But Moore, obviously, can cope and play superb football, too. Much of the sniping at him is pure jealousy and not many have the ability to fit in a successful business career as well.

The vast majority of top footballers, though, spend far more time attending functions (paid or otherwise) than they do trying to make money from football. The invitations seem endless. I get a couple of dozen every week and try to fit in two, three, or even more. If it's within striking distance of Highbury, if the time is right, and if the cause or organisation is reasonable I'll try to get there.

Speech days, women's institutes, bazaars and fêtes . . . the list is endless. It can be time-consuming, but providing I don't have to prepare any complicated lecture I'm happy. I like to keep my brain fairly active, and this sort of engagement makes me more alert. There is satisfaction for me too in working for the Sports Council and making some contribution to the development of sport in the country.

Finally, and often forgotten, is the number of visits to hospitals players make. A couple of requests go up on the Arsenal notice board every week and we don't often disappoint.

That may sound demanding on top of playing football for a living. And it is. That's why on any given day most well-known footballers are glad of a chance to stick their feet up by the fire and watch television or listen to a record.

For much of the time the player is outside the club's influence and the motivation is not constant. That is why the Manager must also expect help from his captain. In training, the captain's attitude can assist the concentration. On the field of play he can be the decisive influence if he has the character and the freedom of action.

Dave MacKay is a good example of a captain who now appreciates the Manager's problems, the importance of the relationship. This has helped him re-establish confidence at Nottingham Forest, where Matt Gillies was booed into oblivion as the team slipped down into the depths of the Second Division. Just before he was offered the job MacKay had brought Swindon to play Forest. He had seen the crowd so intent on taunting the Directors and Manager with being beaten by a farmers' team that they failed to notice the two late equalising goals. MacKay took over at Forest, well knowing his reputation would give him breathing space, but no protection if the team's results were not improved.

As a player he had been an elemental force in football, as irresistible as a runaway tank. It was MacKay's dominating physical presence that caught the eye, masking his shrewdness. That never escaped his Managers' notice. Captain of Hearts, of Tottenham, of Derby, he was the most experienced in the game, his confidence as crushing to opponents as his tackles.

The division of duties was always clear in his mind after an early clash with his Manager at Hearts, Tommy Walker.

> Tommy dropped Bobby Blackwood from the side and this upset the team. As Captain I shared their concern and asked for his inclusion. Tommy made it plain that selection was his job not mine. We lost the match and the selection probably *was* a mistake. But he was right about the responsibility. If he wants to sound opinion he can, but the Manager has to make the decision on who plays, who substitutes, what the tactics

are to be. The Captain has to run play on the field and make any adjustments there. Except for his chance at half-time there's nothing the Manager can do once the whistle's blown. But off the field it's all his. The modern idea that the Captain has a continuing responsibility for the players when the game is over is nonsense. I had enough trouble looking after my own life without having to run other people's.

Few games develop as planned, few players are consistent and the captain must have a feel for the ebb and flow of a match. As a footballer MacKay had that instinct. When he captained Spurs in the 1967 Final, Nicholson had planned that he should stay back while right-back Kinnear pressed up-field to take advantage of Chelsea playing without wingers. 'I was slower and less adventurous by then, well suited to the role of a centre-back. Normally I would still have made a foray or two when I saw the chance and that was planned in the tactics. But our forwards were in wonderful form, having their best game of the season, running Chelsea ragged. So I left them to it and took no chances.'

MacKay had always looked indestructible. Even a leg twice broken and the drop to Second Division football was a mere prelude to his most remarkable achievement in hauling Derby to the heights.

It was a 3–1 home defeat by Manchester City that decided me to quit Tottenham. I was still playing well, though slow for a mid-field man. Then City made us look fools and left me helpless. In my whole career at White Hart Lane we had never before been humiliated in front of our own supporters and I was not going to risk that again.

Brian Clough persuaded me to come to Derby by emphasising the potential of his squad. He could have been bluffing for all I knew but I believed him. He was right. All they lacked was confidence and that was what I could give them because I had never been short of it.

A Captain needs to be popular, needs to be respected if he is to get results from his team. My past reputation made it easy for me at the start, but little things could quickly have undermined it. At Tottenham it was taken for granted that you had new kit cleaned and neatly laid out for everything from training

E*

sessions to matches. The thing that shocked me coming down to a club in a lower Division was that the kit was issued on Monday and you were still making do with it on Friday. But I never complained, or let anyone see it bothered me.

Then the training was never as hard as at Tottenham. That surprised me, though Brian gets good results with his methods and the players are always fit without being pushed. The pre-season work was very hard, particularly the week spent running in the Colwick woods outside Nottingham, but the rest was easy-going. That too I accepted without comment and I never criticised.

While I settled in quickly as one of the team it was Brian who went out of his way to build me up as the superman. Even when I had had a bad game it was others who were criticised. He and Peter Taylor would say, 'you should not have left Dave exposed. Why didn't you cover up for him?' Really it was my job to cover up for them. That was good psychology though, because I could only make the players believe in themselves if they believed in me.

At the start I shared a room with Roy McFarland. He had all the attributes of a great player – strong in the air, fast, fearless, iron hard in the tackle. But he talked about playing First Division football as if it was an impossible dream, something you longed for but couldn't achieve. All my life I had played at the top and it had never crossed my mind that I was of any other standard. With my background there was no difficulty in convincing Roy that he had the ability to play in that grade as of right.

Dave MacKay, with his equable temperament, was the ideal foil for the more volatile Brian Clough.

The players liked having me with them as it calmed the atmosphere when things were going wrong. Brian gets himself and his club a lot of publicity through his abrasive comments, but they are a bit out of character with his normal style as a Manager. He is a shrewd judge of football and expects a lot of his players, but he is usually relaxed with them. However, he can be moody and then he will snap fiercely. That did not often happen when I was with them.

Curiously MacKay looks back in satisfaction at twice breaking his leg.

If I am forgotten for everything else I am always remembered as the man who kept coming back despite the breaks. And they dispelled any fear I ever felt in the game. You cannot help worrying when you see it happen to others. So I was surprised when it was just a sickly sensation, not the searing pain I expected. Now the thought of breaking a leg causes me less apprehension than going to the dentist.

The change to managing meant a change in physical condition. The granite hardness of MacKay the footballer was $12\frac{1}{2}$ stone of bone and muscle. With Swindon he kept close to that weight, ready to turn out for his team at need. Within a few months of moving to Nottingham Forest he had drifted up to 15 stone, despite training with the team, playing in the five-a-sides, playing squash with his Coach, Des Anderson. Mentally there were surprises too.

I was confident I could be an outstanding Manager as I never see myself as an also-ran. I had seen enough of the job to be sure I knew all about it. What I hadn't appreciated was the strain of watching. As a player I was keyed up for games, but never nervous. As a Manager I cannot sit still, making the tackles myself as I sit in the stand. I am developing a permanent twitch and there's this feeling of utter dejection when we lose.

Then I had never appreciated the sudden upsets of the job. Friday morning everything is fine, then John Robertson arrives three-quarters of an hour late for training. He's my best player but to be consistent I have to drop him to maintain discipline and the team and the tactics have suddenly to be re-organised. Next week it will be three men down with 'flu.

Communication with the side is sometimes more difficult than you expect. If we are losing or there's a stalemate I always send on the substitute. It's better to try something than to sit there hoping. But players now can be very touchy about coming off. One game I signalled to the referee that Doug Fraser was to be substituted. When told he said, 'I only go off when the Manager orders me, not the referee. I haven't heard the Boss say anything,' and he stayed out of earshot of me as long as he could.

Even on the field there is no doubt who is 'boss' in most clubs. And it is not the captain. The Manager's all-pervasive influence was given its most public acknowledgement as Sunderland triumphed at Wembley. Stokoe's match, they called it, and it was Stokoe who was chaired in that moment of emotion.

Maintaining the Team

The First Team absorbs much of a Manager's attention. But no matter how good that team it has a short life without adequate backing. So his concern is equally for the medical arrangements, the reserves, the youth teams and the Scouts who can maintain its strength.

'By the end of the century it could be the club Doctor, not the Manager, who will be selecting the team'; Dr David Muckle, Senior Registrar at the Radcliffe Infirmary and Medical Officer for Oxford United, is cheerfully positive about the likely result of biochemical developments.

The biochemistry of a sportsman can already be monitored accurately enough for computer analysis to build up an exact picture of his physical characteristics. In time it should be possible to assess and compare all the special qualities of body and instinct that differentiate the good footballer. Even the 'heart' so important to Managers like Eddie Turnbull may be measured.

David Muckle was himself an amateur footballer of some ability with Whitley Bay. This started an interest not just in sports injuries but in the more positive aspects of fitness. That in itself is unusual for a doctor. In his words, 'For many years doctors concerned with the sick have ignored the fit athlete. This has led to an aura of superstition, apprehension and ignorance amongst sportsmen.'

This attitude was apparent in the evidence to the Wolfenden Committee on Sport that medicine was concerned with illness, not with fitness. The only definition of health that could be given to that committee was 'being unconscious of all those things of which one ought to be unconscious'. And doctors, it seemed, were unconscious of the advances that were possible in this field. Now that more interest is taken the improvement could be striking.

Dr Muckle's positive approach has already had significant practical results. In the 1972/3 season he agreed with Manager Gerry Summers the combined physical training and nutrition programme for the thirty-six hours before a match which would achieve the highest level of stamina in the players.

Over a twenty-match period in which the results were tested, Oxford rose steadily in the table and their performance in the last half-hour was significantly different from other teams and from their own when not using the glucose and mineral solution.

Only one goal was conceded in that final period of the twenty matches, compared with 18 in the first sixty minutes. Of their 24 goals scored 15 were in that last third of the game. The striking contrast with the twenty games in which the glucose solution was not used is clear enough from the charted comparison opposite.

There was also some substantiation of the belief that good muscle tone helps balance, improves mobility and performance, and reduces injury. Certainly Oxford's casualties were surprisingly few and the fact that nine of the side were unchanged throughout helped to validate the experiment by keeping conditions constant.

Fatigue is related to a key biochemical process – the storage of glucose in the muscles. It was on this that Dr Muckle concentrated. In a normal week the players trained to exhaustion on the Thursday and were then fed a drink with high glucose content. On the Friday their diet was mainly carbohydrates with bread, cornflakes, sugar, coffee and milk as part of the staple ingredients. For the thirty-six hours before the match there was no further training, to avoid depleting the supply of glycogen built up to sustain energy. To train shortly before a match can be equated with that story of a bread-eating contest between two Russian soldiers. The favourite failed badly, consuming only five pounds rather than the customary ten. 'I cannot understand it,' said his sergeant, 'we had a practice at breakfast and he ate ten pounds then.'

Care was also taken to keep the players relaxed before a game, since nerves increase the adrenalin flow, using up the glycogen quicker. The nervous footballer goes into the game like a car with the choke out and the petrol tank half-empty.

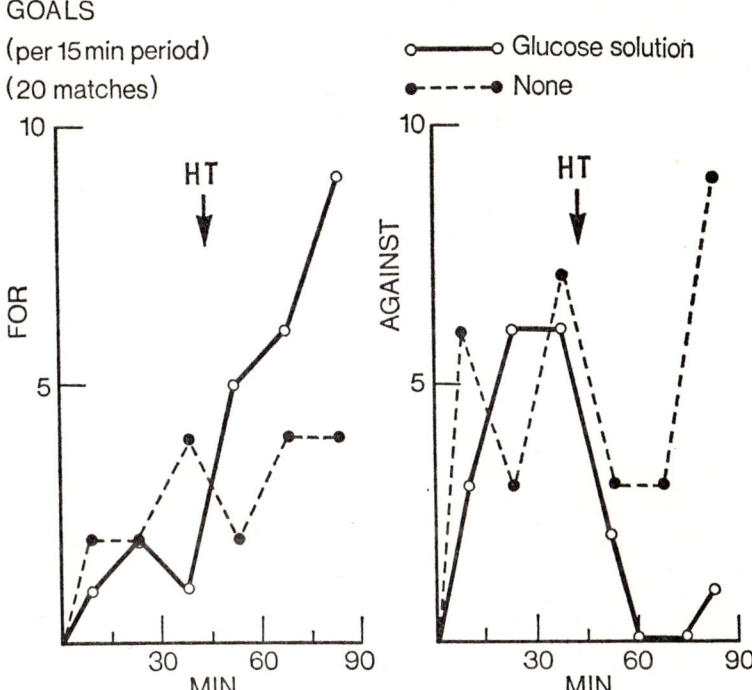

The graph of Oxford United's stamina trial

To avoid this Dr Muckle prefers explanation and reassurance to sedatives or anti-depressants.

Players often follow superstitious rituals prior to an event, like dressing in 'lucky' clothes, carrying charms, or entering the field of play in a set manner. Observations amongst Olympic athletes have revealed a wide variation in the duration of the almost sacrosanct 'warming up' period, from ten to forty-five minutes, with similar intervals given to resting before the event so that any benefit is lost. However, it is agreed that the most outstanding use of these warming-up activities is in occupying the athlete's mind, imparting confidence, and allaying anxiety. It is the same with footballers for it is not unusual for experienced players to be almost paralysed with fear in the moments preceding a match, and during the World Cup, even seasoned footballers suffered from psychological vomiting prior to several Internationals.

Oxford are not the only club to establish a higher level of physical performance through the Manager's cooperation in medical research. At Manchester City Joe Mercer some seasons ago instituted a project with Salford University on a number of aspects of the players' fitness.

Improved recovery rate followed from a study of close relationship between the maximum oxygen intake per kilogramme of body weight and the total time that an individual can run at speed. On the field it is rare to see a player sprint more than thirty yards because of the recovery time he then requires. That expert of the long dribble, Don Rogers, remained a Second Division player for many years despite his dazzling goals because Managers were suspicious of his stamina.

As a result of the Salford work the City players have an enhanced ability to sustain and repeat the explosive sprints that can be so devastating on the field. The study also revealed that Francis Lee and others had a low haemoglobin blood count and needed iron tablets to improve their condition.

Through the constant monitoring of performance in training there was expert advice on whether the players were working to capacity. A typical comment on pulse rates and performance after a work-out by Bell, Marsh, Lee and Summerbee reads, 'The rates show all working hard at least once in the session. Bell may well be working close to his maximum at 183. There are, however, a lot of repeats being done at sub-maximal effort – Bell 141, Marsh 152. Is this wise? I think there is room still to tighten a little on necessary time and sharpen up on longer runs at the beginning.'

Such monitoring allows a Manager to push his players to their maximum effort in training without asking more of them than they are capable of performing.

The medical assistance has become even more vital to Managers over transfers. In the past much money could be paid for a player whose unsuspected physical defects would make him a bad buy. With the vast sums now involved Managers have gone to the other extreme and become too cautious. Asa Hartford, rejected by Leeds, played on for West Bromwich Albion without problem. Freddie Hill, turned down by Liverpool for his high blood pressure, was accepted by Manchester City and was still playing well eight seasons later. Worthington, another Liverpool reject, is challenging for a place in England's team and has helped to revive Leicester.

Gerry Summers' attitude seems the right one for a Manager. He needed a striker and was keen on Hugh Curran, but could not match the £88,000 Huddersfield was prepared to pay Wolves. Curran was then rejected as accident-prone in his medical at Huddersfield. The price dropped to £50,000 and was clearly a bargain if Curran was fit. Summers' instructions to Dr Muckle were, 'Tell me if he is likely to be fit for four seasons of football. That is all I and the club need to know. Don't report to me on what might happen in twenty years. That's his problem and you advise him about the long term not me.'

The standard work of the Trainer or Physiotherapist and of the club Doctor remains the treatment of injury. For footballers the essentials are prompt treatment and a graduated recovery programme so that the player does not lose his athletic potential while nursing the injury. If a cartilage is taken out he should be doing exercises that night, be back on the field in six weeks.

The need for expert knowledge immediately available is not simply for quick recovery. What is lost on the field of play is lost for good. A damaged muscle cannot reunite or regenerate, it scars up. The man who plays on with an injury always risks permanent harm.

That is why Fred Street, the Arsenal Trainer, will never allow pain-killing injections, which destroy the body's danger signals.

Arsenal's philosophy of Management is to appoint the best and delegate the responsibility to them. This applies to the Physiotherapist as much as to the Chief Coach or the Chief Scout. Bertie Mee is an exacting selector and in his own subject he was certain to look for high performance. Street had shared some of his own experience of remedial work in the R.A.F. and as physiotherapist in a London hospital. He had been abroad to work in Australia, then established himself as a successful Trainer at Stoke City.

When Don Howe moved to Albion, taking some of the Arsenal staff with him, Street's recruitment made this a fair exchange. Don Howe's coaching had made a notable contribution to the 'double' success and his loss was the inevitable outcome of aiming for quality. The more able the man the less likely he is to remain a subordinate. Street is an ideal amalgam of the virtues of the old-type Trainer and the new, of the player's confidant and the qualified expert. A quiet, sympathetic personality, an unforced friendliness, help establish the confidence that is the key to the Trainer's relationship with the footballer.

In traditional treatments the myth is quickly separated from reality.

> We try to limit supportive strapping to the ankles. Those bandages on knees are no help. The knee is one of the strongest structures in the body and if that won't stand up to the action a little bit of cotton weave is not going to help. But if the player feels the need of something and it will help him psychologically then we'll give it to him.
>
> We encourage weight-lifting but not solely as a confidence trick. Many of the young footballers come from poor families and are weedy-looking striplings when they arrive – just two legs and a squeaky voice with a coathanger in the shirt instead of shoulders. Weights help build their body, give them a feeling of power. As Charles Atlas used to promise, if you can throw weights around you won't get sand kicked in your face. Footballers must not feel afraid of anyone. But a strong upper trunk is too often disregarded for its importance in relation to football skills. Look at all the great sprinters. They have long tapering legs, but they are all broad at the top. That's where they need the strength to absorb the thrust of the legs. Abdominal power is as important for the footballer – it is the anchor point of his stamina in lasting the game.

Stamina, indeed, has been a feature of the Arsenal play, so many of their matches snatched from tiring opponents in the closing minutes.

The normal bumps and bruises of football demand instant treatment. Street's usual method is ice to shut the system down and limit the swelling, then a pressure bandage to contain the damage overnight. This copes with the commonest injury in the game, the 'dead-leg' which results from a knee in the thigh. The most difficult to diagnose are the knee injuries, with the possibility of cartilage trouble, but so many other alternatives.

Complete rest can be the best initial treatment and for that Street often sends the player to hospital. Footballers are the most impatient patients, unable to keep quiet in their own homes. Bob McNab suffered from a long nagging injury in his groin which only cleared up after confinement to a hospital bed to keep him still.

But most of the remedial treatment is graduated to keep the player active and in condition. It can build up to a greater intensity than for the fit man, since, as at the start of the season, the player has to train back to his peak, rather than just maintain it. Street always leaves ball work to the last, as kicking a football is likely to aggravate a strain.

The Trainer is the man best placed to judge the result of the refereeing revolution of the last few seasons. Firmer refereeing was intended to allow greater scope for the clever player and clamp down on the excesses of physical challenge. If it was effective that should have been reflected in fewer injuries. Street confirms that view.

> My experience is that the game is not so hard. Firstly it's a feeling because I see less of the black-and-blue calves which marked the tackle from behind. Then it's measurable in the number of times I am called on to the pitch. I don't like going on if I can avoid it as this stops the flow of the game. Our boys only go down if they are hurt because they appreciate this too.
>
> Certainly I have been on the pitch much less than in the past, sometimes going three or four games without being called on. This applies at all levels including the reserves. There are not so many hatchet men now as there were a few years ago. From my observation there is an improvement also in attitude with less play-acting and feigning injury. Professionals are realising how unprofessional it is to get a fellow-player in trouble unjustifiably.

Injury has to be expected. One season's breakdown of treatment for a typical First Division club with a staff of thirty shows the wear and tear of the games.

Diagnosis	No.	Average Period (Days) Away from Competition	Remarks
FRACTURES	3	174·3	Nose – 7 days Tibia and Fibula – 173 (Simple) Tibia and Fibula – 343 (Compound) Carried over from last season
JOINT INJURIES	52		
KNEE/DIRECT	1	2	Sub Periosteal Haematoma
KNEE/INDIRECT			
Medial Ligament	6	10·8	
Synovitis	10	8·2	Four incidents following long standing Menisectomy
Menisectomy (Medial)	1	55	
Excision Attached Extra-Capsular Body	1	20	
ANKLE/DIRECT	6	5	
ANKLE/INDIRECT	17	8	Inversion and Medial Rotalis Sprain. No joint effusion
FOOT/DIRECT	4	4·5	
FOOT/INDIRECT	6	6·2	Mid-Tarsal Sprains P.O.P.
MUSCLE & TENDON INJURIES	71		
QUADRICEPS/DIRECT	11	3	
QUADRICEPS/INDIRECT	9	5·4	Rectus Femoris
HAMSTRING/DIRECT	2	3	
HAMSTRING/INDIRECT	11	9·2	
ABDUCTORS/DIRECT			
ABDUCTORS/INDIRECT	12	10·8	
BUTTOCKS/DIRECT	3	2·7	
BUTTOCKS/INDIRECT			
PLANTOR FLEXORS/DIRECT	2	6·5	
PLANTOR FLEXORS/INDIRECT	5	10·8	

Diagnosis	No.	Average Period (Days) Away from Competition	Remarks
TENDON INJURIES/ DIRECT	1	5	
TENDON INJURIES/ INDIRECT	15	15.9	Achilles Tendon 12 Tibialis Posterior 3
UPPER LIMB INJURIES	3	8	Involving two goalkeepers { 1 Rotator Cuff, 1 Acromio-Clavicular, 1 Sterno-Clavicular }
BACK INJURIES	12	14.9	
HEAD INJURIES	2	3.5	Post Concussion
MEDICAL CONDITIONS	22	7.4	
MISCELLANEOUS	6	3	Wounds, abrasions, etc.
Total	171		

That list points the need for adequate reserve cover. Alec Stock of Fulham believes the essential feature of handling a reserve side is to ensure that a senior member of the club is present even for away games that clash with First Team fixtures. Apart from the report on performance there is the need to give encouragement. Stock has emphasised the importance for him of the reserves by appointing Ted Drake to manage them, a man outstanding as a player, successful as a Manager. Ted was not a man ever to be relegated himself to the reserves, but he understands the central problem.

The reserves are a fine grounding for youngsters coming up when they are stimulated by the excitement of working towards the First Team. But for the senior player who is demoted there is a terrible flatness in the near-empty terraces, in the lack of tension and atmosphere. The glory and the savour have gone. It was bad enough for him in my day. It's much worse for the present generation who are more aggressively self-confident and take it harder when their pride is hurt. For them the failure is more bitter and now they suffer more in the drop of money unless there is a squad system which keeps fifteen or so on equal basic pay. These are the ones who need the encouragement and help to get back into the side.

In football so many careers turn sour at the finish, famous footballers ending on the dole, successful Managers declining into failure and obscurity. Ted Drake is a heartening example of a happy personality armoured against adversity. Today he would have made a fortune as player or as the Manager who took Chelsea to their first League Championship. But £8 was his maximum wage with Arsenal, his highest payment as Manager less than £50 per week. He combines a job as representative for an Insurance company with his part-time work for Fulham, and never worries about the might-have-beens. As a player he had an instinctive kindness. An injured knee threatened to keep him out of the 1936 Cup Final. George Allison gave him one game to prove himself – the last League match of the season against struggling Aston Villa. Drake headed home the only goal. But there was no gladiatorial salute of triumph in asserting his fitness. Instead he wheeled instantly to apologise to his dejected opponents, genuinely regretful that *his* goal should have relegated them.

They had much to remember him by that season. At Villa Park he played for the first time in his career with a bandage on his knee, troubled whether he would last the game. He had eight shots and scored with seven of them. 'The eighth hit the underside of the bar and I was certain that it had bounced down over the line. But we never queried the referee's decision.'

Ted Drake admired his Managers, George Kay at Southampton, Allison and Whittaker at Arsenal. 'George Kay had great problems with finance and my transfer for £6,500 averted a crisis. We always worried whether we would be signed on again and a month before the retained list was issued we all used to make an excuse to see George. We would say our boots were worn out and ask for a new pair. Anyone told to make do with those he had knew it was the end.'

When he was himself appointed to manage Chelsea they were £63,000 in the red, still known as the 'Pensioners', still a music hall joke as the experts in brinkmanship.

Drake made some shrewd buys, McNichol, Stubbs and Blunstone costing only £20,000 between them, with no transfer fee for amateurs Lewis and Saunders from Walthamstow Avenue. He clamped down on the wit, gave the club a more purposeful image. 'Look, have you ever won anything?' he asked the players. 'No, Guvnor.' 'What are we going to win, then?' 'We always have a go in the Cup. We have got a chance there.' 'The Cup is just a lottery. If you work hard we will win the championship,' and they did.

But Drake did not survive one bad season and an altercation over the appointment of Docherty as Coach against his wishes. There was no resentment over the parting. 'A Sunday newspaper offered me a large sum to write about it. "You want the dirt?" I asked. "That's right." "Then you are wasting your time." '

'I always enjoyed finding young players and Chelsea have made just over a million pounds from the ones I brought in for nothing. John Hollins was my last signing – not a bad one for a finish.'

The reserves are an important part of the drive to return to the First Division. Ted Drake relishes the success of John Mitchell, a centre-forward with some of his own characteristics – pace, a strong build, a feel for where the goal is, a burning desire to score.

> That was nothing to do with my coaching. Mitchell was promoted a week after I took over. But he shows the value of a good reserve team and it's a change to see a centre-forward of character. This is the hardest place on the field so there are not many candidates for it now, just as there are not many wanting to be fast bowlers at cricket.

The search for players at all levels has put even greater emphasis on scouting systems. Len Richley, Newcastle's Chief Scout, has the varied experience desirable for a job requiring good contacts and sound judgement of a player. He was brought up in the town, but travel has polished and softened the distinctive accent of Tyneside. Signed as an amateur by Sunderland, he moved to Crystal Palace and Hartlepool before becoming Player/Manager of King's Lynn.

> Player/Manager is the hardest job in the game. You are usually beginning to feel your age, but you have always to set the example. You are first out for training and the last in. The whole running of the club is your worry and then you have to keep proving yourself on the field. You always know when you are having a rotten game yourself, but still you have got to drive the others on.

In five years with King's Lynn it was the long Cup runs that brought him most pleasure – especially the defeat of Coventry.

That was typical of a Player/Manager's problems. I had to travel twice to watch them, once down to Bournemouth and once at home to Crystal Palace. Then I decided on unusual tactics. They seemed to have two outstanding men who determined their pattern of play, inside-forward Ronnie Hewitt and the dominating George Curtis at centre-half. A man was detailed to watch Hewitt, which was an obvious move. But I told our centre-forward, Ray Dixon, to reverse his role and mark Curtis all the time without worrying about scoring goals. That upset them and won us a visit to Everton, a great achievement for a small club.

Assistant Manager at Bury, Manager at Rochdale, Richley went on learning in clubs where the job covered anything from tickets to tactics. For Rochdale there was promotion to the Third Division.

Success was based on acquiring men of character and suiting the pattern of play to them. The things I looked for were the will to win and the readiness to work with others. You can spot those who hate losing. They are always going to give of their best.

After Rochdale there was the bewildering experience at Darlington, where the Chairman, George Tait, confidently asserts he can judge a Manager in six months. Richley survived fifteen, which was longer than the rest of his staff, or his three immediate successors. It was then that Harvey invited him to Newcastle as their one full-time Scout.

The first priority is researching the other League teams and following up any tips about non-League players. Richley does not believe in detailed analysis of a footballer. 'You don't want to watch a man too often or you get confused. You have to make up your mind quickly about him as a player and back your judgement. Once you have done that you can spend time researching his background and his character to confirm your choice.'

Most matches Richley watches from the terraces, tapping that always opinionated, often knowledgeable source of information. The crowd's comments are a useful guide on whether a player's form of the day is unusual. Answers like 'you should see him when he has a few pints' may point a necessary line of enquiry.

Jimmy Murphy, that great spotter of talent for Manchester United, used often to disguise himself with false moustache and glasses. Richley and Harvey are more open, although being seen can push up the price when it is clear how keen is the interest. On one scouting expedition in Scotland they stayed thirty miles from the ground, under the impression they were unnoticed throughout the game. Returning to the hotel, Harvey found himself being asked to autograph programmes of the game.

Analysing opponents is not too demanding on Richley's time. 'Most teams in the League play to a standard pattern now so I need only watch them once.'

The search for youth is the responsibility of the part-time Scouts combing the North-East – with Newcastle able to offer sound training as well as local connection.

The North-East is still the main football nursery, every League team aiming to have its Geordie as well as its Scot. Alan Brown tapped this source liberally when he built the strong youth schemes at Burnley, Sheffield Wednesday, and Sunderland. His magic touch as a finder and developer of players is clear enough in the high percentage of footballers in the League who have come through one of these three clubs. And at Burnley the first priority of the Chief Scout is still the wide-ranging search for young talent.

Burnley, with their small catchment area, can never hope to support First Division football from their gates. Yet since the 1930s they have walked successfully on water, keeping their football standards high, their club solvent. The Chester Report rated their achievement unique. It has its roots in a youth policy run in part to maintain the quality of the team, in part to make money from transfers.

Against the £190,000 they received for Ralph Coates, the highest fee they had paid by the end of 1973 was £60,000 for Paul Fletcher. That is a fair comparison of their balance of trade, the exports so much more pricey and more numerous than the imports. Such policy has its risks.

In Jimmy Adamson's first season as Manager a player too many had been sold. O'Neil went to Southampton for £75,000 and the conveyor belt of talent failed to deliver adequate replacement. That was the one time they contemplated a six-figure purchase. As

Burnley slipped into the Second Division only twenty-nine goals were scored all season. When salvation was still possible the Board authorised Adamson to buy a goal-scorer. He knew the one that might work the miracle and approached his club. No sooner was he seen visiting than the player told his Manager he was not interested in going to Burnley.

For the high-priced footballer there is little attraction in a club that cannot pull in vast crowds, does not attract national publicity, brings no perks of fame. So Burnley still concentrate on building a homespun side and a healthy balance through their youth.

For the policy to work they have to be the best in a competitive business and it is Adamson's top priority.

> We go for quality not quantity, usually keeping only ten apprentices, rather than the permitted fifteen. There was a time when Scouts were signing on boys themselves, but this lowered the standards. Judgement is not consistent and the Scouts are naturally keen to be able to say they have found players for Burnley. The Chief Scout and myself always see a boy before we sign him.
>
> £10 a week at 17 is the maximum pay for an apprentice, but the cost of the scouting, the coaching and the incidentals mean we pay out some £70,000 a year on these ten boys. They need to be good to repay an investment like that.
>
> Bill Dougal and Ray Bennion started the interest in youth development in the years just before the war, bringing on players like Harry Potts. But it was Alan Brown who developed the policy, with the backing of the Chairman, Bob Lord. He had this great interest in the young and was always a strong leader. 'You have your say and then we will do it my way' was his method of working.
>
> The purchase of 58 acres at Gawthorpe in 1958 was like locating a goldmine. With four football fields there, one with an all-weather surface, we had the ideal training centre. And we built up the coaching staff to match the facilities.
>
> We could offer such good training that we had the pick of youngsters. It was so easy we got complacent and then our standards dropped. We were slow to appreciate how intense the search had become, how many had joined in the hunt.
>
> Four years ago we reorganised the scouting system, putting

Dave Blakey in charge. Dave had had 600 games with Chesterfield, knew all about football and doesn't mind how far he travels. He's apt to leave on a Monday morning and not get back to Burnley until the Friday. We've given him as big a staff of part-time Scouts as any First Division club and they are fishing in the ponds where the anglers aren't shoulder to shoulder. The production line is rolling again with Docherty, Kindon, Probert, Thomas, Leighton James, playing a major part in improving finances or winning promotion.

That's no mean achievement when competition is so fierce. In the 1950s I saw a Schoolboy International at Wembley and not one player was signed for a club. Recently, when I watched a Lancashire schoolboy's match, 11 of them were signed up although they were only fourteen.

There was a time when Alan Brown had the pick of the youth in the North-East, with only two or three clubs in contention. Now there are ninety others in the hunt and its the same in most other places. That's why we research locally, but also spread our net so wide. That's why I've just travelled 450 miles to convince a parent that Burnley is the right club for his boy. We have to sell the club on its facilities, its opportunities, its coaching and the way we look after our youngsters. We don't make any payments here though we know some do and we have all heard of payments up to £4,000 being made. Ron Greenwood and I have much more in common than both being born in the Burnley area. I have learnt a lot from him and agree with the West Ham policy that if you 'buy' a boy in you are behaving dishonestly and you encourage him to be dishonest and disloyal to his clubs for the rest of his playing career.

In the F.A. Youth Cup last year Burnley were beaten 3-0 by another Lancashire club with an eye on youth – Bolton Wanderers.

In Jimmy Armfield's second season as Manager they have won promotion to the Second Division through his reliance on the young.

Even though we were a trailing Third Division side with gates down to 4,000 I was convinced that a heavy outlay on youth was the way to success. We run four teams and ensure that those with promise get the promotion. That's more than a big club can offer. If Arsenal or Liverpool lose a star they may not be able to gamble on bringing in a youngster. They are more likely to go into the transfer market.

But our sides are home bred and all players have the chance of stepping up quickly into the First Team. In two years my outlay on transfers is only £10,000. When I took an initial look at the team and saw weaknesses in defence I covered them by promoting young players. Two have been outstandingly successful.

Paul Jones is only nineteen and he could become the best centre-half in the country. Don McAllister is the same age and already an accomplished full-back.

Armfield still lives in Blackpool, where he had such an outstanding career on the field. He was one of those players who looked too much the gentleman to be as successful as he was.

Armfield's play was instinct with enjoyment and sportsmanship, a full-back with a forward's flair and a liking for sudden attack which started a new tactical fashion.

He has kept the same principles as Manager.

It takes time to adjust from being a player. In the early months I concentrated on the things I knew I could do well – evaluating the team and changing its tactics, coaching the players, reviving morale.

Bolton had been defensive in method, though the style did not suit the players let alone the spectators. I changed the formation with a specialist winger and adventurous defenders. We set out to attack every team, and it caught a few of them out. We needed success to bring back support, but the way we played was also important. This has helped quadruple the gates to over 18,000 and restore an atmosphere of excitement.

Armfield was another of the former England players to draw inspiration from Winterbottom.

Unconsciously I picked up tips about Managing from all my Managers. But playing is an individual thing. You worry only about your fitness and your form. It was Walter who started me thinking about the game and encouraged me to become an F.A. Staff Coach.

The coaching interest was another essential in transforming the spirit of the club.

You cannot improve morale for long by talking. You have to know how to improve technique and tactics, how to give positive help to players. For most of us that does not come naturally. Only the ignorant criticise the coaching system, dismiss the improved standards, blame it for sterile play. As a qualified coach you are like a qualified teacher – you have the knowledge, but how you develop the class is up to you. If you have a dreary defensive philosophy that's your fault.

Armfield's philosophy is anything but drearily defensive and he has all the bright hopes of youth. His two young sons play together in a particularly successful school team.

I cannot coach them, but they keep me in touch with the enthusiasms of the game and its fresh ideas. They reinforce my own desire to attract young players to the club. As success grows this adds to the advantage I have of being able to tell parents with complete honesty, 'If your boy joins us and tries hard enough he will have every chance to play for the team.' It is a question parents and boys ought always to ask before being dazzled by the glamour of the big clubs. And they should check the record as well.

Some First Division Managers like Ron Greenwood can say, 'If I take you on as an apprentice and you work at your game you will be able to make a reasonable career as a professional footballer. That is my judgement' and be confident that their judgement is rarely wrong. But nearly half of those who have been taken on in the first ten years of the apprenticeship scheme have slipped out of football, and the percentage is rising. In Bertie Mee's words, 'A Manager's greatest moment is when a youngster breaks through. The worst moment is when a youngster breaks down. How do you tell a 16-year-old he hasn't made the grade?' The table overleaf shows how often Managers have had that unhappy task.

The P.F.A. recognised the problem quicker than the League appointing Bob Kerry as their Education Officer. This is the advice he gives boys:

Most boys at some stage or other are attracted by the thought of becoming a professional footballer. However, it must be obvious to most people that whilst football can be a profitable and most enjoyable career there are many pitfalls.

Apprentices Registered 7 May 1960–29 May 1970 (100% sample)

SEASON	1960–61	1961–62	1962–63	1963–64	1964–65	1965–66	1966–67	1967–68	1968–69	1969–70	1970–71
REGISTERED FROM PREVIOUS SEASON	NIL	181	251	354	389	352	375	370	423	482	507
NEW REGISTRATIONS	229	198	253	224	201	286	234	303	322	383	—
APPRENTICES SIGNING PROFESSIONAL CONTRACTS	17	92	112	109	155	171	130	117	117	137	—
APPRENTICES RELEASED	31	36	38	80	83	92	109	133	146	221	—

Number of Registrations: 2,633.
Number of Apprenticeships completed: (2,633 − 507) = 2,126.
Number of Professional contracts = 1,157, 54·42% of the total. The number of releases was 969.
111 Apprentices were given a free transfer at the end of the first season in which they signed professional contracts.

Research by Bryan Smith.

You may be offered a chance to become an 'Associated Schoolboy' in which case you attend the ground for coaching and training sessions and the club has an option on your services when you leave school. Whilst you are an Associated Schoolboy school football must always come before club requirements.

After the age of 16 you may be offered apprenticeship terms, or, at 17, professional terms. This is a much more permanent position involving full-time employment. Opportunities are usually given for you to continue your further education and I must stress that it is in your interest to do so.

In fact it is not often realised just how hard it is to become successful in football. The majority of Associated Schoolboys are not chosen for apprenticeship and only a few apprentices do in fact make a career in the game. The 'drop-out' rate is high so you can see why it is important to do as well as you can at school and prepare for an alternative career.

It is becoming the practice for most young footballers to devote some time to their further education and vocational training. Clubs are nowadays very willing to give boys sufficient time to attend College and to study.

For the boy with good 'O' levels who tries a football career failure is rarely disastrous. But for the other rejects there are limited prospects and the harsh reality is the more bitter after the dreams of glory.

They have missed the chance of a craft training, for a football apprenticeship leaves little time to learn another trade. Managers encourage attendance at College, but the apprenticeship scheme does not compel it.

Brian Hornsby's reaction is not untypical. As an Arsenal apprentice he ignored the encouragement to vocational study. 'For my last year at School I had no interest but football. When it became my profession I wanted to devote all my time to it. If you train to be a motor mechanic you don't study football so why should a footballer study how to be a motor mechanic?' Hornsby progressed quickly to the fringe of the Arsenal squad, but at one stage he was close to becoming one of the drop-outs.

He had been brought up on a small farm near Peterborough and it was city life, rather than study, that distracted his mind from football. A plain-speaking interview with Bertie Mee was the turning-point. But one thought was decisive. 'If I fail as a footballer I will have to get up at 5 a.m. for the rest of my life to milk those bloody cows.'

Hornsby had the ability to make good when he made the effort. Many need an alternative to fall back on. But the most flamboyant and possibly the most capable developer of young players, Pat Saward, would not let them think of failure.

Jimmy Hill, to whom the art of football Management was in correct appointment and proper delegation, gave him a free hand to organise Coventry's youth scheme. Saward set out to develop character and personality.

> All football coaching must be based on repetition. To become perfect in a skill you ask a boy to practise it over and over again. Mentally that's deadening unless he keeps his confidence and his initiative. He needs that belief in himself. In my early days at Millwall the crowd were always on at me, worsening my inferiority complex until I nearly went to pieces. Then I thought 'Am I a failure because I am not good enough, or because the crowd say I am not good enough? Perhaps it's they who don't understand the game, they who are ignorant.' That started me thinking constructively, believing in myself. With confidence I was a capable enough player for First Division Football, for a Cup Winner's medal with Aston Villa. That is the experience that has to be passed on to the young. Once I had learnt this it wasn't enough for me to be a good footballer. I had to be able to hold my own anywhere in society. At Villa Peter McParland and the others couldn't understand why I wouldn't go dancing in the evenings. 'You are good looking and the girls all go for you, why do you waste your time at the Technical College?' I was studying English, elocution and practical psychology because I wanted to be confident in whatever I did.
>
> My youngsters at Coventry didn't have to wait to find this out for themselves as adults. In football you need leadership and initiative on the field and that's what they started learning from me at 13. Look at the sort of players that's produced – Jeff Blockley, Willie Carr, Alan Green, Paddon, Coop, Mortimer, the list runs on and on.
>
> Everyone agrees about continuing youngsters' education while they learn the game, so clubs send them to Technical College on

standard courses that are of no interest to most of them. Willie Carr was learning to be a motor mechanic. What good would that ever be to him? What interest was it?

I had the Technical College develop two day 'Confidence' courses and a personality course. The young players had to write reports on their games and their training. In the hostel we had them stage plays, make speeches.

I told them, 'Son, in three years you may be worth £100,000. You have got to have the personality to go with that, to think big.'

The continued schooling of the apprentice footballer is a concern of most Managements. Arsenal take it so seriously that Bertie Mee refused to sign as an apprentice Paul Fusillo, an Amateur International, when this would have ended his chance of going to University. Fusillo got his degree at Oxford and joined Blackpool.

At Derby, Brian Clough took a different view of Steve Powell, perhaps the most promising young player in the country and with 'A' levels to spare for University entry. When Powell signed as apprentice he was asked if this was not denying him the opportunity of going to Oxford or Cambridge. 'Go to Oxford or Cambridge! When I've had him for a few years he should be able to buy them.'

F

The Money-Go-Round

Transfers demand a nice commercial judgement of Managers. Alan Hardaker, Secretary of the Football League, is astonished at the glib way in which they put a price of one hundred or two hundred thousand pounds on a player. 'My Committee will call me to account over a couple of thousand. But these vast figures are bandied about without concern.'

There is indeed a total lack of logic in the transfer market and it is best treated as a whimsical exercise. This was well expressed as Bert Head talked to Barry Norman about some of Crystal Palace's expensive signings before their match with Norwich.

'If Bert Head were playing Monopoly,' someone remarked with more wit than charity, 'he'd buy the Old Kent Road instead of Mayfair.' Not true at all. He started the week by trying to buy Mayfair (assuming Ted MacDougall at £220,000 can be so described), but Frank O'Farrell landed there first.

Mr Head may have finished up with a package deal of three lesser properties at £280,000 the lot, but it would still be unkind to liken them to the Old Kent Road, begging Millwall's pardon of course.

As it happened, only one of the new Palace acquisitions, Iain Phillip (£110,000 from Dundee), was on display, since Paddy Mulligan (£75,000 from Chelsea) was poorly with a sore throat and Charlie Cooke (£85,000 from Chelsea) was ineligible. Thus Mr Head was in the frustrating position of a gambler limited to putting only a third of his stake on the table. 'Don't equate today's result with the £280,000,' he said afterwards. 'It's not fair.'

Palace had been played on to the pitch with much canned music – though not, oddly enough 'Hey, Big Spender' – and the record of having failed to score in their last six matches.

Yes, said Mr Head later, you could say Palace were still in the market for another player. A striker? 'Call him what you like,' said Mr Head. 'Some bugger who puts the goals in anyway.'

Norwich, actually, were quite well equipped with buggers like that. Bone scored the first after 12 minutes, a corner and a scene of total chaos in the Palace penalty area. Fifteen minutes later Paddon got the second, amid similar panic, with a header.

On the whole, though, he was encouraged by the thought of the players he'd signed. 'Not a bad week's work,' he said. 'Of course, I'm still a bit sore about MacDougall, but he's gone so there's no point in talking about him, is there?'

True. But it was a lot of money he'd spent nevertheless. Didn't it worry him, gambling all that on three players? 'It's the way prices go, isn't it?' he said. 'Of course they're ridiculous – a £100,000 transfer is nothing these days. It's like bananas – they used to be two-a-penny, but they're not any more. No, I'm not worried though. You back your fancy, that's all. It's the occupational hazard of being a manager. The day I lose any sleep through worry is the day I pack it in.'

On the field Norwich had skated the first half and eased up a little in the second when, to do them credit, Palace did look somewhat more businesslike. Even so, just before the end the slow handclapping started, somebody waved a banner saying 'Head Must Go' and Bone came off, being, in the elegant phrase of his manager, 'knackered'.

So once again Palace are in their familiar position near the bottom of the league. 'Well,' said Mr Head, 'we're in the process of building traditions here. I didn't buy these players on a short-term basis, just to get us out of trouble. If you're spending that much money you have to think long-term. You have to think of getting into Europe, otherwise it takes years to get the money back.'

In any case, he said, though he's invested £750,000 in players in the last four years he has got most of it back by selling others. 'Anyway, look at it this way: if I spend half a million pounds this season, which I might, it'll seem an awful lot. But I may not spend any more for another five years. You have to judge it, not week by week, but over a length of time.'

Palace haven't done all that well in the First Division. Wasn't he, perhaps, a little disappointed? 'I'm not disappointed to be here,' he said, 'if that's what you mean. No, you make your own problems just by getting into the First Division. Managing any club is hard – it's a lot harder in this league.'

Cooke should have made a difference, since what Palace lacked, apart from the ability to score goals, was someone with flair who can hold the ball and use it intelligently. Mulligan, too, could tighten the defence, which had been involved in one unscheduled disaster after another in its own penalty area.

Mr Head is naturally aware of this, 'I'd settled with Cooke and Mulligan before I even went after MacDougall,' he said. 'So I certainly didn't get them in place of him. What we need now is a goal-scorer. Once we get one and get over this bad patch, I think we'll be terrific.'

He was not, then, feeling in any way desperate? 'We're never desperate here, mate,' he said. 'We're never desperate here.'

Not desperate certainly, but the worry of survival forced him to go after three more of those elusive goal-scorers. Whittle from Everton, Rogers from Swindon, Possee from Millwall averaged more than a hundred thousand pounds apiece and took the outlay to close on three-quarters of a million. From a business standpoint this read like a chapter from Palace in Wonderland. And when Palace still ended in the Second Division Mr Head's transfer fee into oblivion was £30,000.

The transfer market is not just a subject for irreverent humour and crazy finance. As the prices soar in the top Divisions many clubs in the Third and Fourth can be ruined in the race. If they have aspirations they have to think in terms of buying players of Second and First Division calibre and even the rejects cost more than they can reasonably afford. The shrewd and the lucky can survive. The others are going to the wall with the transfer system pushing them hard against it.

There is a facile and untrue assumption that the money circulates within the League, that no harm is done to the overall finance of clubs; that those in lower Divisions can be helped by transfers.

One season's dealings by Crystal Palace and Manchester United meant the paying out of nearly £100,000 to the players involved for their 5% of the fees. One season's transfer operations in 1972 cost the English League over one million pounds in payment to Scottish clubs. Within the English League itself £6,770,000 was spent on transfers that season with over £330,000 going to the players involved. There is not the cash coming in at the gate to cover such a drain and any case for special help for football is destroyed while clubs can be such spendthrifts.

Transfer-dealing can produce a cold atmosphere at football. When Allison and Jago meet now the conversation is apt to be limited to 'good afternoon' – and all because of Rodney Marsh. In the 1971/72 season Queen's Park Rangers had the best defensive record in any Division. Rodney Marsh was scoring just enough goals for that to be decisive in winning promotion. Then the goals dried up, three matches were lost in succession for the only time in the season. Marsh appeared confused and restless as if aware of Manchester City's interest in him. So Rangers had to put him up for sale at a punitive £200,000. Without him they still finished only two points short of promotion. With him Manchester City took only eight points from their last eight games, narrowly missing the League Championship while the team adjusted to Marsh's unusual skills. Even the gentle Joe Mercer made the barbed comment that it was a lot of money to pay to lose the League. That transfer summed up the worst of a system that can cause disruption and resentment.

A funny thing also happened to Lou Macari on his way to Old Trafford. There he was playing for Celtic, who were already heading for their eighth successive League title and another venture into Europe. Then Tommy Docherty, who lived close to him in Largs, put him in the Scottish team. When the call came for Docherty to take over at Old Trafford, he was lucky about Lou. Macari was one of the many Scottish footballers he wanted. Of course, it is illegal to approach a player to get him to move. You have to approach the club to see if he is available. And Celtic had earlier been approached – by Liverpool. Celtic did not then wish to transfer Macari, and the player did not want to leave. So Liverpool were promised first option if there was a change of heart.

Shortly before Docherty went to United Macari got restless and asked for a transfer. It must have been the thought of all that extra money which helped unsettle him, rather than hopes of football glory. He was getting plenty of that with Celtic.

Macari was so dissatisfied at Parkhead that Stein felt it best to let him go. The price was a small matter of £200,000 and those cautious spenders Liverpool were prepared to exercise their option. Macari had said all he wanted was to play in a League team with fellow Scots. With Shankly as Manager and a team salted with Scottish talent Liverpool seemed a natural home for him. He spent the day at Anfield and everyone put themselves out.

There was Liverpool leading the League, doing well in Europe, and with the keenest following in the country. Somehow the atmosphere did not appeal to Macari and even Shankly's enthusiasm could not rouse him. So Liverpool withdrew from the hunt and Docherty was waiting for him in a Glasgow hotel as he returned.

For all its absurdities the transfer system can be as exciting as the pools, making the fortune of a club or a player.

Roger Davies, Derby's young centre-forward, came suddenly to prominence in their Cup-ties with Tottenham Hotspur. In the home match he equalised in the last few minutes, stabbing the ball home just as the pens were poised to blame Brian Clough for not putting a substitute on in his place.

The replay at White Hart Lane was a night of enchantment with Davies' tall slim figure at the centre of the floodlit stage. In the last ten minutes Derby trailed 1–3 at the end of a game of surging assault and ceaseless challenge. Then Davies scored twice, the saving goal a volley struck on the turn high into the net. In extra time he completed his hat-trick to win the game and a national reputation.

For a First Division centre-forward who can do something old-fashioned like scoring goals no one would start the bidding below £100,000. But only sixteen months earlier Derby had paid Worcester City a modest £14,000 for him. And for Worcester all of this was profit, the prize for their Manager Wilf Grant seeing the potential of a gangling amateur.

Wilf Grant was trying to form a reserve side when he arranged a pre-season friendly on Cadbury's ground against amateurs Bridgnorth. They arrived one short, but he noticed the big centre-forward who had an unusually delicate touch for one so tall.

Later in the season they played Bridgnorth again and he asked his centre-half about Davies. 'I couldn't get near him,' was the reply that confirmed Grant's interest.

He watched him again, but had to wait to the end of the season to sign him. For an amateur there was no transfer fee, but Worcester gave Bridgnorth a gift of £100.

Davies had no reputation as a worker, enjoying his football but not exerting himself unduly. When he turned up for a training session with Bridgnorth before the final of the Welsh Senior Amateur Cup the other players were so surprised they clapped him onto the field.

He was willing enough to train hard with Worcester, and Grant, seeing the potential, set out to eliminate the faults. 'When you lose the ball go and win it back,' was his constant theme with a player who had thought only in terms of goals.

Davies had remarkable ball control, but for a man well over six feet tall he was weak in the air. Grant taught him to run in on the ball to get more power: '*Demand* the ground, make space for yourself.'

To illustrate the point he told Davies to watch how McFarland won the ball in the air, claiming it with confident determination. Within weeks Davies was able to make a closer study of Derby's centre-half.

The interest in Davies was quick to build. Even before the season started Jimmy Bloomfield was asking for him on loan, impressed with his performance in a friendly against Leicester.

The Worcester ground in Flag Meadow Walk, with its ash banking at one corner, its normal gate of a thousand, became the focus of attention as Davies scored with style and regularity. Suddenly there were almost as many Scouts as spectators in the stand.

Davies was not yet the finished product, still a little dreamy. At the crucial point of one hard-fought match he was missing as the centre laid bare the goal.

'Look at the big daft bugger tying up his bootlaces,' shouted Grant in annoyance.

Worcester City were in real financial difficulty, needing £15,000 to clear themselves. And now the firm offers began to come with Davies only just signed professional and costing a mere £10 per week plus £2 appearance money.

Torquay were first with £3,000; then Millwall, with Benny Fenton interested at £5,000; Noel Cantwell was keen enough to get his Chairman off a plane to make an offer of £10,000; Gordon Clark, Arsenal's Chief Scout, was talking in terms of £12,500 with provisos for paying more if Davies was successful at Highbury. But Brian Clough and Peter Taylor came to watch. 'There's something about him that excites me. I want him,' said Clough. Grant had close links with Derby, to whom he had once recommended Alan Durban, the Welsh International. 'They call Durban "speedy" because he is so slow,' he told them, 'but if you want a good football brain go after him.'

Clough and Derby have a reputation for encouraging the skilful player. Grant felt this was the club for Davies, a pure footballer, highly talented, but strong enough not to be knocked off his game.

He told his Board it was time to settle and to give Davies his chance. Most Scouts are instructed not to bother with players over eighteen, and if the moment was missed Davies might stay a non-League player for good. Worcester might lose their profit. So far they had spent less than £50 on Davies in wages in his seven games.

When the discussions started with the Chairman, George Love, Clough's opening bid was £7,000. Throughout the night and into the early hours the negotiations went on. 'I might have given in earlier as I was not sure of Davies' value, but if Clough had come personally to watch him I knew he must be worth a lot. So I held out for the £15,000.' Finally he accepted £1,000 less. 'His father wanted him to go to Derby and we knew he would have a chance to develop there.'

This was still a record fee for a non-League player at the time and it was financial salvation for Worcester. For Wilf Grant there was added satisfaction. 'You share in a player's success if you find him and bring him on. We were emphasising the non-League club's role as a necessary feeder for the League and also showing them that you get late developers in football. You are not necessarily a failure at twenty.'

The battle for talent becomes ever fiercer and such finds as Davies are rare. But they indicate how wide must be a Manager's interest, how developed his scouting system. A few seasons ago a First Division Manager who had the Third and Fourth Divisions researched in depth was likely to find some bargains. Now he must research the non-League clubs as well and even there the competition will be as fierce for the emerging player as it is for the emerging schoolboy.

The transfer market is one of the Manager's main concerns and there are few principles to guide except the need for wide contacts. The circulated list of players available for transfer is of limited help. Herbert Chapman used to go for the player the club did *not* want to sell and that may still be the best principle. Robson worked on it when he made a vital transfer deal with Everton.

All we lacked was a forward of International class. David Johnson at Everton was the man I wanted and we put in a written request for him in August. But Harry Catterick was not interested. Every week I would ask him and every week the answer was the same. But if you are really determined you usually get the man in the end. All Managers have their moods and one day everything may be right. That's how it was when we played Everton.

Royle had just injured himself in training and Catterick was wanting another big powerful man in the centre, not a slight slim one like Johnson. Roderick Belfitt had a fine game and scored a remarkable goal, while Johnson had a real off-day. So Catterick asked for Belfitt and I got Johnson.

Belfitt had been scoring goals for Ipswich and the exchange was not immediately popular.

I had a lot of abusive letters and phone calls. But fortunately Johnson only took two games to settle in. The exchange was of a good average footballer who had been playing above himself for a younger one of outstanding ability. I did not want to part with Belfitt but it was worth it to get Johnson.

Robson savours the new Ipswich stand as tangible proof of successful Management and skilful transfers.

That cost nearly a quarter of a million pounds and most of it came from transfers. There's great pleasure in a successful purchase like Hunter or Johnson. But the deal that has really given me satisfaction was Jefferson. We cleared £80,000 when we had to sell him, and it gave young Beattie his chance. Beattie was a 16-year-old without a sixpence in his pocket when we found him in youth football in Carlisle. For three years I have worked with him, sweated with him, seen him thinking about the game, responding to coaching. Hardly have we launched him than he's of International standard. That's the most rewarding thing that can happen to a Manager.

At Newcastle Joe Harvey too resolved his main problem by transfer, despite the rich seam of local talent. He has yet to revive the glamour of his own playing days, when the club won the Cup in successive seasons, but there has been no lack of excitement at St James's since he brought back First Division football. For him the unwanted adventure was the narrow avoidance of relegation in 1967 and finding himself bottom of the table the following November.

'Those who tell you it's tough at the top have never been at the bottom,' was Harvey's view of those depressing months. Almost he regretted that he had not kept to his decision to give up Management.

Harvey had been the natural captain for Newcastle, appointed soon after his transfer from Bradford City. For ten years he led the team, then coached them to their third Cup victory in five seasons. That heady period was followed by the hard realities of managing Barrow and Workington. At both he had to watch every detail of expense – the boots, the jerseys, the balls, the stamps. The only players he could go for were the ones on free transfer – and even with those there was no affording the wage expense of a mistake. At both clubs isolation was a problem, with no return from scouting expeditions until the early hours, and the time-wasting expense of away games at Exeter or Torquay. With Workington the balance sheet was a first priority, the position in the table a secondary consideration. Every season a player had to be sold to pay the summer wages of the others. It needed cunning, knowledge, and hard work to survive, but Workington was a forcing-ground for Harvey as it had been for Shankly.

Successful deals with players like Charlie Wright and Joe Wilson gave him confidence in working the transfer market. But in 1962 he was ready to give up and go back to his two shops in Newcastle which his wife was running. The club caught him before he could convert to businessman. After the pleasure of taking them back to the First Division came the painful struggle for survival.

Golf and gardening eased the tension, but it was one transfer deal that resolved it. Harvey had long been after Tony Green, but it was only as Newcastle settled at the bottom of the table that Bob Stokoe was at last prepared to release him from Blackpool. £140,000 was the price of salvation, for Green brought instant inspiration to the team.

He was an appropriate saviour in the Newcastle tradition, a Scot and a gifted ball-player. The Scottish connection and style is cherished at Newcastle. Their Scouts concentrate on the North-East and Yorkshire, but the contact with Scotland is direct and continuous.

Joe Mercer stresses the need to be quick and decisive:

> I saw this young inside at Alloa and I liked the look of him. But my Scout warned me he was too frail for English League football. I held off, aiming to watch him again. Then I found that Spurs had stepped in and bought John White, the inspiration of their forward line in the year of the double.

Ron Greenwood recognises the element of luck.

> At Arsenal we were after an outstanding centre-half. We wanted Mel Charles and so did Tottenham. We won, but Mel suffered from a rash of injuries and did us little good. Tottenham had to look for someone else and got Dave Mackay instead. The also-ran turned out to be the real winner.

Jimmy Hill saw the importance of another principle.

> One of my early signings at Coventry did not fit into the team. I had spent a lot of money on him and the great temptation was to go on playing him. Then I realised I would be harming the club twice. Through worrying about the wasted money I would also be damaging my team. So I admitted the mistake and cut my losses instead of doubling them. That is the hardest decision of all.

Charlie Hurley is equally honest about another aspect.

> I tell my team at Reading, 'I was a great player, but I would never buy myself now. I was too unorthodox, too adventurous for the modern game.'
>
> When I buy a player I check his background. That is the value of having connections throughout the game. You can always get the information you want. I was interested in Youlden from Portsmouth and liked his play. Then I found that

he was always the hardest worker in training, was a keen competitor, and had no vices off the field. So I knew I had a bargain.

The excesses of the transfer market were at their worst in Italy. The National side was undermined by expensive foreign imports into League soccer. The football became as sterile as any in Europe. The clubs were manipulated by millionaires.

Allison was once discussing a proposition to take over at Juventus with the Agnelli brothers, who control the club's affairs. On the field was their side costing nearly two million pounds, including Anastasi bought for £440,000, Haller for £298,000. 'We shall tell the President, Malcolm, that you will need to get rid of some of this rubbish.' That seemed an apt final comment on the system.

The Professional Footballers Association office is a long ramble down a tiled corridor winding round the hall of Manchester's Corn Exchange. Push open the outer door and a bell rings stridently as if this was a small sweet shop with the proprietor drowsing in the back parlour.

Cliff Lloyd has been secretary of the 'Union' for twenty years, a cheerful friendly man with none of the abrasiveness of a Scanlon or a Jones. He is the sort of person everyone comes to with their problems, knowing he will help, however busy.

Transfers are a continuing worry for him because of the damage the drain of money can cause so many clubs. Five years ago the Government enquiry into Association Football, the *Chester Report*, foresaw that top transfer fees might double in this time to over £200,000 and stressed that this would be damaging for the game. They recommended a special levy by the League, the percentage rising sharply as the fee rose. This would help to check the escalation, or give all clubs a share in the rising price of success.

The other unaccepted recommendation that particularly concerns Cliff Lloyd is that the club should not retain the option on players at the end of their contract. All contracts between club and player should be for a definite period, at the end of which either party would be free to renegotiate.

The P.F.A. are pressing for this to be implemented, not solely because other workers have the right of free movement at the end of their contract, but because this right might check exorbitant transfer fees. Clubs would not pay out so much for players who could only be retained for the limited period of the contract.

The Chester Committee referred to the harm that the transfer system could do to the game's image. Lloyd is well aware of the pressure it puts on small clubs and of the spendthrift impression it generates.

'A football club cannot be run like a business, but it can be businesslike.' Dennis Piggott, Brentford's Manager-Secretary, is best placed to know. Survival seemed impossible in 1967 for a Fourth Division club with a deficit of £101,525 6s 3d and a demand from the Chairman to repay his loan of £104,000. The club had lost £12,000 the year before and was losing around £500 a week, when Mr Jack Dunnett, the Socialist M.P., asked for his money back. This forced consideration of a take-over bid from Queen's Park Rangers which Mr Dunnett favoured. Fourth Division clubs are not supposed to be able to pay their way on their gates and there was no obvious way of avoiding the merger. But three Directors and Dennis Piggott decided to fight rather than accept the dissolution of a club which had been playing First Division football as late as 1946.

This was not the first crisis to confront the club. Nearly seventy years ago Gibson and Pickford, those two lively historians of the game's early years, wrote, 'A glance at the Brentford club forces home the fact that it has experienced more than its fair share of the "slings and arrows of outrageous fortune" and throws into bold relief the pluck and determination of the Management.' They could say the same about the response of the four brave men, who were soon joined by W. Wheatley and L. F. Davey.

An 'angel' was needed to keep the play running in the short term and it was Ron Blindell who gave this backing, advancing the £104,000 on a year's interest-free loan and buying up Dunnett's £40,000 shares. Later Walter Wheatley took over the loan with £67,000 still outstanding. But the long-term problem remained. How to repay this crippling sum? How to make the club solvent for the future? Within five years the debt was paid off and the deficit had almost disappeared. Mostly this was achieved by an attack on costs rather than a drive for extra income. The reserves and youth teams were immediately disbanded, the professional staff reduced from twenty to fifteen. The last reserve match was against Gillingham, the win giving the twelve players a bonus totalling £24 compared with the £21 gate takings. Abolishing the reserve team saved £17,000 a year in wages apart from reduced expenses on travelling, kit, referees, lighting and all the other incidentals. Other economies were exploited to the full – travelling by coach instead of train, staying fewer nights in hotels, having the ground prepared once a fortnight by contract instead of keeping a full-time groundsman.

Income was boosted in two ways. Dunnett had limited the issue of share capital to 51% in order to retain control himself. This ban was removed and the remainder of the shares issued.

Dividends are limited to 7½% by F.A. regulation. None had been paid since 1937 and none was likely for many years. Yet there was enough goodwill for the club for all to be taken up.

The Brentford Pool runs separately, but the annual donation from this and the supporters club was increased, as were other fund-raising activities. In the first year the loss was changed to a profit of £18,000. By 1972 the profit was running at £27,000, the same figure to which the deficit balance had been cut. Working to a limit of fifteen professionals backed by six signed amateurs gave no obvious playing problems. In the previous five years Brentford had won promotion from Fourth to Third Division then slipped quickly back again. At the end of five years without reserves they achieved promotion again but again slid swiftly back.

Only Portsmouth, Carlisle and Aldershot ran the same way, but it is hard to see why other clubs in lower Divisions afford the luxury of the extra teams when they are losing money. It makes sense as an insurance policy for the rich clubs like Arsenal or Liverpool, even though the big Italian clubs never find it necessary to have more than seventeen or so on the staff. If Inter-Milan want their squad reinforcing they buy the best, rather than bring them through the reserves.

Looking back, Dennis Piggott sees the main purpose of the Brentford Reserve side as giving a game to the four or five First Team reinforcements. For a club in such financial problems, nearly £20,000 a year was a high price to pay for this practice.

The careful club can still exist on its own efforts even in the Fourth Division of the English League. There is a bleaker outlook in Scotland.

Kilmarnock is one of the best run provincial teams, the last club to win the Scottish League championship before the Celtic monopoly and semi-finalists in the European Cup Winners' Cup in 1967.

Only four years after that rich run in Europe their losses for the year were £13,612. That was in a season in which they reached the semi-final of the Scottish Cup and began saving wages by phasing-out full-time players.

The Directors in their report said: 'It is inevitable in a year when no players have been transferred that the accounts will show a substantial loss.' Except for Rangers and Celtic all clubs are faced with the same problem of balancing the books from ordinary income. Kilmarnock's loss was kept within bounds only by the Cup run and by converting players to part-timers training two or three times a week. With the dwindling gates often below 4,000, self-sufficiency is an impossible dream.

The cash infusion from transfers to the English League remains the life-line for many Scottish clubs. For the players it is the one prospect of moving quickly from the life-style of the semi-detached house and the worry over bills.

Billy McNeill, the Celtic captain, was probably the only Scottish player to earn £10,000 a year. For most First Division players the 1972 basic pay was between £30 and £35 a week. Bonuses could add £10 a week to this, but the Scottish Football Association rules have in the past officially confined these to £3 for a win and £360 in total if the team takes the Scottish Cup.

Fear of relegation or desire to beat Celtic or Rangers has been known to push up the bonus, as much as £500 being paid to avoid the drop to the Second Division.

The unrealistic clause 'a reasonable wage for a player of the First Division club shall be not less than £624 per annum for full-time players' is not quite so dated in Scotland as in England. But though he may be on three times this salary at twenty a footballer can in Scotland spend the rest of his career without increase.

Under the rules the club need only pay £300 to a player sold for transfer, though most have their ways of ensuring this does not apply.

As in England the club retains an option on the player for a further twelve months at the end of his contract, which is normally limited to a year.

Of nearly a thousand professional players in Scotland nearly half are dependent on the game for their living. While Willie

McLean, Secretary of the Scottish Professional Footballers Association, fights to improve the conditions, he and the Managers know the available cash is limited.

Rangers' Manager, Willie Waddell, says,

> The majority don't earn a living wage, but it remains better than that of the ordinary working-man. Given a chance anyone would prefer to be a footballer, rather than a joiner. It's a job with some magic. It opens up doors to him that would be closed to the average person.
>
> I don't think the game can do much more. There isn't the money about. But it gives young men a grounding and character training and it's up to them to make the most of it. The rules clubs operate should help them observe the rules of society later in life.

Football does demand a more disciplined life than most jobs and has a greater attraction. As a Celtic player commented, 'I fight hard over contracts and feel I'm worth more than I get. But let's be honest. If I had to pay my own fare to Parkhead and bring my own boots I'd be there. It's not like actually earning a living is it?'

The real living is to be earned in England and for many of the better players this will always be the great attraction. Joe Harper, asking Aberdeen to put him on the transfer list that led to Everton, made his ambition clear: 'I must seek financial security for my wife and a future family.' For the successful there can be more than security in the English League.

The normal pattern of footballers' earnings is £2,000 to £2,500 in the Third and Fourth Divisions, £4,000 in the Second, £5,500 in the First.

In winning First Division teams the bonuses take pay far higher. Yet Bob Wall looking back over the years still rates the footballer as best off relatively when the maximum wage was first £8 in winter and £6 in summer, three times the craftsman's wage of 50s a week.

He recalls there were no disputes over contracts then, only anxious enquiries if they would be renewed.

It is a beguiling but fallacious picture of the footballer better off under the old system. The relative value of the maximum soon declined when it was 'frozen' for twenty years. Indeed in 1931–2 only the intervention of John McKenna, Chairman of the Management Committee, stopped it being arbitrarily reduced to £6. When it was ended in 1963 the maximum was only £20 per week. The maximum's inhibiting effect had eroded the previous differential, though the craftsman himself had risen in the social order. Now that there is free bargaining, the First Division footballer has improved his position, and his social equivalents in money terms are Britain's Managers, not craftsmen.

Of the two main arguments against ending the maximum wage the most popular was that it would destroy teamwork. Clearly this has not happened because the chief complaint against modern football is that there is too much 'method', too little flair and individualism. One reason for this is that clubs have in general differentiated more by the success of the team than the ability of the individual. Herbert Chapman, so often ahead of his time, wrote in the 1930s:

> Some men may believe that their value is greater than that of other members of the side and that they are a big box office attraction, but they are dependent on others for their success, and they cannot be treated differently. I certainly would not like to operate a system under which financial or other distinctions were made between players in a team except as laid down by rule.

Some big clubs now operate within this formula that the guaranteed basic pay for the First Team squad of fifteen or so is identical, but that players' success makes the differences in specified bonuses. Some pay extravagantly for the star.

At one end of the scale is Brentford, with a total wage bill for staff and players of £57,000, at the other end Leeds United paying £275,000, with Don Revie earning over £15,000 and five players over £10,000 in a season in which the 'double' was so nearly won.

But the effect of success is most clearly seen by comparing Arsenal's 'double' team of 1971 with the following season when they again reached the Final, but finished fifth in the League. In 1971 the bill, including the Players' Benefits (the accounts name for their loyalty bonus), was £337,797 for players, trainers and staff. In 1972 it was down to £255,052. Liverpool that year were third, a point off the League Championship, but with no success in the Cup, and their payment was only £209,322.

Team success is still a more paying proposition – and always a greater draw for crowds – than individual ability.

The Business Game

In football it is a case of 'winner take all' off the field as well as on it. Three-quarters of the clubs are in dire financial difficulty, facing the problem of whether to aim at solvency or success, whether to invest in the future, or save in the present by cutting out reserve teams, paying only the rate for the Division, taking on part-time players. Yet the successful can coin money on the prestige of their name. No club has exploited this so well as Rangers in Glasgow. Each year their Pool brings in more than three hundred thousand pounds profit and pays more than half a million pounds to the Exchequer in betting duty. On a sample week in January 1973 there were 618,000 entrants at a stake of 6p with prize money of £12,238 for the winners of the five separate pools.

Manchester United and Celtic are not far behind in the size of their pools operations, but for most clubs twenty thousand pounds profit is a fair target.

These pools are run on a simple system of allocated numbers that requires no calculation on the entrants' part. In theory he can keep choosing and changing the set of numbers that allocate teams to him. In practice this is so rarely done that these pools have been judged games of chance with the clubs given another three years to work out a solution that conforms to the Betting

Act. But for the present the club pools still bring millions of pounds into the game.

Rangers have also exploited the commercial possibilities of their crest and their name, a separate company drawing royalties from firms who use the insignia to sell anything from carpets to cards.

The driving force behind these Rangers enterprises is David Hope, a perfectionist who has not yet had to pay out on his offer of cash prizes to any colleague discovering a mistake in his planning. His is a remarkable story of persistence and initiative. Coming from a poor family in Glasgow he started work as a labourer in a foundry, educated himself, then walked to University to study Maths and Physics.

Setting up a radio shop without capital he built the business to a size that finally attracted a bidder's interest. He had no intention of selling out, but each refusal drew a raised offer. After the third time his family suggested that if the bidder raised again no Scot could refuse such an exaggerated profit. When the man returned with a final offer Hope shook hands, picked up his coat, and walked out of the shop for good. He was sixty-four and planned to spend the rest of his life fishing and enjoying his retirement. It was then that Rangers asked him to have a trial run at organising the Pool for them. Hope had been a life-long Rangers' supporter and had played football for eighteen years himself, keeping goal with Ashfield. He was known to Rangers' Directors as an expert mathematician and an organiser of outstanding ability. He redesigned the whole system of the Pool, from the cards to the different coloured plastic trays in their Dexion racking which enable the winner's name to be located in thirty seconds.

The profits from the Pool have embellished the Ibrox Ground and been used to build the unique Rangers' club with its 20,000 members and its larger waiting list. Rangers' social club contrasts with the common English practice of looking on football as a ninety-minute game, with clubs bolting and barring their grounds as soon as they can hurry the spectators out.

David Hope is the companionable guide to the club, who can discourse endlessly on every detail from the special dye for the Rangers blue of the Boardroom chairs to the 34 tanks with their 180 gallons each of beer piped instantly to the bars above. The gadgetry and the electronics for the Stage in the main restaurant is his special love, the facilities attracting artists such as Lulu and

Shirley Bassey. It is a sobering thought for those who feel that the football branch of the entertainment industry is overpaid, that their fee for a week would pay most footballers for a year.

At Ibrox the money from the Pools has also gone to a great increase in seating in the Stadium. Apart from the comfort of spectators this is the best method of combating violence on football grounds. The more seats there are, the less chance of trouble.

In the big club the Manager can be left free to concentrate on football while others look after the commercial projects. But in the smaller his range is as wide as in any business. It is in the lower Divisions that techniques familiar to industrial management are being tried out. Ron Tindall of Portsmouth used 'Management by Objectives' to chart his course; Tony Waiters at Plymouth Argyle turned to job description to define responsibilities through the club; John Bond at Bournemouth has tried the 'Coverdale Management Training'.

Rational business methods can be applied to football, but its dreams and hopes defy realistic analysis. As a hard commercial proposition it is an unacceptable risk for teams like Bournemouth or Brighton to aim at the First Division. But if a man or a town will back them with adequate funds then anything is possible.

A part of the Coverdale training is the definition of aims, and Bournemouth's are far from limited. The eight results for which Bond is working sum up the intentions of all ambitious Third Division clubs: to reach the First Division in five years; to make the club pay its way; to have a progressive and productive youth development scheme; to think on the same lines at all levels of the club; to coordinate the playing staff all with the same basic ideas; to get an average gate of 20,000 and over 25,000 on special occasions; to build the image of the club locally and nationally; to make the ground of First Division standards in all respects.

Bournemouth's special aim is to be the first League club to run professionally a sports complex based on the football ground. Already their rebuilding programme is advanced and their eager young staff plan to make the stadium an entertainment centre open throughout the week. But everything will hinge on the football success and on overcoming the initial frustrations of promotion missed by a point and transfer payments far exceeding transfer returns despite the £200,000 received for Ted MacDougall.

Bournemouth could not aim so high without the backing of a wealthy chairman. It is the same at Brighton and Hove Albion.

Pat Saward impresses on young players that they must think big, and that reflects his own outlook. As Brighton dropped down to the Third Division the new plush offices were going up. For him that was no contradiction.

> I never talk about *trying* to do anything. You must always believe you *can* do it. That is what I tell the youngsters and that is how I act myself. We won promotion as soon as I came without any sizeable expenditure and without the resources for Second Division football. The success came quicker than I expected and the excitement of it coupled with a good start to the season obscured the problem for me. When we began to lose I kept thinking the next match would go right. But the more we lost, the more players lost confidence. The drastic action was delayed too long. That was a mistake, but it does not change the future plans. We are building a group of young players who will bring us sustained success. Everyone says you don't find footballers on the South Coast. There will be a lot of red faces when I prove them wrong because in this area I am finding boys as good as Jeff Blockley and Willie Carr when they came to me. I will show they can be developed, take Brighton to the First Division, then move out of football within ten years. Football Management should only be a step in a career, not a lifetime's work.

Saward's plans will not lack financial support. Part of the drastic action was a Board change which made Mike Bamber joint-chairman with Len Stringer. Bamber has launched with another Director, Norman Hyams, a property company in which the Football Club has a 49% stake. Nearly half the profit will go to Brighton. Such resources are not available to the average Manager, nor will he have had the business experience to handle them.

The need for more training of football Managers is explicit in the problems men like Noel Cantwell faced when suddenly confronted with the overnight change from player to Manager.

The first Football Club Management Studies Course, sponsored by the F.A. and the League, was only recently completed in a belated attempt to meet the requirement. This was a three-year programme with the sixteen course members spending a fortnight each summer at Loughborough University and working on projects on return to their clubs. Those selected were Managers, or likely to become Managers, such as Jimmy Adamson and his Burnley Chief Coach, Joe Brown, or Malcolm Musgrove, the Coach of Manchester United before becoming Torquay's Manager.

The course centred on business management, rather than football. It covered management styles and motivation; job analysis and target setting; facility planning, public speaking, financial management, law, psychology and organisation.

The main case-study was of a mythical Third Division team, Hanford Albion, with fading support, a sizeable overdraft and a small supporters club. That example was certainly topical and the lessons appreciated even by experienced Managers. End-of-course comments concentrated on the need felt for further practical help in the understanding of a Manager's job. Going to the heart of the matter were the requests for advice from the most successful motivators of footballers – Jock Stein, Matt Busby, and Bertie Mee the interesting choice – rather than theoretical psychology, and for an illustration of contrasting styles of Management, with Bertie Mee picked as the expert in delegation, Leicester's Jimmy Bloomfield as the believer in doing it all oneself. On the details of management they wanted more instruction on apprenticeship schemes, on the selection and training of staff and on the organisation of medical facilities, with Ian Adams, the Leeds medical officer, regarded as the main authority. This was a sensible appreciation of the needs of a Manager and of the priorities of his job.

One of those priorities is the relationship between Manager and Chairman that is the vital link in the power structure of a club. On day-to-day matters most Managers deal direct with the Chairman if there is any point on which they need a decision. And in most football Boards the Chairman is the decisive influence. Nothing would ever happen at Burnley that did not meet with Bob Lord's approval, or at Charlton against Michael Gliksten's wishes, or at Darlington if George Tait disagreed.

When the colourful Malcolm Allison finally took over from Joe Mercer he could not have done so without the support of Eric Alexander, the Manchester City Chairman. A year later, with the team in disarray and the supporters disenchanted, Alexander was quick to agree when Allison asked to break his contract and try his luck with Crystal Palace on a new five-year contract at £13,000 a year. A major shareholder was reported as saying, 'If I had had the chance I am sure I could have talked Allison into staying.' It would have needed more than silver-tongued oratory to stop Allison leaving, but it was significant that he had had no opportunity to try to dissuade him. Certainly there was no doubt that the Chairman of the club he joined would have his way. Raymond Bloye bought Crystal Palace for quarter the price of a good player – some £37,000. The Matthews Holdings Group, of which he is Chairman, acquired 51% of Palace's equity. The aim was to include it in the Company's leisure division, but City comment did not approve of such an unstable asset as a football club. So Bloye bought out the shares at the same price to take control himself. Clearly, Allison's job is dependent on satisfying the Chairman. But with a five-year contract that is hardly the sort of risk that leads to the poorhouse.

Derrick Robins was one of the more forceful Chairmen, the total commitment that has brought his business success best symbolised by the *two* telephones beside his bed. He is unusual in being himself a notable sportsman and one who has made a major contribution to cricket as well as to football. One of the liveliest pairings in soccer was his relationship with Jimmy Hill, a Manager who could match him for sharpness of wit, for drive, for business acumen and self-confidence. Robins rates Hill as the ablest Manager he has met in a long career in the game.

> You could never win an argument with Jimmy, but there were times when I had to say 'I know I am right so this is how we will do it'.

Hill appreciated the need for a good relationship between team and Directors. Before he came the players would not have recognised most of them by sight and felt only antagonism. But Hill told his team to get to know the Directors and to appreciate that many of them were eminent men in their own field worth respecting for their other talents if not for their football knowledge. However busy I was he always made sure that I knew what was going on and involved myself. If he went to sign a player he made sure I came with him not just to approve the transfer, but for the chance to talk over the club's affairs on the journey.

Jimmy Hill is now a sports consultant advising a number of football clubs and drawing on his own experience.

> They are surprised when I tell them that the first step to success is to get a good loudspeaker. But you have to think of football as entertainment. When I took over at Coventry I could see we would achieve nothing worthwhile without the money for new players. How do you get money when you are a struggling Third Division side whose football is not likely to draw the crowds?
>
> You have to attract them by making them feel part of the club. The loudspeakers on most grounds are quite inaudible and used to tell people they have left their car engines running. We used the speakers to inform them about players, to identify them with the team, to amuse them. The broadcaster was always a personality – first Godfrey Evans, then a trained professional.
>
> Where other clubs shepherded the spectators out as quickly as possible we tried to get them to stay, to use the catering services, to feel at home.
>
> Long before the League hired out its special supporters' train we ran one for the fans with myself and the Directors explaining all we could about the match, the team, the club.

Hill also appreciated that the players needed some amusement. At Fulham he had once gone for treatment to an injury only to find Charlie Mitten's greyhound on the table being massaged by the elderly trainer. That had caught the fancy of the team and the memory helped him ease the tension at Coventry as he was pushing the players hard for promotion. When they returned from a training session they found the passage blocked by Hill's hunter with the horse being rubbed down by the masseur. Football is big business but there is no reason why it should not still be fun.

It's Tough at the Bottom

Peter Sillett, the former Chelsea and England full-back, was once warned, 'Never take over as Manager of a Southern League club or you will never get back in the Football League.'

Malcolm Allison, Ron Saunders, or Frank O'Farrell could disprove that advice, but not Sillett.

For eight seasons he has managed Ashford without attracting attention. Only in 1970 could the club win promotion to the Premier Division of the Southern League and at once it slipped back again.

Yet last season they reached the semi-finals of the F.A. Challenge Trophy and were on the verge of one of those Wembley days that can make a Manager. The club has a professional staff of twelve, augmented by two amateurs. The wage bill is under £150 a week and a thousand spectators is an event. To win the main trophy for non-League clubs might have launched Sillett on a new career. But Scarborough scored the goal that mattered in a tight game and the dream dissolved.

'Don't start at the bottom. Cut yourself in at the top.' That is also the advice of Alec Stock to aspiring Managers. His own managerial career, covering a quarter of a century, has been at its most successful in the lower reaches. There he had remarkable achievement with Yeovil, with Leyton Orient and with Queen's Park Rangers. The flirtations with First Division football have never been so rewarding – an early parting with Arsenal, disappointment in Italy. Now he has picked Fulham up from the depths of the Second Division and may soon be trying his luck again on the peaks.

For him football is a game of climbing mountains.

> When you win promotion you have built yourself another mountain. The Directors say 'Go climb it' and you look round and think desperately 'with what?'

Football Management is a lonely job. There is no one to guide you, no football advice available to a Manager. If you have been successful in the Third Division all you are is an expert on Third Division football. You know those teams intimately, their players, their standards, their styles. You know almost nothing about the higher levels.

The Manager is insecure as well as isolated. Whatever you do you know you will never run your own business, or be your own master. However pleasant the Chairman and Directors, however confident in you, they are still human. If things go wrong for a spell, as they do in any business, the public pressures quickly become intolerable in football. You can never be sure in advance how they will stand up to them. What has been achieved in the past may count for nothing in a present problem.

Stock can speak with feeling from his Rangers experience. He led them to victory at Wembley in the League Cup, the first Third Division side to win a major Final there. Then he took Rangers to the First Division.

> The strain made me ill. But whereas a professional footballer would have had special treatment I was left in the public ward of a public hospital. Then I was sacked under the pretext that I was sick. I was certainly sick to be treated like that when on the point of recovery, as my future performance with Luton and Fulham was to show.

Bobby Charlton, looking ahead to Management, spoke of his hopes to have the offer of a First Division club. Stock's premise is not that one should start managing at that level, but should begin there as Coach or Assistant. The ideal preparation indeed may well be to manage a non-League club, then coach a First Division side.

This was the route for Gordon Milne, managing Wigan Athletic then moving on as Team Manager of Coventry, or of Ron Greenwood starting with Eastbourne, like Gordon Jago later, then becoming Assistant at Arsenal.

Stock's own brief stay at Arsenal was a traumatic experience.

At Leyton Orient the Manager was totally involved with all the details of finance and football. I liked everything to be exact, players to be punctual, discipline to be good. When I went as Tom Whittaker's assistant the nature of the job was not clearly defined to me and I never felt fully occupied in so big an organisation. The players seemed to have a more casual attitude than we had been able to afford at Orient and it was difficult to establish a sympathetic relationship. We did move up the table from near the bottom to near the top, but I was never at ease. My impression was that the real reason I had been invited to come in was not as possible successor to Whittaker, but to get the best out of one of the characters of the Arsenal side, Vic Groves.

Groves, a jellied-eel salesman of cheerful disposition, had played inside me in the England Amateur team before his bustling enthusiasm and considerable talent took him to Arsenal via Orient.

After a few months a chance meeting with the Orient team ended Stock's stay. On his way to watch a reserve match against Aldershot he happened across them. His unease was sensed, his affinity with Orient appreciated and the Chairman, Harry Zussman, asked him back. While he was considering the proposition the evening paper headlined his acceptance and the decision was made for him.

Stock has always been one of the shrewdest judges of a player. Three of today's most prolific and exciting goal-scorers were let go by Fulham – Marsh, Macdonald and Clarke – and Stock picked up two of them at a derisory price. Marsh fascinated him for the contrast of delicate control backed by thirteen stone of formidable power. He kept on at Vic Buckingham until he caught him one morning when irritated by Marsh's waywardness. That was the foundation of Rangers' success.

MacDonald he brought to Luton for £18,000, seeing, in a fullback, a forward's potential. He played him first at outside-left, then inside, then used the human tank to cleave through the centre.

No doubt Fulham asked me to take over to stop any drain like that happening again. The football Manager's job is a jigsaw with some pieces always missing. But when you get the great player you want to make sure you don't lose him. In the lower Division that is very difficult with the First Division wages forcing one to pay more than one can afford and affluence making players independent.

Stock came of a mining family, but his bright intelligence launched his career in a London Bank. His amateur football began with Wilmington Total Abstainers and brought him to Tottenham's notice. In 1935, after working overtime on the German Ledger, coping with the rush for foreign exchange for the Berlin Olympics, he trained at White Hart Lane. It was in a practice game there that he impressed the visiting Jimmy Seed who signed him for Charlton.

After war service with the Tank Corps, reaching the rank of major, his football interest impelled him to answer an advertisement for a Yeovil Manager. He soon made this sloping pitch nationally known with a Cup run that took Yeovil to a fifth-round match at Old Trafford before a crowd of over 80,000.

Yeovil was as well organised as any League Club, but the limited playing staff gave problems. The previous round we played First Division Sunderland. My goalkeeper was a landscape gardener from London and in training he dived on a bottle top and cut his hand. The only reserve was an amateur, Victor Dyke, working in a Solicitor's office. It seemed to be asking too much of him to play his first game in the tense atmosphere of a fourth round Cup-tie, but he treated it as a joke and was largely responsible for Sunderland's defeat.

Stock has felt the lowly start a drag on progress. Noel Cantwell has the other view, his managerial career launched at the top with Coventry before demotion to Fourth Division Peterborough.

You cannot resist the offer of a First Division club, and if you do start lower down you may be stuck there for good. But there is no doubt which is the right way of learning the job. No one makes you Manager of the Bank of England overnight, but in football terms that was what happened to me. I walked off the field one Saturday and the following Tuesday I was Manager of a First Division team.

As a player one thinks one knows the Manager's job and problems, but they are quite different from what one expects. Looking back I can see the main mistake I made. Jimmy Hill had rushed Coventry up from Third to First Division and given the club the organisation and support for top-level football. Yet in a playing sense we were short of the strength to make an impact. My own special interest was in developing young players and that was an exciting experience with Pat Saward.

What was needed, however, was action this day with the First Team. That ought to have been a total priority when most of my effort went to the future. There were some solid achievements in building up the facilities at the Ryton training-ground, in starting the hostel for young players and speeding the flow of those now proving themselves. The ideas were sound, the timing was wrong.

When I came to Peterborough the message was too clear to miss. They had only five points from thirteen games and were bottom club in the League. Winning points and winning back spectators at once was what mattered.

Cantwell's arrival soon doubled the gates to a healthy 7,000, while the team climbed rapidly out of danger. Only three new players were acquired – Keith Bradley from Aston Villa, John Cousins from Notts County, and Eric Young on a season's loan from Manchester United.

The main problem was that the players had lost confidence in their own ability, and so had the fans. I could see they were much better than their position and my belief was easily communicated. John Barnwell, the Coach, and I had so much First Division experience between us that they could respect our judgement. The training had also been ineffective and dull – too much lapping, too little functional work. We were able immediately to bring enjoyment and purpose into that and the players then began to develop their potential.

System is just as important in the Fourth Division as in the First. But with the players not so precise in their passing or immaculate in their control, system doesn't necessarily win matches. And it is unwise to assume that all of them will readily follow complicated tactics. Some will just be confused by them. You have to make the best of the players as they are and not expect the impossible.

There are three real differences between managing a Fourth Division and a First Division club. You take on more yourself, you are freer from the harsh pressures, but you have more problems over money.

Peterborough had had their problems over money in the past. When they were elected to the Fourth Division after many stirring battles in the Cup they shot at once to the top of the table. In that 1960/1 season they scored 134 goals, something no other team has achieved in the history of the League. Next year they failed by four points to slip through the Third Division at a stroke.

The confident start encouraged too great expectations. When they became enmeshed in the Third Division, inducements were offered to players beyond the basic pay and bonuses specified in the contracts. That is against League rules and Peterborough were demoted to the Fourth Division. The affair cost the club the confidence of the town.

The past had proved that Peterborough could support a thriving side, but as the deficit built up the prospects became even bleaker. This was a situation familiar to many lowly clubs, in which they could only be rescued by the new Directors or the community.

The Board's appointment of Cantwell and their readiness to back their judgement with cash has revived the glad confident spirit of the early days in the League.

> It was a brave decision to appoint me at a substantial salary when they were in financial difficulty. And only the fact that they have put in £5,000 of their own money gives me a real chance to be successful. Since I came no team has looked significantly better than us and we should get promotion next season.
>
> But one needs money for emergencies. Eric Young has to go back to United so I cannot plan round him and will have to find a replacement. We will be aiming at Second Division Football in the foreseeable future, and even with increased support we cannot finance that through the gates. But if we are successful the development funds and the commercial ventures can then

bring in the extra money. Without the Directors' personal contribution we could not have made the start.

One further step will help balance the books and improve performance. The Reserves play in the Eastern Counties League, but that does not provide the right type of opposition. We need to be truly professional and by transferring to the Mid-Week League we will be against the reserve sides of other Leagues. This will also save travel costs and allow me to have a smaller staff of players, since some of the First Team can play in mid-week games.

Peterborough's past performance is not untypical of the success of the few non-League clubs allowed in. Hereford United is the latest to make instant impact on the League. Their motto 'Our greatest glory lies not in never having fallen, but in rising when we fall' might more suitably be applied to Peterborough.

For their own progress has always been upright and sedate, until the accelerating pace of the last five seasons. The club, formed fifty years ago, became a limited company and entered the Southern League in 1939. For twenty years their application to join the League was rejected, although they had an unrivalled record in the F.A. Challenge Cup, only once failing to reach the first round proper in twenty-five successive seasons.

The wheels of election grind very slow, with the League clubs supporting each other in distress and barring more vigorous applicants. Of the trickle of entrants Oxford, Cambridge, Peterborough and Hereford all point the moral that a larger infusion of new blood would give greater virility to the lower Divisions.

Consider what Hereford had to offer. As a non-League club their gates averaged 5,224 compared with the Fourth Division average of 4,959. Their estimate that League football would improve attendances to over 8,000 was confirmed in their first season.

The population of Herefordshire is 140,000 and this is the only professional club in the county. The nearest League ground is Newport County, forty-two miles distant. Hereford was capable of a profit of £15,000 in the year it joined the League, when so many complain of the struggle to survive.

From near bankruptcy five years before they had surged ahead to reflect the fervour and support of the town. The Corporation converted a loan of nearly £14,000 into a gift, reflecting both their backing for football and their judgement that receipts from their car park outside the ground would recoup any loss. From two uncovered terraces, with the team changing in the public baths behind the ground, the Edgar Street facilities had been improved to match any in the Fourth Division.

A new stand was built, tiled dressing-rooms and modern medical facilities added, and more than 90% of the accommodation was covered. The soaring income from the development fund gave money in hand for further improvement.

John Charles, the outstanding Welsh player of the generation, the idol of Italy when he played for Juventus, had been happy enough to come to Hereford. As Player/Manager Charles built a formidable team, his work further developed by Colin Addison.

Hereford's playing strength was clear for all to see when their substitute, George, stabbed home the shot that sent Newcastle United slithering out of the Cup. That extra-time goal confirmed their superiority in two tense matches, before West Ham too were stretched to a replay.

Yet the voting for Hereford's entry was as close and protracted as the Cup-ties. Their main non-League rivals, Wigan Athletic, could point to a Cup performance of similar quality in the narrowest of defeats by Manchester City at Maine Road. Wigan's excellent case was lost through over-eagerness, excessive publicity antagonising the League representatives and undermining support. But Barrow, eleven times applicants for re-election with average gates of less than two and a half thousand, were so nearly voted back in Hereford's place. After a tie at 26 each, Hereford at last nosed home by 31 votes to 23. At once they proved there was nothing exaggerated in their claim to be 'an ambitious club, financially buoyant and fortunate in their choice of Manager'.

Colin Addison had been one of Bertie Mee's first transfers to Arsenal, but not one of his shrewdest. A poised, clever inside-forward with York City and Nottingham Forest, Addison never fitted smoothly into the Highbury style, though an admirer of Mee's methods. Moving on to Sheffield United, he had dropped out of the First Team when Hereford approached him.

'Addio', as the supporters acclaim him, is neat and tidy in dress and mind, a serious forward-looking young man. Hereford are too absorbed in the future to look back to a past triumph, but he recalls the Newcastle game with conscious effort.

Going to play at St James's Park could have been unnerving. If I had gone through all the big names from Tony Green to Bobby Moncur and had a plan for each I would have only scared and confused the players. So we made just one simple adjustment. Malcolm Macdonald is a left-footed player who likes to move to his left and we made sure the right-back came in to cover this route to goal. Otherwise there were no special instructions. 'Don't clutter up your players with unnecessary knowledge' is one of my rules. We followed our usual style; keep it simple and to the point; be positive with all players looking for goals, even the centre-backs from set-pieces; keep working.

'Keep working' was also the response to entry into the League. The part-time professionals were converted to a full-time staff of sixteen. Half the winning side were replaced. Tyler had so impressed West Ham that they acquired him for the highest fee paid for a non-League footballer. The £15,000 received gave Addison the money for the transfers. Tommy Naylor from Bournemouth, Henry Gregory and Dave Rudge from Aston Villa, Kenny Wallace from West Ham, George Johnston from Fulham, Colin Tavener from Trowbridge, centre-forward Eric Redrobe from Southport, cost only £20,000 the lot.

The early matches were a strain for Addison, out of form himself in the field and with only nine points from fourteen games. 'We played good football, but got little return. The improvement came as we became more professional, that little bit harder. Not dirty – just harder.'

Addison is not given to humour, but he also relates the subsequent run of success to the breaking of his leg. He makes it clear he is joking, but it was not necessarily coincidence. The Player/Manager, like the part-time player, has too much asked of him by League football. From the touchline Addison could give more thought to the planning and direction.

Hereford have most of the attributes for the more lively approach to League football that would dispel the Cassandra cries of doom. The town looks on the football club as a civic amenity. The Chairman, Frank Miles, has played for the club's colts and knows his soccer as well as his business of running a chain of carpet shops and a finance company. Reg Tidball, the Secretary, who once managed the Hereford Co-operative Society, has been chairman of the City's Finance and Planning Committee, confirming the close link between club and City Council. Development schemes treat the football ground as an entertainment centre, with the plans including a restaurant, a bowling alley and a Sauna bath. Hereford's initiative extended to taking Jim Finney, the World Cup referee, on the staff. This is a source of football knowledge and administrative ability too rarely tapped by League clubs. They could also copy his careful indoctrination of players in the rules of the game when it is too often erroneously assumed that professional players are word-perfect in them.

If Hereford have been so invigorating an addition to the League it is reasonable to assume that Wigan and many others in the queue could be as effective. Gordon Milne's experience with Wigan, Noel Cantwell's with Peterborough, make them confident that the best of the non-League clubs can offer more than some of the old teams, drained of energy and support.

Even the top-class amateur clubs are close to League standard. Cantwell has much respect for Bishop's Stortford, who held Peterborough to a draw in the Cup. Three Isthmian League clubs reached the second round proper of the F.A. Cup that season and I visited Bishop's Stortford after the win that took them to the confrontation with Cantwell's team.

This was the high point in the ninety-eight years of the club's history, so it was hardly surprising that the social club over the changing room had a forlorn look, as if still suffering a hangover from the previous night's junketings.

Every successful amateur club has an honorary secretary like Brian Bayford, his spare time wholly devoted to its welfare for his fourteen years in the job. With him was Gordon Atkinson, a player for fifteen years and Manager for two, then promoter of their Pool – a full-time job.

Atkinson looked a typical left-back to me, the strongly built sort who left you on the floor in the first minute. But he was much milder and kinder than the types I used to run into. Why had he given up managing? 'The pressure to win was too much for me. They talk about the problems of professional clubs. It's just as intense for amateurs. You've got to be successful or no one wants to know.'

In Stortford's annual report was a page of humorous definitions, one of which read: 'Football Coach – an animated ulcer.' In the circumstances it did not seem very funny, but there was nothing ulcerous about Atkinson's present job.

> We have 8,000 contributors to the Pool, and last year we passed over £3,500 to the club. We run a lot of other money-spinners.
>
> Why so many changes in the playing staff? When Ted Hardy took over as Manager last year a lot of the Dagenham players wanted to stay with him. Three came last season and three this.
>
> We are glad to get Ted because we know he is the best manager in the amateur game. No one gets many goals against a side Ted manages. If anyone scores against us there's a real inquest into what happened.

Unbeaten at home this season, the 'Bishops' had conceded only eight goals in eighteen games, so the court-martials had not been too frequent.

Ted Hardy works in the Borough Market from 4.30 a.m. to 10.30 a.m. which, as he says, leaves him free to devote the rest of the day to the problems of football Management. Square and compact, as if squashed by carrying those baskets on his head, he doesn't look like the man with whom to start an argument. Ted was with Arsenal until a smashed kneecap and cartilage trouble forced him to leave for the amateur game, starting with Hendon.

Before coming to Bishop's Stortford he had taken Dagenham to two Amateur Cup finals at Wembley, the only place where success eluded them.

> What changes did I make? We train together two evenings a week. Some preferred to train on their own, but discipline is important and working together is important. I had to sort out a player who thought it was too far to come from Harwich to train.
>
> We aren't defensive. We usually play 4–3–3 but that's the same as in my Arsenal days when forwards played the old W formation. Then the insides lay deep and there were still only three up.
>
> We do play tight at the back. *Very* tight. In important matches you can't afford to give away a goal.

How big is the gap between top-class amateur clubs and the Fourth Division?

Negligible! They are nearly as good as us.

The difference in approach was clearly just as negligible. With the amateur distinction about to be ended, some clubs like Bishop's Stortford may also be pressing for League recognition.

Looking to the Future

Since the War more than eight hundred Managers have left their English League clubs. That makes the average 'life' of a Manager three years, a bleak prospect at first sight.

But security has never been the name of this game – and those who have it as their first priority should not be professional footballers or Managers. Without success there is no support and no contract will ever paper over the divide of failure. Nearly all Managers have been footballers themselves, aware that the best team must always be picked with a ruthless disregard for sentiment. That is their own approach to the players they manage. They understand the same hard logic applying to their jobs. And the players' reaction is always *the Manager is dead; Long live the new Manager* – for whom they nearly always turn on an unusual performance in welcome.

Longer contracts will bring no greater permanence. Frank O'Farrell, Noel Cantwell, Alan Ball and the rest were unprotected by them. The S.F.A. Contract with Docherty did not assure them of his services when a higher-paid job was offered, nor did Manchester City's contract keep Malcolm Allison. It is a two-way traffic. Movement is inevitable and Dave Bowen has a point that a club may need a new Manager every five years or so if the players are not to become complacent.

Shankly, or Stein, or Revie may surf along on the tide of success.

The big clubs can freshen their approach with an influx of new players or a new Coach, but a change of Manager will often give new stimulus to the ordinary team. The coming of Stokoe and Armfield has rejuvenated Sunderland and Bolton. Of such is the excitement of the game.

The contract's main importance to Managers is to give some financial security and advice is available to them from the Managers and Secretaries Association or the F.A. Most contracts run for more than a year and that is a considerable advance on the average businessman's. It is the Coaches, the Scouts, the Assistants for whom there needs to be more emphasis on contracts. At present many have no proper agreements, but are even more vulnerable than Managers. When the Manager changes they are likely to go too, for the new man will wish to work with people he knows.

The training of Managers is a more obvious need than better contracts. Thirty years ago there was little coaching and an assumption that players would instinctively find the right methods. Now the value of coaching is accepted and the system highly developed.

But Managers are still expected to be players one day, masters of a complex business the next. The change is more difficult than they expect and many are poorly prepared for it. The F.A.- and League-sponsored course is being continued at Lilleshall, rather than Loughborough, and now there is another to supplement it. In June 1973 the P.F.A. organised at St Helens their own course for players with a Management career in mind. This is a welcome recognition of the need by the players themselves. As Derek Dougan, Chairman of the Professional Footballers Association, commented,

> The emphasis is on those problems which beset a Manager in his early years in the job – problems which in the past have produced unhappy experiences for young Managers. It is worth recalling that 800 Managers have been dismissed since the War and many of those have undoubtedly suffered from a lack of preparation for the job. It should be obvious to all footballers that any improvement in the training of Managers must also be a good thing for the players they will eventually have under their charge, and therefore a course such as this will eventually benefit us as well as helping individuals in their transition from player to Manager.

There has been a tradition of laying all blame for the turnover of Managers on wayward Boards or the ruthless drive for results. Dougan rightly accepts that sometimes the cause is the inexperience or ineptitude of Managers appointed without training and usually without the detailed selection techniques that industry would use.

The value of the P.F.A. course is that it will not only give some preparation for the player who wants to try Management, but will give him a chance to reflect whether the change is one he can make. Before accepting his Middlesbrough appointment Jack Charlton commented, 'I have enjoyed my freedom as a player. I have to be quite sure that I am prepared to accept the total involvement and the work that is an inescapable part of football Management.' Not all players realise in advance what the change means. Bobby Charlton was just as sensible joining this first course as his induction to Management. International fame as a footballer had been no help to Billy Wright in converting to Manager.

As with coaching, more intensive training of Managers can raise the general standard, though it can never be a substitute for the character and judgement that makes some naturally outstanding, whether trained or not.

The Managers should also be taking a greater part in shaping the playing future of the game. The F.A. took a realistic step in this direction, ending the rule that barred professional players from the Council and making a former Charlton player Secretary.

But still it is the Chairmen and the Secretaries who decide the future of League football, with Managers and players having no vote and little say. That must change.

Alan Hardaker was himself an amateur player with Hull and his views are forthright: 'I did not know enough about football to tell a professional how to play. While they were learning that trade I was studying administration and they don't know enough about that to tell me what to do.'

The League and the Managers are now facing the same problems which beset cricket twenty years ago. When the county grounds were packed in the 1940s we never dreamed how deserted they would be twenty years later.

In part the drift of spectators has been the inevitable result of wider car ownership, a wider range of sporting interest and a demand for more instant entertainment. But a contributory factor was the county cricketers' absorption with method, making the game look like a job and a rather boring job at that.

Cricket has regained its health, but the resurgence of interest came only after fundamental changes. There are useful guidelines for football in the study of the expedients tried by a sister sport.

Continual tinkering with the rules was the most popular and the least effective of the solutions. Not only did this fail to enliven the First-Class game, it antagonised the mass of club cricketers who had none of the professionals' problems.

Other measures inspired the revival. A positive award for attacking play forced captains to be more adventurous in tactics as they searched for bonus points. To accommodate more Cup competitions with their compulsive attraction the run-of-the-mill County Championship matches were substantially reduced. The loss of gate money was more than covered by getting the maximum return from T.V. and sponsorship. Limited-over cricket helped players rediscover the spirit of excitement that enthuses crowds.

All these have relevance for football, which has the same ills and opportunities. The game itself is still healthy enough, as the numbers playing rise steadily to two million adults and three-quarters of a million schoolboys in England and Wales alone. Sunday football grows apace and so does the interest of women in playing the game. Televised football draws ever larger audiences and football promotions proliferate. The problems are only in some League clubs' ability to attract spectators or equate their growing expenses, now to be increased by at least a million pounds of V.A.T., with their rising payments and costs.

The defensive tactics of the planners is one cause of the alienation that has lost three million spectators in the past season. There was a time when they were criticised for the outbursts of emotion in kissing each other after scoring a goal. Bill Nicholson was asked whether he was concerned that his 'double'-winning team of the 1960s should indulge in such display. 'It is when they have nothing to kiss about that I will be worried', was his realistic answer.

A recent survey commissioned by the League and the *Evening Standard* traced the decline in League goals and attendances, recording that 19% of those sampled gave the lack of goals and skill as their reason for ceasing to watch.

LOOKING TO THE FUTURE

Season	Matches	Goals	Attendances	Min. Adm.
1937–38	1848	5441	28,139,933	5p
1938–39	1848	5787	Not recorded	5p
1946–47	1848	6055	35,604,606	6½p
1947–48	1848	5292	40,259,130	6½p
1948–49	1848	5254	41,271,424	6½p
1949–50	1848	5126	40,517,865	6½p
1950–51	2028	6110	39,584,987	6½p
1951–52	2028	6376	39,015,866	7½p
1952–53	2028	6362	37,149,966	8½p
1953–54	2028	6443	36,174,590	8½p
1954–55	2028	6453	34,133,103	8½p
1955–56	2028	6702	32,744,809	10p
1956–57	2028	6887	32,744,405	10p
1957–58	2028	6841	33,562,208	10p
1958–59	2028	6823	33,610,985	10p
1959–60	2028	6732	32,538,611	10p
1960–61	2028	6982	28,619,754	12½p
1961–62	1982 (Accrington resigned)	6537	27,979,902	12½p
1962–63	2028	6642	28,885,852	12½p
1963–64	2028	6219	28,535,022	12½p
1964–65	2028	6500	27,641,168	12½p
1965–66	2028	6499	27,206,960	20p
1966–67	2028	5774	28,902,596	20p
1967–68	2028	5716	30,107,298	20p
1968–69	2028	5196	29,382,172	25p
1969–70	2028	5243	29,600,972	25p
1970–71	2028	5029	28,194,146	30p
1971–72	2028	5255	28,700,729	30p
1972–73	2006	4689	25,151,934	40p

At the end of the 1961 season 6,982 goals had been scored in the four Divisions. By 1972 the total was down by more than 25 per cent to 5,255. The next season it dropped below 5,000 for the first time. The kissing had not stopped, but the opportunity had been sadly reduced.

Goals are not the only attraction for spectators. In Germany the scoring is freer, the fall in gates more pronounced. In Italy a goal is a rare event yet attendances and receipts rise despite the barren 'technical' football. The essence of a spectator's enjoyment is atmosphere, purpose and a shared excitement.

Coaching and planning have improved technique, stamina and efficiency, but at the expense of spectacle and self-expression. The points system rewards defensive expertise and the off-side law is being exploited to channel play into a dull duel within twenty yards of the half-way line. The growing stalemate is best broken by giving the planners sufficient inducement to take risks. Eight points for a win, three points for a draw and one point for every goal scored would bring a new attacking emphasis into the play. Such a system would also keep alive for longer the interest of middle-of-the-table teams whose position could change dramatically in a few games.

Only in the final resort should there be any major change in the structure of the rules. C. W. Alcock once wrote, 'One of the greatest contributories to the general popularity of football today is its simplicity. What attracts thousands of spectators is the readiness with which every detail of the game can be, if not thoroughly understood, at least followed and appreciated by the spectator of ordinary mental attainments.' That remains true nearly a hundred years later and the less the game itself is altered and complicated the better.

Incentives should be tried first, but if they fail the deadlock could be broken by one major change – total abolition of the off-side rule. This would give the players the space they are denied by restrictive formation and by the speed of the modern tackling. It would also end the main source of disputed decisions. Alf Ramsey tried out the 'no off-side' experiment with the England squad at Lilleshall and found that a team playing in an ordered formation still had the advantage over the other using any device such as leaving two men up on the goal-line. But League soccer must be a lot sicker before such drastic remedy is tried, since the present rules give no problems to the enjoyment of those two-and-three-quarter million ordinary players.

The most pressing problem for League football in Britain is the transfer system. It is a cause of friction, an encouragement to disloyalty, a drain on the resources of clubs who claim to be financially embarrassed. Only part of the money circulates within the League. Over a million pounds is passing annually from England to Scotland. In the 1972/3 season £6,770,000 was paid out in transfers and of that £338,500 went to players, mainly the higher paid. If Ted MacDougall can get £17,500 from two moves in one year it must be a great temptation for a good player to change clubs, if he can.

The Professional Footballers Association sees the ending of the club's options on their players as a way of reducing the size and are pressing for players to be free to move at the end of their contract. This must happen soon. The P.F.A. has never lost a battle yet and if it decides to fight this one seriously it has all the arguments. The Chester Committee recommended this development back in 1968 and the option system contravenes normal industrial practice and individual rights. But while this change will come, the desirable results may be for the higher-paid players and not for football or the generality of professional footballers.

When the maximum wage was ended the playing standards and the pay of the top-class player surged ahead. But the number of professionals in the English League has dropped from over 3,000 to under 2,5000. The trend will be accelerated when options are ended.

The best players will be able to auction themselves profitably at the end of their contracts, but the danger is that the clubs will no longer invest money in young footballers from whom they may get no return. Burnley thrive on the present system and have one of the best youth schemes. Jimmy Adamson's comment will be echoed by many others: 'If the club's option is ended we would disband our youth scheme. Why should we pay out a lot of money to develop players for other teams with no gain to ourselves?'

The majority of Scottish clubs have come to depend on selling a player to England to balance the books, even with expenses cut to a minimum and players engaged part-time. To have players free to move at the end of their contracts without fee for the club might prove a crippling loss. Clubs impatient of success will still buy players in mid-contract, but many more will move at the end of their term without gain to the club that has trained them.

No attempt to limit the size of transfer fees has ever been proof against the determination to buy success in the glory game. The control should be by limiting the number of players a club may sign on transfer to three during one year and by bringing forward the close season for transfers from March to December. This would force clubs to develop their own playing staff and prevent the mad rush for new signings by clubs threatened with relegation.

When he was writing about the future of the English League, Herbert Chapman proposed in the 1930s that eleven clubs should be promoted or relegated each year to lessen the inhibiting fears of relegation so harmful to the style of play. It is an intriguing thought that the whole Second Division should change each season, half promoted, half relegated. Such upheaval hardly seems practical, but the system of four up and four down was one of the excellent proposals by the League Management Committee that needs rapid adoption, rather than being toned down to three.

The reduction of the number of clubs in a Division is also inevitable, though individual fears will delay the process.

The ideal shape of the League is two premier National Divisions of sixteen teams and four Regional Divisions of twenty teams.

The English League now prides itself on being the toughest and most competitive in the world; but the long grind puts undue pressure on the best players and reduces the quality of the football.

Thirty League fixtures a season would cure any staleness in players and the boredom of spectators with run-of-the-mill games. It would allow the home Internationals to be reinstated in the season, with proper time for preparation, instead of dying in limbo as at present. The Regional Leagues would allow another twenty teams into the League, cut travelling expenses and sharpen the local rivalry that adds to gates.

Another sponsored Cup competition could be run, confined to the clubs in the two Premier Divisions. This would be on similar lines to cricket's Benson and Hedges, but drawn in eight zones of four clubs. This minimum of three, maximum of six, extra matches would replace the lost twelve League games and could well cover any drop in revenue.

The old 'Test' matches should also be revived, the four promotion candidates playing off against the four threatened with relegation to determine whether they went up or not. These clearly would provide compulsive watching and if the temper of the matches might be suspect with so much at stake the same applies to all vital games from the European club championship to the World Cup games.

Entry into Europe will not make the movement of players between countries any freer than at present and should not inspire any 'Super League' of Europe. On a continuing basis football interest is parochial. More than eighty years of League football have not yet sparked any desire for a combined English and Scottish 'Super League' and the attraction of a European League will be as remote.

When Herbert Chapman was looking into the future, many of his guesses, such as the development of floodlighting, were prophetic. But his comments were caustic on an architect who called to see him with a plan to make Highbury unique by lifting the playing surface eight feet and running underneath a series of water pipes to keep the turf heated in frosty weather. The price of this, together with an underground garage and store, would have been £13,000. Chapman sent him packing.

He would have been surprised to know that that £13,000 would have saved Arsenal ten times the cost later outlayed on their under-soil heating. Whether he would have approved the installation is another matter. This has ensured Arsenal never have to play a home match in dangerous ground conditions, but it is doubtful if it has saved games from being cancelled. The one time Arsenal could have proved the point, when all other games in the area were off and their ground was in perfect condition, a blizzard blew up in the interval forcing the abandonment of the match. Joe Mercer was once stopped on his way to Highbury by a friend who told him cheerfully, 'The pitch is flooded, the game is off, but at least the water is hot!' Whatever the economics the prime consideration is that the heating has improved the playing surface. Today's equivalent of the under-soil heating on which Chapman frowned is the artificial turf pitch.

Astro or Tartan synthetic turf pitches have been developed in America and are approved by FIFA as proper surfaces for football. The installations in Islington and Hackney in the last three years are forerunners of many more in the London area. They have proved their worth as utility pitches capable of staging forty-nine games a week instead of the two or three that is all the wear a grass pitch can endure. The Astro turf has been chosen as it is quicker draining and remains immediately playable in any weather conditions except driving snow.

The Astro turf is laid on compacted soil with hard core at the base and topped by a layer of asphalt properly graded for drainage. The underpad is bonded to the asphalt with the Astro turf giving a true and unchanging bounce in all weathers and all parts of the pitch. The fibres of the pitch produce more burns and abrasions than grass, but the give in the surface reduces the number of serious injuries. It also allows the use of shorter, rounder studs, cutting down this type of injury. The cost is currently £200,000 for an installation.

Within ten years the top League clubs should have changed to this type of pitch. The six million pounds to equip thirty-two grounds in the two Premier Divisions suggested could be found from Pools or development fund revenue. The advantages would be immense, apart from playing in perfect conditions in all weathers. There would be no excuse left for the myth that it is so much more difficult to play in an away game, since surfaces would be identical. The playing season could be adjusted to suit the needs of football instead of being controlled by the needs of reseeding. The World Cup showed the attractions of summer football and such pitches would allow this to be exploited.

Commercial possibilities are also increased as the stadia, now idle for much of the year, can be fully exploited for other sports and other attractions staged on a surface that would suffer no damage.

With or without synthetic pitches the Commercial Manager will become a more essential part of football club Management. The interest in successful clubs is invitation to a whole range of commercial ventures in line with Jimmy Hill's concept of a football club as entertainment centre or David Hope's business projects for Rangers. The Manager of a football team should not be diverted from his main function and it needs other skills to exploit these opportunities to the full.

With the money from the turnstiles rarely covering the players' wages, League football needs to exploit to the full the cash available from sponsorship and TV. This has been cricket's sensible approach to the decline in gates which is an inevitable trend from changed social habits and wider choice.

The present campaign against TV can only be harmful. It is TV that proves and fosters the deep and widespread support for the game. Over-exposure to soccer's highlights may be a minimal influence in keeping down attendances at Barnsley or Darlington. But this is of little significance compared to the money it is bringing and can bring into football and all that it does to popularise the sport. The aim should be to get the maximum return from TV rather than to fight it.

This is financial sense. Such is the attraction of TV that if it ceases to concentrate on soccer the other sports it will cover instead will gain in interest and support at soccer's expense.

There is also a social obligation to the old and infirm who cannot easily watch matches, but who get such pleasure from televised football. What a loss of enjoyment there would have been for the country had the Cup Final not been televised, only witnessed by the privileged 100,000.

You cannot compel spectators to come to the grounds, but the necessary cash for the support and improvement of the game is easier to tap. Apart from TV and sponsorship the pools are the obvious source.

The big clubs can find the money from their own development organisations, but the help for the smaller League clubs must come from the pools companies. The Pools Levy Board proposal being canvassed might return to football some of the £60m a year taken in tax. But if the Government returns some of the pools tax money to football, it will be for the game as a whole, not just the Leagues.

That very astute businessman, Derrick Robins, now Coventry's President, has pressed for a higher percentage payment to the Leagues from the major pools companies. At present some £700,000 goes to the English League and £225,000 to the Scottish. This is from a pools' turnover exceeding £150m and profits above £40m. The contract has seven years to run, but this is a derisory contribution when so much is taken out of the game. Past history makes it difficult for the League to complain. Before the War, offers of a gift from the pools companies were twice spurned. The present payment is the sum agreed for the copyright of the fixture list and the League has always been apprehensive of the outcome if there was an appeal against the judgement in their favour over this copyright.

But whether through the Government or the direct contribution from the pools, revenue from this source should be increased to at least £3m a year within the next ten years (even that being less than 2 per cent of turnover). This is the money that could be devoted to improving grounds, extending seating, and experimenting with new playing surfaces.

The provision of seating is the most likely method of reducing the violence on the terraces that the League and *Evening Standard* survey confirmed as the main cause of declining attendances. This is the only long-term solution of the problem that reflects the attitude of an age. Only the First and Second Division clubs may be able to afford it – but they are the ones that attract the crowds and the hooligans.

For a season in which attendances at League matches declined by some three million and at Cup games by some three hundred thousand, 1973 still had more of hope than concern for the future of British football.

Liverpool, Leeds and Derby all performed with distinction in Europe. Liverpool in particular continued our dominance of the UEFA Cup with the sixth successive win by an English team in this or its Fairs Cup equivalent.

Their home victory over Borussia Munchengladbach in the first leg of the Final was soccer at its most attractive, the football flowing and clever, the excitement intense.

The Lancashire teams that made a clean sweep of all four Divisions – Liverpool, Burnley, Bolton, and Southport – were all entertaining and adventurous in their play.

In Scotland, while Celtic took their eighth successive League title, Rangers restored the balance in their centenary year by winning the Cup Final in a magnificent duel studded with goals and watched by 134,000.

But it was Sunderland's win at Wembley that gave the game its greatest stimulus and best expressed its enchantment. There is not much amiss with football when one match can set the whole country talking. Not for forty-two years had a Second Division side won the Cup, and it was the forty-two-year-old Manager, Bob Stokoe, who was the decisive influence on their success. Other Finals have gone down to history linked with a player's name, like the Matthews' Final of 1953. This was the first to be remembered for a Manager – Stokoe's Match.

A Manager's influence can easily be overplayed. Once, in Italy, the weak Lucchese team was about to play the strong Juventus side when the Manager died. On the way to the match another was impressed into service, watching from the touchline without speaking to the team. The game was drawn and the delighted team chaired him round the ground.

At Wembley the Sunderland players hoisted Bob Stokoe on their shoulders before they chaired the Captain, Bobby Kerr. But that was better deserved, though Stokoe still accepts his dependence on his players: 'I am paid a handsome salary, but they earn it for me.'

Yet his own impact was too dramatic to be belittled. When he came the team was loitering in the lower reaches of the Second

Division, the last ten matches lost. The next ten were won. Within six months Sunderland was transformed into a side that had beaten Manchester City, Arsenal, and Leeds on merit.

This was an instant miracle, but Stokoe had had a long apprenticeship as Sorcerer. As he moved from Bury to Charlton, to Rochdale to Carlisle to Blackpool, his one set-back was dismissal at Charlton. That never shook his confidence. At Rochdale he made a clean sweep of most of the staff, leaving himself with only five players and a bank balance of £8,000. From free transfers he built a side that won promotion to the Third Division for a club that had three times had to apply for re-election. While he gained in experience and reputation Stokoe always hankered to return to the North-East and its 'special' breed of footballers and football fanatics. It was there that he had his roots and had made his name as Newcastle's centre-half in the 1955 Cup-winning side. He had watched with regret as the gates at Roker Park slumped to little more than ten thousand.

> There was that special feeling for the game in Sunderland and I knew that all they were waiting for to come flooding back to the ground was evidence that the team was playing attractive football.

Stokoe soon gave that evidence by developing the adventurous talents of Tueart and Hughes, by converting Watson into one of the best centre-halves in the country, by acquiring Luton's discarded centre-forward Halom to give new thrust to his forwards. Above all, he communicated to the players his own relaxed approach to the game, the strong determination to win never soured by tension and hardness.

He is a players' Manager, putting their interests first. His close identification with them was neatly and publicly expressed when he led out his team at Wembley in the red track-suit of Sunderland, rather than the sober clothes of a Manager.

Stokoe took over from Alan Brown, whose remarkable record of developing the young has never been matched by equal results on the field. Brown was a strict disciplinarian and the players responded to Stokoe's less formal approach. He encouraged them to enjoy their football and their social life, provided always that they were unstinting of effort on the field.

Before the Cup Final he let them relax in the luxurious

atmosphere of Selsdon Park Hotel and to attend the Football Writers' Dinner, against advice and tradition. The mood was set. Stokoe's crucial contribution was not the tactical gambit of keeping Kerr back to mark Eddie Gray out of the game, but his briefing, 'Enjoy yourselves. Go out to win and don't worry if you get beaten.' That won them the match and the admiration of the public.

Cricket lost its hold when the players became so 'professional' they ceased to look as if they were enjoying themselves. Football has been in the same danger. No wonder Sunderland, who started the Cup as 250 to 1 outsiders, became everyone's favourite.

'Nice guys never win anything' is the maxim that has caused such damage in sport without even the merit of being true. It set the trend for gritty determination with all the emphasis on the result rather than the means or the mental outlook. Stokoe will have helped to reverse that thinking. Winners set trends. Even Leeds, so strained at Wembley, put six past Arsenal with uninhibited relish a few days later. Sunderland had found their new Messiah and the game a fashion to be copied.

Appendix

Plymouth Argyle Job Descriptions

(Two samples: Team Manager and Chief Scout)

TITLE OF JOB: Team Manager

NAME: A. K. WAITERS

In a sentence describe the job:

The overall responsibility for Team affairs including the preparation, selection and recruitment/termination of all staff.

WHO ARE YOU RESPONSIBLE TO?

Chairman/Board of Directors

WHO ARE YOU RESPONSIBLE FOR?

1. Coaching Staff
2. Playing Staff
3. Scouting Staff
4. Ground Staff

LIST, IN ORDER OF IMPORTANCE *(as far as possible)*, ALL YOUR DUTIES AND RESPONSIBILITIES

1. Preparation and selection of First Team.
2. Recruitment and development of Senior Professional players.
3. Press and TV relations.

4. Overall responsibility for prevention of injuries, treatment of injuries and remedial work of injured players; the medical welfare of the Players and Staff.
5. Overall responsibility for the playing and training areas and the staff involved.
6. Overall responsibility for the recruitment and development of young players (Schoolboys, Amateurs, Apprentices and Junior professionals).
7. Overall responsibility for preparation and selection of Reserves and Youth Team.
8. The employment structure and the organisation and delegation of responsibilities and duties.
9. The administration, and delegation of administration, within the department.
10. Overall responsibility for training and playing kit, maintenance etc. of training and playing facilities – including dressing-room areas.
11. Travel and accommodation arrangements for matches.

ARE THERE ANY OTHER DUTIES/RESPONSIBILITIES YOU FEEL YOU COULD AND SHOULD DO?

1. Better liaison leading to greater contact with communications media.
2. Closer contact with ground staff.

ARE THERE ANY DUTIES/RESPONSIBILITIES YOU HAVE, BUT FEEL YOU SHOULD NOT BE DOING?

Less involvement in general office administration – need for Secretarial assistance.

ARE THERE ANY DUTIES/RESPONSIBILITIES WITHIN OUR DEPARTMENT EITHER NOT BEING DONE OR BEING NEGLECTED?

1. Amateurs/Schoolboys – poor development through deficiencies in coaching organisation and through lack of facilities.
2. Patchy scouting network and system of information.
3. Development of Apprentices/Young Professionals unsatisfactory. Necessity for improved facilities and an additional Coach.

APPENDIX 215

4. Improved system of house acquisition for new players.
5. Better remedial work for injured players.
6. Improved opportunity for Further Education.

WORKING CONDITIONS:

HOURS: Unlimited.

HOLIDAYS: Three weeks ideally. Practically – who knows!?

EXPENSES: Club improvements etc. – £50 maximum at Team Manager's discretion.
Above that with Directorate permission.
All running expenses of car.
Accommodation, Meals, Second-class rail travel.

TITLE OF JOB: Chief Scout and Assistant to the Manager

NAME: ELLIS STUTTARD

In a sentence describe the job:

To assess players at all levels, organise and administer the club scouting system, and assist the Team Manager in team administration.

WHO ARE YOU RESPONSIBLE TO?

The Team Manager – and ultimately to the Board of Directors

WHO ARE YOU RESPONSIBLE FOR?

1. The Club Scouts
2. In the absence of, or as directed by, the Team Manager, the coaching, playing and ground staff

LIST, IN ORDER OF IMPORTANCE *(as far as possible)* ALL YOUR DUTIES AND RESPONSIBILITIES

1. Scouting organisation.

2. In liaison with the Reserve Team Manager the recruiting of Schoolboys, Amateurs and Apprentices.
3. Scouting reports.
4. Organisation of trial games.
5. Assessing First Team opposition.
6. Expenses etc. involved in Scouting organisation.
7. Administration of Team Affairs as directed by Team Manager including:
   (*a*) Expenses
   (*b*) Lodgings for Apprentices/Professionals
   (*c*) Filing system
   (*d*) Youth Team administration

ARE THERE ANY OTHER DUTIES/RESPONSIBILITIES YOU FEEL YOU COULD AND SHOULD DO?

Other duties arise at different times and unexpectedly.
Prepared to have a go at any of them.

ARE THERE ANY DUTIES/RESPONSIBILITIES YOU HAVE, BUT FEEL YOU SHOULD NOT BE DOING?

No.

ARE THERE ANY DUTIES/RESPONSIBILITIES WITHIN OUR DEPARTMENT EITHER NOT BEING DONE OR BEING NEGLECTED?

The Club Scouting System has been neglected in the past. A concentrated effort and greater financial commitment is necessary.

WORKING CONDITIONS:

HOURS: Unlimited.

HOLIDAYS: Three weeks per annum.

EXPENSES: Club Car and running costs.
Second-class rail travel.
Meals and accommodation whilst on club business.

Index

Aberdeen, 93, 102, 176
Adamson, Jimmy, 46, 153-5, 182, 203
Addison, Colin, 192-4
Ajax, 63
Alcock, C. W., 118, 202
Aldershot, 40, 174, 187
Allchurch, Ivor, 54
Allison, George, 29, 150
Allison, Malcolm, 18, 96, 106, 114-16, 119, 129, 172, 182
Alloa, 171
Anderson, Des, 139
Anderson, Jimmy, 76, 77
Armfield, Jimmy, 155-7, 198
Armstrong, George, 125, 135
Arsenal, 11, 14, 24, 31-4, 63, 68, 106-7, 108-109, 114, 124-8, 130, 145-7, 161, 168, 177, 185-6, 192, 195, 204, 209, 210
Ashford, 185
Aston Villa, 12, 39, 75, 111, 150, 160

Ball, Alan Snr, 197
Ball, Alan Jnr, 124
Banks, Gordon, 13
Bamber, Mike, 181
Barnsley, 206
Barnwell, John, 189
Barrow, 170, 192
Bastin, Cliff, 30

Bates, Billy, 109
Bates, Ted, 47, 108-10
Bath City, 130
Baxter, Jim, 13
Bayford, Brian, 195
Beattie, Andy, 55, 56, 59
Belfitt, Rod, 169
Bell, Colin, 115, 144
Benfica, 12, 63, 94
Bennion, Ray, 154
Best, George, 12, 61, 71, 88
Birmingham City, 14, 24, 33, 40, 41
Bishop Auckland, 8
Bishop's Stortford, 194-5
Blackburn Rovers, 19, 34, 156, 171
Blackpool, 19, 34, 156, 171
Blackwood, Bobby, 136
Blanchflower, Danny, 60, 74-81, 99
Blakey, Dave, 155
Blockley, Jeff, 106, 124, 160, 181
Bloomfield, Jimmy, 167
Bloye, Raymond, 183
Bolton Wanderers, 155-8
Bond, John, 17, 119, 180
Bournemouth and B.A., 16, 17, 113, 119, 180-1
Bowen, Dave 44, 52-5
Bowles, Stan, 110-11
Boycott, Geoff, 119
Bradford City, 39, 170
Brazil, 42, 46, 50

INDEX

Bremner, Billy, 106
Brentford, 123–4
Bridges, Barry, 112
Bridgnorth, 166
Brighton and H.A., 22, 103, 180–1
Bristol City, 60, 123
Broadbent, Peter, 37
Brooking, Trevor, 101
Brown, Alan, 153–5
Brown, Bill, 78
Brown, Bobby, 13, 56
Brown, Joe, 182
Buckingham, Vic, 8, 187
Buckley, Frank, 34–6
Bull, Walter, 30
Burnley, 35, 99, 111–12, 117, 153
Bury, 19, 40, 152
Busby, Sir Matt, 12, 27, 29, 39, 70–4
Butler, Jack, 32

Cameron, John, 28
Cantwell, Noel, 95, 181, 189–91, 194, 197
Carlisle United, 19, 174
Carnegie College, 45, 89
Carr, Willie, 103, 160–1, 181
Carver, Jesse, 42, 121
Catterick, Harry, 38, 92–4
Cavanagh, Tommy, 71
Celtic, 23, 31, 63, 81–5, 102, 165, 175–6, 208
Channon, Mike, 107
Chapman, Herbert, 27, 29, 30–4, 51, 98, 107–8, 118, 125, 169, 203, 204, 205
Charles, John, 35, 36, 54, 192
Charles, Mel, 54, 171
Charlton Athletic, 7, 111, 188
Charlton, Bobby, 12, 48, 64, 186
Charlton, Jack, 69
Chelsea, 14, 19, 27, 81, 91, 103, 106, 135, 137, 150, 185
Chester Committee, 153, 172–3, 203
Chivers, Martin, 107, 113
Clark, Gordon, 89, 168
Clemence, Ray, 66
Clough, Brian, 16, 32, 93, 94–6, 100, 137, 161, 168
Collins, Bobby, 69
Cooke, Charlie, 163–4
Cooper, Terry, 70
Cormack, Peter, 65, 66

Coventry City, 18, 26, 33, 42, 71, 94, 96, 103, 106–7, 114, 119, 160–1, 171, 188–9, 207
Craig, Jim, 85
Crawford, Ray, 50
Crayston, Jack, 29
Crerand, Pat, 71
Crewe Alexandra, 67, 92
Crystal Palace, 114–16, 151–2, 162–5, 182
Cullis, Stanley, 34–8
Curran, Hugh, 145
Cush, Wilbur, 68
Czechoslovakia, 60, 62

Darlington, 152
Davies, Roger, 166–8
Deeley, Norman, 37
Derby County, 15, 33, 65, 88, 94–6, 137, 166–8, 208
Dickinson, Jimmy, 20
Docherty, Michael, 111
Docherty, Tommy, 9, 44, 55–9, 71, 93, 101, 104, 151, 165–6
Doherty, Peter, 60, 74, 76, 79
Doncaster Rovers, 42, 43
Dooley, Derek, 18
Dougal, Bill, 154
Doyle, Mike, 115–16
Drake, Ted, 149–51
Dumbarton, 23, 24
Dunfermline Athletic, 82
Dunnett, Jack, 173
Durban, Alan, 168
Dyke, Victor, 188

Edwards, Duncan, 12
Eggleston, Tommy, 94
Eire, 62
England, 13, 42, 44–56, 59
Eusebio, 12
Everton, 28, 92, 94, 105, 169–70, 176

Fenton, Benny, 8
FIFA, 205
Finney, Jim, 194
Finney, Tom, 21, 50, 65, 110
Fletcher, Paul, 112, 153
Football Association, 15, 48, 27, 199
Foulke, William, 28

INDEX

Fraser, Doug, 139
Freeman, Reg, 105
Fulham, 149–51, 184, 186, 188
Fusillo, Paul, 161

George, Charlie, 88, 127–8
Germany, 55
Giles, Johnny, 69
Gillies, Matt, 136
Givens, Don, 110–11
Gliksten, Michael, 182
Graham, George, 125
Grant, Wilf, 47, 166–8
Gray, Eddie, 68, 106, 210
Greaves, Jimmy, 78
Green, Tony, 171, 193
Greenock, Morton, 28
Greenwood, Ron, 23, 91, 100, 119, 129, 155, 157, 171
Grimsby Town, 115
Groves, Vic, 187

Hancocks, Johnny, 37
Hardaker, Alan, 162, 199
Hardy, George, 32
Harper, Joe, 93, 176
Hartford, Asa, 145
Hartlepool, 95
Harvey, Joe, 91, 170–1
Head, Bert, 162–4
Hearts, 136
Hereford United, 122, 192–4
Herrera, Helenio, 31
Heslop, George, 105
Hewitt, Ronnie, 152
Hibernian, 91, 101–3
Hill, Jimmy, 8, 26, 32, 119, 171, 183, 206
Hockey, Trevor, 55
Hollins, John, 151
Hope, David, 178–80, 206
Horn, Graham, 24
Hornsby, Brian, 159–60
Howe, Don, 145
Huddersfield Town, 30, 31, 145
Hulme, Joe, 30
Hull City, 33
Hungary, 53, 54
Hunt, Roger, 65, 92
Hunter, Alan, 169

Hunter, Norman, 55
Hurley, Charlie, 62, 171

Ipswich Town, 42, 49, 50, 78, 79, 131–3, 169–70
Ireland, Northern, 33, 44, 59–62, 77

Jago, Gordon, 7, 110–12, 165
James, Alex, 31
James, Leighton, 55, 112, 155
Jeffery, Alick, 42, 43
Johnson, Dave, 93, 169
Johnstone, Jimmy, 58, 84
Jones, Bryn, 25
Jones, Cliff, 54
Jones, J. L., 28
Jones, Mick, 14
Jones, Ron, 7
Juventus, 42, 172, 192, 208

Kay, George, 150
Keegan, Kevin, 65
Kendall, Howard, 93
Kennedy, Ray, 125
Kelly, Hugh, 109
Kelly, Sir Robert, 82
Kelly, Theo, 92
Kiernan, Billy, 8
Kilmarnock, 86
King's Lynn, 151–2

Law, Denis, 58, 64
Lazio, 42
Leadbetter, Jimmy, 49, 50
Lee, Francis, 115–16, 144
Leeds City, 30
Leeds United, 23, 63, 68–70, 81, 94, 100, 104, 106–7, 109, 131, 145, 208, 210
Leicester City, 13
Liverpool, 7, 11, 14, 23, 46, 63, 72, 89, 91, 92, 106, 117, 131, 165–6, 208
Llanelli, 82
Lloyd, Cliff, 172
Lloyd, Larry, 65
Lochhead, Andy, 111–12
London Combination, 31
Lord, Bob, 154, 182

INDEX

Lorimer, Peter, 95
Love, George, 168

Macari, Lou, 100, 165–6
MacDonald, Malcolm, 71, 187
MacDougall, Ted, 113, 162–4, 180
MacKay, Dave, 78, 136–9, 171
Mahoney, John, 55
Mansfield Town, 94
Manchester City, 12, 13, 15, 18, 65, 72, 77, 81, 89, 96, 99, 106, 114–16, 137, 144–5, 165–6, 192
Manchester United, 12, 26, 63, 64, 70–3, 81, 87, 105, 119, 165–6
Margate, 113
Marinello, Peter, 125
Marsh, Rodney, 115–16, 144, 165, 187
Matthews, Stanley, 12, 21, 41, 50, 119
McCracken, W., 29
McFarland, Roy, 95, 138
McGarry, Bill, 91
McIlroy, Jimmy, 59, 99
McLintock, Frank, 106, 125, 128
McNab, Bob, 135, 147
McParland, Peter, 12, 160
McWilliam, Peter, 29, 38
Mee, Bertie, 11, 16, 29, 87–90, 106, 124–8, 145, 159
Mercer, Joe, 18, 52, 54, 64, 91, 105–7, 121, 144, 165, 171
Middlesbrough, 95–6
Milburn, Jack, 14
Miles, Frank, 193
Millwall, 7, 160
Milne, Gordon, 18, 106–7, 114, 187, 194
Mitchell, John, 151
Mitten, Charlie, 184
Moore, Bobby, 106, 131–5
Morley, H. H., 27
Moscow Dynamo, 86
Moscrop, Edwin, 117
Muckle, Dr D., 141–4
Mullen, Jimmy, 35
Murphy, Jimmy, 153
Musgrove, Malcolm, 182

Nagy, Imre, 53
Neill, Terry, 33, 44, 61, 62
Newcastle United, 68, 91, 151–3, 170–1
Nicholson, Bill, 8, 18, 74–81, 137

Nordahl, Bertil, 43
Norman, Maurice, 77
Northampton Town, 30, 52, 54
Nottingham Forest, 15, 16, 45, 65, 136–9, 192
Notts County, 189
Norwich City, 34, 162–3
Nulty, Geoff, 111

O'Farrell, Frank, 71, 100, 162, 185, 197
O'Neil, Brian, 153
Orient (Leyton), 104–5, 185, 187
Ormond, Willie, 49, 59, 101
Osgood, Peter, 135
Oxford United, 120–4, 141–2

Paine, Terry, 107–8
Panathinaikos, 92
Parker, Tom, 108
Pegasus, 7
Pelé, 13, 42
Peterborough, 24, 190–1
Professional Footballers Association, 26, 172
Phillips, Ted, 50
Pickard, Alf, 35
Piggott, Dennis, 173–4
Plymouth Argyle, 28, 112, 180
Pointer, Ray, 23
Poland, 53
Portsmouth, 12, 13, 19–25, 174
Portugal, 94
Powell, Steve, 161
Prentice, John 56
Preston North End, 65
Price, Peter, 24

Queen's Park, 28
Queen's Park Rangers, 7, 57, 110–12, 185–6

Radford, John, 125
Raisbeck, Alexander, 64
Ramsey, Sir Alf, 13, 27, 38, 39, 44–52, 93, 99, 106
Rangers, Glasgow, 28, 63, 81, 85–7, 175–6, 178–80, 206, 208
Raynor, George, 39, 40–3

INDEX

Reading, 171-2
Real Madrid, 63
Revie, Don, 13, 14, 26, 29, 68-70, 93, 94, 177, 197
Richley, Len, 151-3
Riggs, Les, 113
Roberts, 32
Robertson, Jimmy, 126
Robertson, John, 139
Robertson, J. T., 27
Robins, Derrick, 26, 96, 183, 207
Robinson, Peter, 67
Robson, Bobby, 131-3, 169-70
Rochdale, 19, 91, 152, 209
Rotherham United, 40
Rowe, Arthur, 8, 38, 39, 47, 76
Royle, Joe, 93, 94
Rous, Sir Stanley, 40

St John, Ian, 14, 67
Sammels, John, 16
Santos, 63
Saunders, Ron, 30, 123, 185
Saward, Pat, 160-1, 180-1
Sawyer, Eric, 66
Scotland, 13, 49, 55-9, 72, 101, 118
Scunthorpe United, 65
Seed, Jimmy, 7
Sefton, Alan, 20, 21
Sexton, Dave, 89, 91, 103-5
Shackleton, Len, 15
Shankly, Bill, 11, 23, 29, 63-6, 92-3, 110, 117, 165, 197
Shankly, Bob, 91
Sheffield United, 40, 105, 192
Sheffield Wednesday, 18, 45, 94, 153
Shelley, Albert, 64
Sillett, Peter, 185
Simonsson, A., 42
Simpson, Peter, 128
Skegness Town, 42
Slater, W., 37, 120
Smith, George, 19
Southampton, 28, 47, 107-10
Southend, 35
Southern League, 20, 31, 113, 185
Spartak Trnava, 90
Spurdle, 14
Southport, 117, 193, 208
Stein, Jock, 23, 82-5, 99, 197
Stephenson, Alan, 23, 24
Stepney, Alex, 13

Stiles, Norbert, 51-2
Stock, Alec, 9, 106, 155-9
Stockport County, 67
Stoke City, 46
Stokoe, Bob, 15, 19, 140, 171, 198, 208-10
Storer, Harry, 33
Storey, Peter, 124
Storey Moore, Ian, 15
Struth, Willie, 86
Summerbee, Mike, 115-16, 130, 144
Summers, Gerry, 103, 120-4, 133, 145
Sudell, Major, 27
Sunderland, 15, 19, 70, 112, 151, 153, 171, 198, 208-10
Sweden, 39-42
Swift, Frank, 12
Swindin, George, 29
Swindon Town, 136, 139
Switzerland, 41, 55
Symon, Scot, 86

Tait, George, 152, 182
Taylor, Eric, 18
Taylor, Peter, 96, 138
Taylor, Tommy, 101, 131
Tidball, Reg, 193
Tilson, Fred, 12
Tindall, Ron, 19-24, 180
Thompson, Peter, 64, 65
Torquay United, 47
Toshack, John, 55, 65
Tottenham Hotspur, 7, 8, 28, 29, 38, 39, 63, 67, 74-81, 87, 99, 113, 136
Turnbull, Eddie, 29, 91, 101, 119, 129, 141

Veitch, Colin, 29, 38
Vizard, Ted, 37

Waddell, Willie, 85-7, 176
Waiters, Tony, 112, 180
Wales, 42, 44, 52-5
Walker, Billy, 45
Walker, Tommy, 136
Wall, Bob, 16, 176
Walsall, 35
Walthamstow Avenue, 150
Waterlooville, 19

Wembley, 8, 11, 12, 15, 19, 44, 46, 59, 73, 186, 195, 209
West Bromwich Albion, 8, 89, 145
West Ham, 23, 77, 81, 91, 100, 131, 155, 157
White, John, 78, 99, 171
Whittaker, Tom, 29, 33, 150
Whittle, Alan, 93
Wigan Athletic, 114, 187
Wilson, Bob, 95, 128, 134–6
Wilson, Ray, 92
Winterbottom, Walter, 26, 45–6, 104, 130, 133, 155

Wolverhampton Wanderers, 13, 34–8, 44, 45
Worcester City, 47, 168
Workington, 65, 170
Wright, Billy, 29, 35
Wright, Charlie, 170
Wright, Pat, 20

Yeovil Town, 111–12, 185, 188
York City, 192
Youlden, Thomas, 23